Singapore Cinema

This book outlines and discusses the very wide range of cinema which is to be found in Singapore. Although Singapore cinema is a relatively small industry, and relatively new, it has nevertheless made an impact, and continues to develop in interesting ways. The book shows that although Singapore cinema is often seen as part of diasporic Chinese cinema, it is in fact much more than this, with strong connections to Malay cinema and the cinemas of other Asian nations. Moreover, the themes and subjects covered by Singapore cinema are very wide, ranging from conformity to the regime and Singapore's national outlook, with undesirable subjects overlooked or erased, to the sympathetic depiction of minorities and an outlook which is at odds with the official outlook.

The book will be useful to readers new to the subject and wanting a concise overview, while at the same time it puts forward many new research findings and much new thinking.

Liew Kai Khiun is an Assistant Professor at the Nanyang Technological University, Singapore.

Stephen Teo is an Associate Professor at the Nanyang Technological University, Singapore.

Media, Culture and Social Change in Asia

Series Editor: Stephanie Hemelryk Donald

Editorial Board:

Gregory N. Evon, University of New South Wales
Devleena Ghosh, University of Technology, Sydney
Peter Horsfield, RMIT University, Melbourne
Chris Hudson, RMIT University, Melbourne
Michael Keane, Queensland University of Technology
Tania Lewis, RMIT University, Melbourne
Vera Mackie, University of Melbourne
Kama Maclean, University of New South Wales
Jane Mills, University of New South Wales
Laikwan Pang, Chinese University of Hong Kong
Gary Rawnsley, Aberystwyth University
Ming-yeh Rawnsley, School of Oriental and African Studies, University of London
Jo Tacchi, RMIT University, Barcelona
Adrian Vickers, University of Sydney
Jing Wang, MIT
Ying Zhu, City University of New York

The aim of this series is to publish original, high-quality work by both new and established scholars in the West and the East, on all aspects of media, culture and social change in Asia.

47 Youth Culture in Chinese Language Film
Xuelin Zhou

48 Green Asia
Ecocultures, Sustainable Lifestyles and Ethical Consumption
Edited by Tania Lewis

49 Eastern Westerns
Film and Genre Outside and Inside Hollywood
Stephen Teo

50 Singapore Cinema
New Perspectives
Edited by Liew Kai Khiun and Stephen Teo

Singapore Cinema
New Perspectives

**Edited by
Liew Kai Khiun and Stephen Teo**

LONDON AND NEW YORK

First published 2017
by Routledge
2 Park Square, Milton Park, Abingdon, Oxon OX14 4RN

and by Routledge
711 Third Avenue, New York, NY 10017

Routledge is an imprint of the Taylor & Francis Group, an informa business

© 2017 selection and editorial matter, Liew Kai Khiun and Stephen Teo, individual chapters, the contributors

The right of Liew Kai Khiun and Stephen Teo to be identified as the authors of the editorial material, and of the authors for their individual chapters, has been asserted in accordance with sections 77 and 78 of the Copyright, Designs and Patents Act 1988.

All rights reserved. No part of this book may be reprinted or reproduced or utilised in any form or by any electronic, mechanical, or other means, now known or hereafter invented, including photocopying and recording, or in any information storage or retrieval system, without permission in writing from the publishers.

Trademark notice: Product or corporate names may be trademarks or registered trademarks, and are used only for identification and explanation without intent to infringe.

British Library Cataloguing in Publication Data
A catalogue record for this book is available from the British Library

Library of Congress Cataloging in Publication Data
A catalog record for this book has been requested

ISBN: 978-1-138-92525-0 (hbk)
ISBN: 978-1-315-68387-4 (ebk)

Typeset in Times New Roman
by codeMantra

In memory
Toh Hai Leong (21 March 1956–15 January 2014)

Contents

List of figures		ix
Foreword		x
CHUA BENG HUAT		
Acknowledgements		xii
Contributors		xiii
Introduction		xvii
LIEW KAI KHIUN AND STEPHEN TEO		

PART I
Cine-pasts   1

1	Malay cinema's legacy of cultural materialism: P. Ramlee as historical mentor	3
	STEPHEN TEO	
2	Singapore cinema: Connecting the golden age and the revival	20
	EDNA LIM	
3	Convergence and slippage between film and history: Reviewing *Invisible City*, *Zahari's 17 Years* and *Sandcastle*	37
	LOH KAH SENG AND KENNETH PAUL TAN	
4	Independent digital filmmaking and its impact on film archiving in Singapore	51
	KAREN CHAN AND CHEW TEE PAO	

PART II
Cine-citizenry   65

5	Jack Neo, conformity and cultural materialism in Singapore film	67
	STEPHEN TEO	

viii *Contents*

6 Sensuous citizenship in contemporary Singapore cinema:
A case study of *Singapore GaGa* (Tan Pin Pin, 2005)   84
SOPHIA SIDDIQUE HARVEY

7 Popular music and contemporary Singaporean cinema   94
LIEW KAI KHIUN AND BRENDA CHAN

8 Off with the shaking heads! Reel-ising the "Singapore
Indian" in the local Tamil films, *My Magic* and
Gurushetram – 24 Hours of Anger   104
NIDYA SHANTHINI MANOKARA

PART III
Cine-cityscapes   **127**

9 Singapore v. Foucault: Biopolitics and geopolitics in
contemporary queer films   129
JUN ZUBILLAGA-POW

10 Mapping Singapore's cinemas   144
CHARLEY LEARY

11 Going to the movies in *Pardes*   156
ANJALI GERA ROY

Index   173

List of figures

2.1	Examples of shots from the opening sequence of *12 Storeys*	23
2.2	Melvyn and Vynn are dwarfed in the heartland	27
2.3	Melvyn and Vynn in the playground	27
2.4	The boys in front of City Hall	28
2.5	Tattered clothing in the *kampong* vs. formal wear in the city in *Bujang Lapok*	31
8.1	Mohan, sons and social worker in L-shaped flat	110
8.2	Prakash's interrogation scene	111
8.3	Marsiling Warriors dancing during X-plosion Nite dance competition	113
8.4	Prakash and Subra looking at "snow"	114
8.5	Vinod restraining Prakash with a bicycle chain	115
8.6	Dead bodies floating on pond	115
8.7	Opening scene with Francis and bartender	117
8.8	Francis and Raju in the L-shaped flat	118
8.9	Close-up of needle piercing through the skin	119
8.10	Electricity being passed through Francis	119
8.11	Raju with the framed photograph of his young parents	120
8.12	Francis and Raju sleeping in the dilapidated building	121
8.13	Prakash and Subra boarding a train at Tanjong Pagar Railway Station	122
9.1	Film still from *Sisters* (2011)	133
10.1	Rex Cinemas, 2010	146
10.2	Faith Community Baptist Church, formerly Liberty Cinema, 2010	148
10.3	Map of Singapore's cinemas	153

Foreword

Watching Singapore films as national duty

Chua Beng Huat

Growing up in the 1950s in Bukit Ho Swee, an *attap*-house community at the edge of the colonial city that was Tiong Bahru, I had very easy access to movie theatres. Closest was the King's Theatre at Kim Tian Road; and within walking distance was the Great World entertainment park which housed the Sky Theatre and the Atlantic Theatre. The Oriental Theatre and the Majestic Theatre in Chinatown, which screened Mandarin movies and occasional Hokkien-dialect films, were only a 5 or 10-cents bus ride away. Coming from a small-business family, I always had discretionary cash to go to the movies. The price of a ticket for the Saturday or the Sunday morning matinee was 50 cents, and that for regular afternoon or evening screenings were 1 dollar for seats closer to the screen, or 2 dollars for the back rows, and up to 2.5 dollars or 3 dollars for "circle" seats on the second floor. Until today, I cannot bear to sit in the front half of the movie house. The ticket prices at each theatre were determined by whether it was air-conditioned and whether it had plush "velvet" seats or thin plywood seats, which were often infested with bed-bugs.

The first morning matinee would start at 9am, the second at 11am. I would regularly sit through both movies, usually at King's, if I were on my own; but frequently, I went with my elder sister to see Mandarin movies at the Oriental or the Majestic. I was quite indifferent to what was showing but they were generally Hollywood westerns with cowboys and "Indians" or Hong Kong melodramas from Shaw Brothers or the Great Wall Studio. By the time I started secondary school, the movie theatres of choice were the Capitol, Odeon and the Cathay in the vicinity of North Bridge Road, all within walking distance of each other. Hanging out after school, one activity was sitting through a 3pm screening in any one of these cinemas. All these "downtown" cinemas screened Hollywood movies, and beyond the action movies, the films were mostly incomprehensible to me but it almost did not matter. Movies were one of my major leisure activities. Meanwhile, unknown to the boy who spent so much time in movies was the fact that there was a movie production studio making Malay-language films. I do not remember at all watching any "Singapore" movies.

Then, in 1995, came Eric Khoo's *Mee Pok Man*, a film that foregrounds the "underbelly" of successful Singapore. This was followed by Jack Neo's *Money No Enough*, which transformed the everyday grumblings of Singaporeans into a social critique laced with humour. Under the political conditions of the time, all professional associations (such as the Law Society) were legally constrained to stay within their narrow professional interests and civil society organisations were constantly at risk of being de-registered. Aesthetic cultural practices, such as caricature drawings and theatre performances, carried a disproportionate social responsibility to critically reflect on the social and political conditions, in spite of the fact that such practices were subject to state censorship on different grounds. Films are no exception. This continues to be true, as in the most recent banning of Tan Pin Pin's film, *To Singapore with Love* (2013) for commercial release, while the fate of Eric Khoo's most recent "erotic film", *In the Room* remains in limbo at the time of writing.

In any case, since the mid-1990s, Eric Khoo has become the renowned auteur whose films are "must see" for the arthouse crowd, while Jack Neo's output based on a one-film-a-year production schedule has been hugely popular with large numbers of Singaporeans who come to see and laugh at themselves being "caricatured" on the big screen. Perhaps the success of Neo and Khoo at both ends of the movie spectrum engendered a sense of filmmaking as a "viable" if unstable profession and "persuaded" liberal-minded middle-class parents to permit their children to go to film schools. A short string of filmmakers with their breakthrough first films followed: Kelvin Tong and Jasmine Chan with *Eating Air* (1999); Royston Tan with *15* (2003), the short and long versions; Boo Junfeng with the banned short-film *Tanjong Rhu* (2009) and his feature film *Sandcastle* (2010); and in the documentary field, Tan Pin Pin's *Singapore Gaga* (2005). These filmmakers and their works stand as evidence and affirmation of something called "Singapore Cinema". But this cinema has a disrupted history. If one were to cast a glance backward in Singapore film history, we may discover the "Golden Era" of the Malay film studios and its films, which remain mostly unrecognised, therefore compelling a need to reconnect with this history. So we now have a discontinuous history, a constellation of recognised filmmakers from our contemporary era, who, in spite of their relatively young age are "pioneers"; a National Film Commission that provided public funding; and, with recent academic analyses of the history and the filmmakers and their work, including this collection of essays, all the essential elements constitutive of Singapore Cinema and a "film industry" now in place, ready for further development. For myself, watching Singapore films has become something of a "national" duty, regardless of what the reviewers say. And, I urge all Singaporeans who are into movies to do the same, lest the fledgling industry fizzles out, again, for lack of audience, and the same tragic history of discontinuity may be re-enacted twenty-five years from now.

Acknowledgements

The editors would like to thank the following organisations and individuals without which this publication would not be possible. For organisations, this includes the Nanyang Technological University Centre for Liberal Arts and Social Sciences (CLASS) and the Asia Research Institute (ARI) of the National University of Singapore for funding the workshop on Singapore Cinema in October 2011 that brought together the contributors of this book, as well as the Wee Kim Wee School of Communication and Information for financially supporting the preparation of the manuscript. As for individuals, we would like to acknowledge the participation of Professor Chua Beng Huat and Associate Professor Adam Knee as part of the committee involved in the selection of the relevant papers, and Ms Sharon Loo for her meticulous proofreading services.

Contributors

Chan, Brenda is an independent scholar with research interests in Asian popular culture, particularly Chinese-language cinema, Chinese-language popular music and Thai popular culture. She teaches in the Singapore Management University as adjunct faculty and was formerly an assistant professor at the Wee Kim Wee School of Communication and Information in Nanyang Technological University.

Chan, Karen is the Executive Director of the Asian Film Archive (AFA). Since 2006 she has overseen the growth, preservation and curation of the AFA's collection. Under her leadership, the AFA has since expanded its staff strength and had its first collection of films inscribed into the UNESCO Memory of the World Asia-Pacific register. She also teaches film literacy and preservation courses and serves on the Executive Council of the South East Asia-Pacific Audiovisual Archive Association.

Chew, Tee Pao is an Archivist at the AFA and works with the Executive Director in strategising the Archive's key preservation and outreach programmes, while promoting AFA's advocacy and preservation efforts. A filmmaker himself, his short films have been screened at local and international film festivals, including the Singapore International Film Festival and the Hong Kong Independent Short Film and Video Awards.

Chua Beng Huat is Provost Chair Professor, Faculty of Arts and Social Science, and received his PhD from York University, Canada. He is concurrently Head, Department of Sociology, Convener Cultural Studies Programmes, FASS and Research Leader, Cultural Studies in Asia Research Cluster, Asia Research Institute, National University of Singapore (NUS). Before joining NUS, he was Director of Research at the Housing and Development Board. His research areas include housing and urban studies, cultural studies in Asia, East Asian pop culture and comparative politics in Southeast Asia. He is a founding co-editor of *Inter-Asia Cultural Studies*.

Leary, Charley is Senior Lecturer in the Faculty of Cinematic Arts at Multimedia University (Malaysia). He received his PhD from the Department of Cinema Studies at New York University's Tisch School of the Arts. He previously

xiv *Contributors*

worked at the National University of Singapore's Asia Research Institute. His research interests include Chinese-language film, American independent film and the cultural heritage of Borneo.

Liew Kai Khiun is an Assistant Professor with the Wee Kim Wee School of Communication and Information at the Nanyang Technological University. The courses he has taught include Film and Television in Singapore as well as Television and Cultural Studies. His research interests covers that of the transnational circulation of popular culture flows within East and Southeast Asia and cinematic heritage in the regional contexts.

Lim, Edna is a Senior Lecturer with the Department of English Language and Literature at the NUS where she primarily teaches film for the Department's Theatre Studies Programme. Her research interests span a range of issues in contemporary Hollywood cinema, adaptation studies, Asian cinema and Singapore film. She is currently working on a monograph on Singapore cinema.

Loh Kah Seng is Assistant Professor at the Institute for East Asian Studies in Sogang University, South Korea. His research investigates the transnational and social history of Southeast Asia after the Second World War. Loh has been author or editor of six books, including *Squatters into Citizens: The 1961 Bukit Ho Swee Fire and the Making of Modern Singapore* (NUS Press & ASAA 2013); and *The University Socialist Club and the Contest for Malaya: Tangled Strands of Modernity* (co-authored, Amsterdam University Press & NUS Press 2012).

Manokara, Nidya Shanthini was conferred her PhD in Theatre Studies from NUS in 2014. Her primary research interests include evolving Asian practices and affective registers in performance. She is also a trained Bharata Natyam dancer. In her doctoral thesis, she investigated the performance of love within the practice of Bharata Natyam. She has presented conference papers inspired by the dance practice, at international conferences including *International Federation for Theatre Research* (IFTR) and *Performance Studies International* (PSi). The Singapore Tamil Theatre and Media industry are her secondary areas of research.

Roy, Anjali Gera is Professor in the Department of Humanities of Social Sciences at the Indian Institute of Technology Kharagpur, Anjali Gera. She has published several essays in literary, film and cultural studies. Her books include *Cinema of Enchantment: Perso-Arabic Genealogies of the Hindi Masala Film* (Orient Blackswan 2015), *Bhangra Moves: From Ludhiana to London and Beyond* (Ashgate 2010), *Imagining Punjab, Punjabi* and Punjabiat in the Transnational Era (Routledge 2015), *The Magic of Bollywood: At Home and Abroad* (Sage 2012), (with Chua Beng Huat) *Travels of Indian Cinema: From Bombay to LA* (Oxford University Press 2012) and (with Nandi Bhatia) *Partitioned Lives: Narratives of Home, Displacement and Resettlement* (Pearson Education 2008).

Siddique, Sophia Harvey holds a PhD from the University of Southern California School of Cinematic Arts. Her research interests include Singapore cultural studies, representations of trauma and memory in Cambodian, Indonesian and Thai cinema, and the impact of new media on Southeast Asia's moving image culture. She teaches film history, contemporary Southeast Asian Cinemas and seminars (such as, *The Cinema of Satyajit Ray*; *Cyborg Cinema*, and *Sensuous Theory*). Her most current projects include a book: *Screening Singapore: Sensuous Citizenship Formations and the National* as well as an anthology about horror: *Transnational Horror: Bodies of Excess and the Global Grotesque* (co-edited with Raphael Raphael, Palgrave Macmillan 2017). She is an Associate Professor at the Department of Film, Vassar College.

Tan, Kenneth Paul is Associate Professor and Vice Dean at the Lee Kuan Yew School of Public Policy, NUS. Building on insights from political science, public administration, cultural and media studies, and urban studies, he has written widely on various aspects of Singapore's transition from a developmental state to a global city. His publications include *Cinema and Television in Singapore: Resistance in One Dimension* (Brill 2008) and *Renaissance Singapore? Economy, Culture, and Politics* (NUS Press 2007).

Teo, Stephen is currently Associate Professor in the Wee Kim Wee School of Communication and Information, Nanyang Technological University. He is the author of *Hong Kong Cinema: The Extra Dimensions* (BFI Publishing 1997), *Wong Kar-wai* (BFI Publishing 2005), *King Hu's A Touch of Zen* (Hong Kong University Press 2007), *Director in Action: Johnnie To and the Hong Kong Action Film* (Hong Kong University Press 2007), *Chinese Martial Arts Cinema: The Wuxia Tradition* (Edinburgh University Press 2009), *The Asian Cinema Experience: Style, Space, Theory* (Routledge 2013). His next book is *Eastern Westerns: Film and Genre Outside and Inside Hollywood*, to be published by Routledge.

Zubillaga-Pow, Jun obtained his PhD in Music History from King's College London. He is a musicologist and cultural historian specialising in global Beethoven reception and Asian culture. He is the co-editor of *Queer Singapore: Illiberal Citizenship and Mediated Cultures* (Hong Kong University Press 2012) and *Singapore Soundscape: Musical Renaissance of a Global City* (National Library Board 2014). He has published in *Music and Letters*, *The Musicology Review*, *Sexualities*, and *South East Asia Research* and is currently editing two volumes on Schoenberg studies and Sinophone musics.

Introduction

Liew Kai Khiun and Stephen Teo

The small nation state of Singapore, fifty years old in 2015, has generally stimulated interest in its style of governance and economic management, but not so much in its arts and culture. This new volume of essays is an attempt at redressing the tendency to neglect more serious discussion on Singaporean arts and culture, particularly its film culture. It is a contribution to a small but growing literature on Singapore cinema. The volume is the result of a workshop held at the Asia Research Institute, National University of Singapore, in October 2011. Since then, it would be true to say that Singapore's film culture has clocked some significant new achievements in the form of more landmark productions impacting the film community in Singapore and the world. As 2015 marks Singapore's 50th year of separation from the Malaysian Federation, the Golden Jubilee was dubbed "SG50" in the mainstream media, and film was one of the key media tools mobilised to mark this commemorative year. While SG50 demonstrates the extent to which Singapore has grown and matured as a nation state, and the country rallies its filmmakers to celebrate the commemoration, it brings attention to the fact that Singapore did not have a film industry for the first twenty-five years of its existence as an independent state. Singapore's most immediate interests were focussed on nation building, the economy, industrialisation and urbanisation. It was not until the early 1990s that filmmaking came to be recognised as an industrial and artistic enterprise worthy of development in a new country. Eric Khoo's *Mee Pok Man* (1995) and the Jack Neo comedy *Money No Enough* (1998) were milestones in this emerging film culture and industry. Though the industry is very small by comparison to those in other Asian countries, it is vibrant, diverse, contrasting, and not without contradictions and paradoxes – very much like Singapore itself. As a major global city in Asia, Singapore films attract attention in the same way as its other achievements in business and governance; but perhaps more than any other sector of industry, Singapore cinema genuinely reflects the cultural state of the country. The city-state thrives on its inter-Asian mixture of Chinese, Indians, Malays and Eurasians living together on a small island. Singapore cinema reflects the strengths of this multiculturalism (and multiracialism), which needs to be more celebrated than it is, if it is to be understood in its proper context.

One of the oft-stated axioms about Singapore is that it is a clean but sterile city-state, its people pliant and conformist, and its culture heavily subjected to the censorious hand of the state. However, as demonstrated in this volume, Singapore films are far from sterile, pliant or conformist. They offer a vision of the country that is much more complex than is otherwise thought. As Singapore cinema is not a conception entirely constructed by government officials or ministers, unlike the city-state itself, the idea of a Singapore cinema must be examined more closely in connection with civil society. However, rather than suggesting that the cinema is entirely infused with criticisms of the state, this implies Singapore films are much richer in content, and filmmakers function in their capacity to critically observe the hopes and despair of modern Singaporeans. Singaporean films display a range of genres from comedy to tragedy, social melodrama to documentary, and horror to action; such a range reflects the spectrum of emotions and thoughts. Therefore, Singapore films are both expressions of its people and its artistes.

The view of a tightly controlled Singapore with its filmmakers eagerly conforming to government control and censorship is outdated and critically untenable. Singaporean filmmakers know that Singapore cinema must also function as a national cinema; and recent developments of the ties between filmmakers and the state surrounding the SG50 celebrations show the evolving sophistication of the relationship between the cinema and the state, despite the occasional lapses where the state resorts to heavy-handedness. As filmmakers adhere to benchmarks and yardsticks, and conform to mainstream values, this ultimately shows the national and social significance of Singapore films. While the artistic standards of Singapore films are occasionally recognised by international film festivals, there are patterns and principles in the filmmaking that are not often taken into account when we think of Singapore cinema. If we adhere to the view that Singapore cinema virtually sprouted from nowhere in the 1990s, it has etched a very distinctive character over the last two decades, and it has produced some memorable works in that period for a young cinema. The perception that its filmmakers (most of whom were born in the post-independence era) were hard put to express themselves freely is not borne out by the empirical evidence of the films. Singapore films are definitely worthy of scholarly review. Filmmakers inscribe critiques into their films more than we think. Such critiques need to be excavated and opened to scrutiny.

In the years since our workshop in 2011, a consensus between filmmakers and the state apparatus revolving around the politics of history, memory and remembering has developed. All these factors were behind the SG50 commemoration. If the relationship between the filmmakers and the state was characterised by the politics of public morality in the 1990s and early 2000s, the period of the Golden Jubilee celebrations was marked by the negotiations around the politics of the past. The demands of wholesomeness framed in the protection of the "cultural and familiar values" of the "conservative heartlands", particularly in the area of sexual identity and gender concerns, have not ebbed at the point of this publication. Among the more prominent cases in recent years is Ken Kwek's *Sex.Violence. FamilyValues* (2012), a work that was almost completely banned days before its first screening because complaints were made about its seemingly offensive sexual and racist content. As 2015 drew closer, portraying the past increasingly became a contentious subject on which the state was keen to take control in order to shape the narrative of the past and the present, rather than leaving it purely to the imaginations of the filmmakers.

For Singapore cinema, the prequel to the celebratory mood of SG50 came in 2013 with Anthony Chen's *Ilo Ilo*. This was a narrative about a Filipina domestic worker employed by a Singaporean family who are themselves struggling to keep up their middle-income lifestyle. The film is set in the 1997 Asian financial crisis. It bagged the Caméra d'Or award at the 2013 Cannes Film Festival, in addition to winning four out of six nominations at the Golden Horse Film Awards later that same year, including the Best Picture – a rare honour for a Singapore production. *Ilo Ilo* brought Singapore cinema to unprecedented heights in the international film circuit, and with it, a new level of recognition for local directors. Within the realm of popular culture, Jack Neo's three instalments of *Ah Boys to Men*, released between 2012 and 2015, found a commercially lucrative model of cooperation with the government in its nationalistic, yet tongue-in-cheek, vision of military service that Singaporean citizens are compelled to undertake upon reaching the draft age. With a totally new corps of young artistes who gained their limelight from the social media, the trilogy was generously supported by the military and the government, including the unprecedented use of the city's downtown area as a war zone. The box office returns for Neo's trilogy even outperformed that of Hollywood blockbusters in Singapore.

Away from the commercial cineplexes, prominent Singaporean filmmakers have also been leaving their mark albeit through commissions from the state to produce short films to front SG50 projects. This included Boo Junfeng's *Things That Make Us, Us* which launched the whole project, and Royston Tan's *Old Friends*, made for the nation-wide Singapore Memory Project (SMP) film festival. Tan had earlier made two other works in the same vein, *Old Places* (2010) and *Old Romances* (2011), commissioned by the Media Development Authority (MDA) and released on television. Emphasising the affective dimensions of nostalgia, heritage and communitarian bonds in the otherwise ordinary "heartlands" (the public housing estates in which the majority of the population live), the commissioned works of Boo and Tan fitted well with the efforts of the state to merge the "hardware" of the prosperous cityscape with the "heartware" of its citizenry. Nonetheless, in the same way that the state claims to protect public morality and "family values", it also shows the same fervour towards ensuring the dominance of its foundational myths. Apart from commissioning and funding films, the MDA also functions as the state's regulatory body overseeing censorship, and has consequently often been in dispute with artistes and filmmakers, particularly when they are perceived to question or challenge some of the foundational myths. A case in point is Tan Pin Pin's *To Singapore with Love* (2014), discussed in Loh Kah Seng and Kenneth Paul Tan's chapter in this volume. Tan's film has been effectively banned from public screening. A documentary told from the perspectives of Singaporean leftwing activists living in exile in Southern Thailand and Malaysia as well as in Europe and America, Tan's film has obviously touched a raw nerve on the politics of the past, from the government's

xx *Liew Kai Khiun and Stephen Teo*

perspective. Viewed as a "revisionist history", the restriction placed on the film serves as a sign that the authorities and local filmmakers may not share the same politico-cultural trajectory even as filmmakers (including Tan Pin Pin herself) are mobilised to celebrate SG50.

The film community's assertion of its artistic autonomy was perhaps reaffirmed over the tributes paid to film critic turned independent filmmaker Toh Hai Leong, who died on 15 January 2014 at the age of fifty-eight after battling diabetes for close to a decade. Although known as an eccentric, Toh's commitment to Singapore's film culture was undeniable, and the cinema fraternity has acknowledged this. His only film, *Zombie Dogs* (2004), portrayed the psychopathological dimensions of anomie and alienation in Singapore. Even though censors and cinema operators did not endorse it, it was critically acclaimed for its raw and unrestrained cinematic treatment of that which Toh saw as the zombified, tranquilised citizenry of Singapore.

As it unfolded, the year 2015 became highly significant; first, for the outpouring of public sorrow in the week-long funeral for former Prime Minister Lee Kuan Yew on 23 February 2015; and second, for the commemorative events marking SG50, climaxing in the largest National Day Parade on 9 August 2015 that the nation had ever seen. Banking on the public mood, the People's Action Party (PAP) government called a general election in September 2015, and was ultimately rewarded with a landslide victory of 69.9 per cent of the popular vote – a result that surprised even the ruling party who had expected further backlash from simmering public frustrations over several pressing issues such as the high cost of living, immigration and public transportation woes.

In this respect, Singapore screen culture came to mirror the developments taking place on the political front of the Golden Jubilee celebrations and Lee's passing. Beginning with his 90th birthday in 2013, a series of commemorative books and documentaries on Lee Kuan Yew were produced by both state and private initiatives, obviously foreshadowing the eventual demise of the great man. After his death, a stage musical *LKY* was virtually rushed into production, performed by local theatre, film and television actor, Adrian Pang. The production would not have been possible when Lee was alive. The iconoclastic Lee was openly disdainful of the vanity of post-colonial leaders of his generation whose images were displayed in statues and monuments. On the cinematic front, another re-enactment of the late statesman's public persona was seen in *1965*, the first attempt at a historical epic in Singapore cinema, directed by Randy Ang and Daniel Yun. The role of Lee Kuan Yew was played by theatre and television veteran Lim Kay Tong. Barely lasting a week at the local box office after it opened before National Day, *1965* was generally perceived to be a media-historical flashbulb event marking SG50, but the critics saw it as a shallow cinematic depiction of the historic year of 1965. Lim's characterisation of Lee Kuan Yew was perhaps the only memorable conceit in the film, being one more in a seemingly endless inundation of images of the elder statesman in the years just before and after his passing, and fitting into the official narrative of Singapore's development "From Third World to First", to quote the title of a book of memoirs by Lee, published in

2000. The other memorable happening emanating from the film was its premiere, held at the newly refurbished art deco-designed Capitol Theatre, a longstanding icon of Singapore architecture going back to the 1930s. The classy Capitol undoubtedly added another spark of memory to the SG50 stream of nostalgic reminiscences. However, *1965* proved to be entirely negligible; and if it remains unforgotten in the future, it would be mostly remembered as one of the media events commemorating SG50.

Meanwhile, a more autonomous initiative was emerging in the area of short films, moving away from reconstructive histories and constructed memories of the dominant narrative. Short films constitute a medium in which Singaporean filmmakers have excelled. Historically, the resurgence of a local cinema in the early 1990s was based on the making of short films that went on to win recognition in the Singapore Film Festival and international film festivals. To commemorate SG50, seven prominent local directors, all of whom made their names through short films and were associated with the evolution of Singapore films as national cinema, came together to produce *7 Letters*. The directors were Eric Khoo, Boo Junfeng, Royston Tan, K. Rajagopal, Jack Neo and Kelvin Tong, each of whom contributed a short film to the anthology. The individual films serve as reminders of the cultures, languages, places and peoples that have been lost in the five decades of nation building. The short films of *7 Letters* are flashbacks to a more colourful past, offering glimpses of the golden age of Singapore cinema (Eric Khoo); the elegantly ornate colonial houses constructed around the former Naval Base in the 1960s (Rajagopal); the rustic *kampong* communities of the 1970s (Jack Neo); multicultural musical encounters in the more dated public housing apartments of Queenstown slated for demolition (Royston Tan); and amnesic sojourns between Singapore and Malaysia (Tan Pin Pin, Boo Junfeng and Kelvin Tong). Quietly supported by the Singapore Film Commission, the film was initially given a limited run at Capitol Theatre from 24–26 July 2015. However, due to popular demand, the cinema operator Golden Village distributed the film in its commercial circuits, and it had a run of approximately one month. The seven directors of this feature demonstrated the more autonomous role of Singapore cinema by using its resources for introspection, retrospection and providing soft critiques of Singapore's history of the last fifty years. In this example, Singapore cinema is more personal and human, and not necessarily serving to project the hegemony of the state.

The filmmakers in *7 Letters* have earned their places in pioneering contemporary Singapore film, and are part of the project to build a national cinema over the twenty years since the screening of Eric Khoo's *Mee Pok Man* in 1995. Despite the ongoing tensions with state censorship and funding, the works of these filmmakers are now more likely to be institutionally archived and enshrined as part of the canon of Singapore's national cinema. The present era of the internet and cyberspace notwithstanding, these filmmakers continue to direct for the more formal and public traditional cinema attended by physical audiences that had emerged in the late nineteenth century. With a more amorphous audience arising from changing patterns of viewership as a result of new media, the evolution of

Singapore cinema in the next twenty-five to fifty years towards the republic's centennial year of independence in 2065 remains to be seen.

As part of its reopening, Capitol Theatre, in collaboration with the Asian Film Archive (AFA) and relevant government ministries, re-screened several restored films that were produced and shot on location in Singapore between the 1950s and 1970s. These included *Lion City* (1960), one of the very few Mandarin films produced in the island-state; and the Hokkien opera movie *The Taming of the Princess* (1958), an even rarer instance of a film produced and shot in a Chinese dialect in Singapore that is reputed for its Mandarinisation policies in the 1980s. These films provoked both remembrance and enchantment from the audience. Would *7 Letters* be given the same reverence five decades from now should it remain unforgotten? Or, will the more critical and provocative role of Singapore cinema be superseded by an emerging generation of teenage video loggers (vloggers) like Amos Yee, who was incarcerated for causing offence to religious sensitivities for posting a YouTube video on the occasion of Lee Kuan Yew's passing, comparing the statesman to Jesus Christ? Come what may, it is certain that over the last twenty years or so (and longer if we consider the prior Malay film industry based in Singapore before it became fully independent), Singapore cinema has functioned as a medium in providing parallel multicultural cine-scapes alongside the rapidly evolving landscape of the republic.

This volume reflects the fact that scholarly and general interest in Singapore cinema has tried to keep pace with the development of its film industry and culture. From books splashed with pictorial illustrations to academic journal articles, most publications thus far have focussed on the empirical on the one side, and critical commentary on the other. Concerned more with revealing and reconstructing the historical evolution of cinema cultures, the former is substantially laden with factual and empirical details of events, places, films, production houses and audiences from the early beginnings to the world of Malay films at the dawn of Singapore's independence (see Uhde and Uhde 2010; Chung 2009; Fu 2008; Millet 2006). In the case of the latter, film studies have been related to the broader sociological and cultural critiques of the hegemonic apparatus of state power in Singapore in suppressing the narratives of both the socially marginalised and those attempting to visualise such marginalities. Here, the discourse has been heavily framed by the sociological dimensions of Singaporean film representations as well as the ways in which they speak or do not speak to different socio-cultural segments in the republic (see Loh 2011; Gomes 2011; Tan 2010; Chan 2009; Woo 2008; Tan 2008; Harvey 2007; Khoo 2006; Tan *et al.* 2003; Chua and Yeo 2003; Ravenscroft *et al.* 2001). For the past decade, both amateur and scholarly efforts have relied on textual and filmic records as material evidence to unearth and mirror a proto-authentic history and social reality of Singapore as seen through the mechanical lens of the cinematic apparatus.

Our volume presents a renewed focus on Singapore cinema that will hopefully bolster the knowledge and information gained from the existing literature with an updated and comprehensive outlook of the ongoing development of Singapore cinema. It will offer analytical discussions of various topics in order to establish

Introduction xxiii

a serious academic perspective of Singapore cinema. The aim is to strengthen the wider discourse on Singapore cinema and support its identity as a subject deserving more serious discussion, commensurate with Singapore's global identity as a city and an Asian model of governance and growth. Singapore cinema as a field of culture remains understudied and underappreciated. To this extent, we hold that Singapore cinema is worthy of serious assessment and study on the same level as other Asian cinemas.

The volume presents chapters covering the range of major talents in Singapore filmmaking today, while taking into account the historical legacy of the film industry. It submits a newly revisionist historical perspective, first, to reaffirm the connections between present Singapore film and the Malay-language films produced in the island during the 1950s heyday, as epitomised by the more iconic films of P. Ramlee. This idea of revising cinematic history to take account of past accomplishments and their contributions to the present is one of the guiding motifs in the book, and it serves as a means of re-conceptualising the overview of Singapore cinema and challenging the average perceptions. The historical association between Malay cinema and the present Singapore cinema becomes meaningful in so far as both cinemas have elicited parallel perceptions. Malay films of the 1950s, particularly those featuring P. Ramlee, were similarly seen as light entertainment and hopelessly parochial because they were meant solely for the Malay audience. This critical stance is no longer taken seriously, and is now treated as redundant and strictly non-academic.

Many scholars have already attempted revisionist studies of Malay cinema and its greatest icon, P. Ramlee. Our volume offers our own rendition of this revisionism within the renewed outlook of Singapore cinema. It is an opportune time to do so, given the nation's attainment of its golden anniversary as an independent state, and the fact that its filmmakers are becoming more mature and more tendentious. The international award-winning success of *Ilo Ilo* has brought renewed attention to Singapore cinema, and stimulated a push towards more support for the film industry from government and educational institutions. Polytechnics and universities will have more incentives to teach Singapore cinema as well as its development in the past, present, and future.

A note about the chapters

Divided into three segments of Cine-pasts, Cine-citizenry and Cine-cityscapes, this anthology comprises eleven chapters. In the first part, four chapters angulate cinematic texts within the politics and methods of remembering and history in the republic. In Chapters 1 and 2, Stephen Teo and Edna Lim examine both the ideo-historical conditions and representations of P. Ramlee and the golden age of Malay cinema as the prequel in framing the genesis of Singapore's national cinema. Addressing the use of film in featuring Singapore's troubled political past of arbitrary detention and the exile of leftist opposition activists, Loh Kah Seng and Kenneth Paul Tan compare the different historical hauntings in both conventional historical studies and film representations in Chapter 3. In Chapter 4, film xxiv *Liew Kai Khiun and Stephen Teo*

archivists Chew Tee Pao and Karen Chan track the expansion of digital technology within the republic's film industry in facilitating the preservation of film materials critical in keeping cultural memories alive.

Stephen Teo extends his discourses on conformity and cultural materialism on P. Ramlee to Jack Neo in the second part on Cine-citizenry in Chapter 5. In Chapters 6 and 7, Sophia Siddique Harvey as well as Liew Kai Khiun and his co-author Brenda Chan delve into the sonic-visual elements of Singapore-produced independent and commercial films that are part of the republic's "sensuous vernacular" ethnolinguistic soundscapes. Nidya Shanthini Manokara explores the depiction of ethnicity in Singapore cinema in Chapter 8 by analysing the struggles of the Singaporean Indian minority to take ownership of their filmic identity so as to rise above the racial caricatures predominant in local commercially successful productions.

Moving on to the third part on Cine-cityscapes, Jun Zubillaga-Pow locates the tensions in the corporeal performativity of sexuality within the heavily scripted landscapes of Singapore in the films of Boo Junfeng, Loo Zihan, Lincoln Chia, Eric Khoo and Royston Tan in Chapter 9. In Chapters 10 and 11, both Charles Leary and Anjali Gera Roy forward new dimensions of mapping the evolution of the Singapore cinema spaces shaped by advancements in geo-mapping technologies as well as migratory patterns. Leary deploys the new media of digital satellite images in Google Earth to map the evolution of cinemas in the republic, while Roy trains her insights into the actual cinematic space of Jade Cinema to thread the demographic evolution of the Indian community in Singapore.

References

Chan, Brenda. "Gender and Class in Singaporean Film *881.*" *Jump Cut: A Review of Contemporary Media* 51 (2009). www.ejumpcut.org/archive/jc51.2009/881/text.html (accessed 20 August 2012).

Chua, Beng Huat, and Wei Wei Yeo. "Singapore Cinema: Eric Khoo and Jack Neo – Critique from the margin and the mainstream." *Inter-Asia Cultural Studies* 4, no. 1 (2003): 117–25.

Chung, Stephanie Po-Yin. "A Chinese Mogul and the Transformation of his Movie Empire: The Loke Wan Tho Family and the Cathay Organisation in Southern China and Southeast Asia (1915–2000)." *Asia Europe Journal* 7, no. 3 (2009): 463–78.

Fu, Poshek, ed. *China Forever: The Shaw Brothers and Diasporic Cinema.* Chicago: University of Illinois Press, 2008.

Gomes, Catherine. "Maid-in-Singapore: Representing and Consuming Foreign Domestic Workers in Singapore Cinema." *Asian Ethnicity* 12, no. 2 (2011): 141–54.

Harvey, Sophia Siddique. "Nomadic Trajectories: Mapping Short Film Production in Singapore." *Inter-Asia Cultural Studies* 8, no. 2 (2007): 262–76.

Khoo, Olivia. "Slang Images: On the 'Foreignness' of Contemporary Singaporean Films." *Inter-Asia Cultural Studies* 7, no. 1 (2006): 81–98.

Loh, Kah Seng. "Film and the Making and Keeping of Singapore History and Memory: A Dialogue with Martyn See and Tan Pin Pin." In *The Makers and Keepers of Singapore History*, edited by Loh Kah Seng and Liew Kai Khiun, 272–87. Singapore: Ethos Books and Singapore Heritage Society, 2011.

Millet, Raphaël. *Singapore Cinema.* Singapore: Editions Didier Millet, 2006.

Ravenscroft, Neil, Steven Chua, and Lynda Keng Neo Wee. "Going to the Movies: Cinema development in Singapore." *Leisure Studies* 20, no. 3 (2001): 215–32.

Tan, Kenneth Paul. *Film and Television in Singapore: Resistance in One Dimension.* Leiden: Brill, 2008.

Tan, Kenneth Paul. "Pontianaks, Ghosts and the Possessed: Female Monstrosity and National Anxiety in Singapore Cinema." *Asian Studies Review* 34, no. 2 (2010): 151–70.

Tan, See Kam, Michael Lee Hong Hwee, and Annette Aw. "Contemporary Singapore Filmmaking: History, Politics and Eric Khoo." *Jump Cut: A Review of Contemporary Media* 46 (2003). www.ejumpcut.org/archive/jc46.2003/12storeys/text.html (accessed 20 August 2012).

Udhe, Jan, and Yvonne Ng Udhe. *Latent Images: Film in Singapore.* Singapore: National University of Singapore Press, 2010.

Woo, Yen Yen Jocelyn. "Engaging New Audiences: Translating Research into Popular Media." *Educational Researcher* 37, no. 6 (2008): 321–9.

Part I
Cine-pasts

1 Malay cinema's legacy of cultural materialism

P. Ramlee as historical mentor

Stephen Teo

Malay cinema in Singapore

For more than twenty years in its fifty years as an independent nation, Singapore did not have a film industry. The best that one could say about this lack is that it was a transitional phase in which a dormant Singapore cinema was waiting for the right moment to rise up. This occurred in the 1990s, beginning with an outburst of short films (Harvey 2007, 266–8), and with long feature film productions by mid-decade (Eric Khoo's *Mee Pok Man*, released in 1995, is generally seen to be the milestone). Historically, Singapore had a film industry focussed on the production of Malay-language films. Singapore functioned as the Mecca of Malay film production. The first Malay talkie *Leila Majnun* was filmed in Singapore in 1933 (Uhde and Uhde 2000, 3). However, an industry did not flourish until after the Second World War. Two production studios, Cathay-Keris and Shaw Brothers' Malay Film Productions, dominated the entire feature film production of Singapore at the time. Over 200 Malay films were produced in total. Its heyday extended from the 1950s to at least the mid-1960s. This coincided with the period when Singapore's political destiny was very much connected with the independence movement in Malaya and the emerging nation state of Malaysia with which Singapore merged in 1963.

Thus, Malay cinema was an ethnic cinema that had aspirations to become a national cinema. However, Singapore separated from Malaysia in 1965 to become an independent nation, thus throwing Malay cinema's nationalist narrative askew. Though Malay films continued to be produced in Singapore until 1972, the industry was already fading by the end of the 1960s. Economic costs and union problems contributed to the eventual demise of the industry. Malay films appeared outdated when contrasted with the modern offerings of Hollywood and Hong Kong, which dominated the market for film entertainment. More importantly, it no longer seemed credible for the newly independent country with a Chinese majority population to maintain a film industry producing Malay-language films. Although Malay was recognised as the national language of Singapore, it was not much used in daily life by the majority of Singaporeans, and senior commentators still find it necessary to exhort Singaporeans to learn and speak the national language (Mahbubani 2014). Arguably, had Singapore remained in Malaysia, it

4   *Stephen Teo*

might have continued to function as the base of Malay film production. Malay films gave Singapore an identity when it was still an integral part of the Malay world. When Malay film production ceased, it lost not just an identity, but a whole industry.

The disappearance of Malay cinema meant that, for a long time, Singapore existed as a nation without a national cinema. However, a Singapore cinema did eventually emerge and it grew with a separate identity from the historical Malay cinema which had given Singapore a prior cinematic identity. With the growth of new Singapore cinema, a question arises: how should one appraise Malay cinema? Philip Cheah has said that the cinema in Singapore had "always been dogged by a struggle for national identity" (Cheah 2001, 157), by which he might have actually referred to Malay cinema as a fitting example of the quandary. Does it really belong to Singapore? Or does it more appropriately belong to the Malaysian national context? This kind of quandary over ownership has been addressed by other scholars, notably Alfian Bin Sa'at, who goes on to say that the Malay cinema's studio era remains essentially "peripheral to the consciousness of not only Singaporean audiences, but filmmakers as well" (Alfian 2012, 36). Malay cinema was an ethnic cinema whose narratives "were characterised by an increasingly communalistic Malay ethnic-cum-racial exclusivism" (Kahn 2006, 128). This communalism was at variance with the new national ethos of Singapore under the leadership of the People's Action Party (PAP), which sought to create a multi-cultural, multiracial society. Malay cinema therefore poses a historical paradox in the Singapore context.

Malay cinema has, however, bequeathed an undeniable heritage to Singapore cinema. This heritage has been recognised by historians, and perhaps by the public. Most commentators point to P. Ramlee as the single most representative figure of Malay cinema. The films of P. Ramlee constitute practically the Malay cinema's golden age, cherished by all the races of Malaysia and Singapore. They are artefacts of the Malay imagination, typified by the sublime *Ali Baba Bujang Lapok* (1961), which epitomised Malay cinema as social practice as well as leisure practice. At the same time, Malay films elucidated the aspirations of the Malays and their social conditions as well as the urge for nationalism. Joel Kahn sees "images and representations of Malay-ness" in P. Ramlee's films "that have their origin in the conservative discourse of Malay nationalism" (Kahn 2006, 128). Timothy Barnard (2006) considers Malay films as a marginalised form of "literature" in which to read the contexts of its times. He "reads" the texts of P. Ramlee's *Penarek Becha* (*The Trishaw Man*, 1956) and *Labu dan Labi* (*Labu and Labi*, 1962) as sources "for gaining a better understanding of the vibrant social and cultural currents of the 1950s and 1960s in a Malaya that faced modernization and decolonization" (Barnard 2006, 167). Syed Muhd Khairudin Aljunied (2006) views Malay films as an alternative historical and archival source providing "an illuminating insight into the social history of the Malays" (Khairudin 2006, 115). He analyses *Seniman Bujang Lapok* (*The Nitwit Movie Stars*, 1961) as a "study of Malays in Singapore during the post-war years" (Khairudin 2006, 116). For Khairudin, the film showcases the Malay community's concern for "having to

Malay cinema's legacy 5

maintain traditional Malay values whilst at the same time, keeping up with the coming of modernity" (Khairudin 2006, 117). This reaction to modernity is echoed by Malaysian critic Hassan Muthalib, who declares that P. Ramlee "extolled traditional Malay culture and values, believing that they were not at odds with living in the city with all its modernity" (Hassan 2013, 59).

Many of P. Ramlee's films are now valued for their primary social content as much as for their enduring capacity to entertain. Khoo Gaik Cheng had inferred that Malay cinema is nowhere near a radical form and practice of cinema (like Third Cinema), and that it has "a long history … as entertainment" (Khoo 2006, 98). According to Hassan Muthalib, one of the outstanding features of Malay films was "that there were absolutely no expressions of anti-colonial sentiments whether openly or subtly" (Hassan 2013, 52). Malay films are probably best seen as falling into that which Khoo has called the "grey area between unqualified assimilation and remembrance" (Khoo 2006, 99). Though Khoo does not elaborate on the grey area, I take it to mean that Malay films are highly suggestive of a communal vision of life and a faintly nostalgic style of living because Malays have assimilated themselves to modernity. A film such as *Seniman Bujang Lapok* may actually be exemplary of this grey area. The film thrives on the entertaining performances of the three principal actors – Aziz Sattar, S. Shamsuddin, and P. Ramlee – as bachelors trying to rise above their stations. The narrative, such as it is, unfolds on a very loose and relaxed structure relying mostly on situation comedy, slapstick, song interludes and melodramatic exuberance.

The structure is influenced by a kind of multi-media theatre, *bangsawan*, the traditional home of Malay performers who were later employed in the film industry. Barnard claims that *bangsawan* actors were responsible for "developing the techniques, traditions and ideas that would dominate the glory days of Malay filmmaking in Singapore in the 1950s and 1960s" (Barnard 2010, 57). It is not difficult to see that the actors in *Seniman Bujang Lapok* evoke these very same *bangsawan* practices. The actors are essentially playing themselves, as untrained actors seeking employment in the Malay Film Productions studio. They follow the director's instructions and fit into the system of film production and performance. Thus, it shows the Malays adjusting themselves to the modernity of the cinema. They do so in the only way they would know how – through their familiarity with *bangsawan* performances. Thus, *bangsawan* implicitly engenders the remembrance of Malay tradition. Meanwhile, they carry on with their ramshackle lives in the *kampong* (the Malay word for village), determined to make something of themselves as actors so that they can marry the women they court in the *kampong* and become men of substance.

The unassuming narrative structure and the threadbare production standards contribute to the movie's charm. The austerity of the production conveys the innocence of a style and standard of living among the Malays that has now expired (at least in Singapore). The film opens with touristy shots of urban Singapore in the early 1960s. The camera follows an advertising truck carrying a huge poster of a Malay film cruising around the city streets. It then goes into the *kampong* showing the three Malay protagonists of the title still ensconced in a rural setting,

6 Stephen Teo

providing a contrast with the metropolitan views of the city seen earlier, and indirectly reminding viewers that Malays are traditionally associated with the *kampong* and its rural lifestyle.

The *kampong* is a potent symbol of remembrance to Singaporeans today. Politicians constantly invoke the *kampong* "spirit" by reminding Singaporeans of a time in which a communal spirit united the various communities. There is no doubt that the film's significance for a scholar such as Khairudin lies in this remembrance conjuring a contrast of lifestyles. He analyses the protagonists' journey into the city to become movie stars as a way of earning a living, overcoming their backwardness and engaging with the "challenge of modernity that Malay society was grappling with in the 1950s and 1960s" (Khairudin 2006, 120). Hence, the protagonists are assimilated into the system (that of the film industry and, indirectly, of society), allowing them to confront the modernity impacting their lives.

This chapter will draw on P. Ramlee's films to illustrate principles of intrinsic social values and norms that are transparent in the films themselves. These values and norms guided the Malays as they assimilated into modern society and determined the pattern of behaviour that I will postulate here as cultural materialism, and which I will go on to address in relation to the films of P. Ramlee. In effect, P. Ramlee depicts a culture of materialism showing the Malays going about the business of assimilating into modern living, wherein materialistic needs are always primary concerns. In this process of presenting a culture of materialism, the remembrance of a traditional lifestyle (the *kampong* spirit) is often evoked, thus becoming a factor in the affective behaviour of cultural materialism. It may serve as a counter-response to the culture of materialism. Cultural materialism may be misinterpreted to imply a crass or corrupting form of behaviour but the keyword is on the *cultural* implying that materialism, while it may be inherently corrupting, is moderated and arbitrated by ethical values popularised within the Malay community. These values are in turn mediated by the interventions of the creative talents of P. Ramlee, such that they become part of the cinematic and cultural language of Malay cinema. The films themselves are treated as classic texts of cultural materialism.

In its application to Malay cinema, cultural materialism reflects Malay society's concern over poverty and social marginalisation. In the films of P. Ramlee, such a concern is expressed in harmony with the materialistic instincts of Singapore as a rising nation within the geopolitical context of the Cold War throughout the 1950s and 1960s. This was exactly the period in which the Malay film industry thrived in Singapore. Materialistic values were offered as the most effective way to combat communism, which threatened the security of both Malaysia and Singapore at the time. Singapore grew as a port city, a financial centre, and a place in which multinational corporations could do business and find a base for manufacturing. Malay cinema developed in tandem with this political environment that cherished materialism.

At the same time, the materialism evident in the films of P. Ramlee is in complete harmony with the commercialism of the Shaw Brothers-owned Malay Film Productions studio in Jalan Ampas (and later the Merdeka Film Studio in Kuala

Lumpur where P. Ramlee was also employed and spent his last years). Kahn notes that the Shaw Brothers ensured the films "were commercially viable" and that they "would play to local audiences" (Kahn 2006, 128–9). In the local milieu, the materialism portrayed would have been informed by cultural features and attributes of the larger community of Singapore and Malaysia. The films often followed the plotlines and conventions of storytelling found in Chinese and Indian films. Interestingly, though Chinese and Indian characters are not usually featured, whenever they appeared, such characters are usually pawnbrokers, businessmen or *towkays* in the case of the Chinese, and moneylenders (or *ceti*) in the case of the Indians. Thus, their roles illustrate nothing more than the tendency of cultural materialism prevalent in the community.

Given the pre-eminence of music in P. Ramlee's films, we might note that music plays a role as an indicator of cultural materialism. Nightclubs are a commonplace setting in P. Ramlee's films. Here, culture, in the form of song and dance, and business are interlinked; and the lifestyle that revolves around the nightclub is the very manifestation of cultural materialism. The nightclub becomes a hub for a more liberal form of cultural materialism in the Malay cinema of that period, a sign of the easy and unforced Malay assimilation into Western modernity. Sex and drink are acceptable practices of this setting, startling now in view of the rise of Islamic fundamentalism in Malaysia and the imposition of *Sharia* law. The nightclub, clearly a symbol of cultural materialism incompatible with the spirit of Islamic values, must be understood as a symptom of the Malay aspiration towards modernity. It is not the only symbol of cultural materialism, but it is perhaps a key symbol complementing other symbols that seem more natural to the Malays, for example, the *kampong*.

In Malay cinema, cultural materialism is custom-made to fit and adapt to the Malay sense of religious and cultural propriety. In this way, there is a certain sense that materialism itself is tempered by the spiritual qualities of Malay tradition and the ethical norms regulating the lifestyles of Malays. The *kampong* spirit is definitely significant to the cultural materialism of the Malays, and the *kampong* is as much a cultural setting as the nightclub. Kahn tells us that "normal *kampong* life is the very definition of Malay virtue" (Kahn 2001, 103). A ramification of this statement would suggest that the nightclub, so ubiquitous in the Malay cinema of P. Ramlee, would be the very definition of Malay vice. The Malays have been so overwhelmingly identified with the *kampong* that the nightclub assumes strength of symbolism for its commercialism and the materialism that the Malays aspire to. Hence, the nightclub is primarily noteworthy for generating a greater sense of urbane materialism and integrating the Malays into a multicultural hub of materialism in a way that a *kampong* could not. Because materialism is universal in Singapore, Malay cinema's display of cultural materialism shows the influences of Western modernity as well as other Asian (particularly Chinese) forms of cultural materialism.

It is not the purpose of this chapter to spotlight the ethnographic or social history of the Malay community and its concern over the collision of modernity with tradition. It seeks instead to denote Malay cinema's kinship with the present

8 *Stephen Teo*

Singapore cinema to which it is normally thought as having no connection at all. Younger generations of Singaporeans do not usually make the link between present Singapore films and the past cinema of the Malay film industry. Yet we may detect a link between the past and the present through the films of P. Ramlee and the present-day films of Jack Neo, for example. This is a proposition that I will explore in another chapter. Neo can be regarded as the modern P. Ramlee. In fact, we can see P. Ramlee as the cultural mentor of Neo. The link between them transcends the historical paradox that is at the heart of Malay cinema's relationship to Singapore. Alfian Bin Sa'at has asserted that there are "traces" of the Malay cinematic heritage that can be found in contemporary Singapore cinema (Alfian 2012, 36). I concur with him although what Alfian considers "traces" differs quite radically from my interpretation of the same. Alfian refers to the connection between Singapore and the Malayan hinterland as an abiding vestige of the Malay cinema and points to a sense of nostalgia in which Singapore, as the metropolitan centre, looks keenly at the Malay hinterland as "a repository of certain conservative cultural and moral values in contradistinction to the chaotic liberal relativism of the city" (Alfian 2012, 37). This affective urge to share cultural and moral values is indeed part of the legacy of the Malay cinema but I will frame this legacy through the lens of more economic and materialistic values. Indeed, I assert that it is cultural materialism that provides an ideological connection binding the historical Malay cinema and the present Singapore cinema. A cultural determination of economic materialism offers a bonding between the Malay cinema of the studio era (the "golden age") and the contemporary Singapore cinema. This can then be seen as the cinematic language of Singapore.

Cultural materialism as dominant tone in P. Ramlee's films

Cultural materialism can be defined as a process in which culture becomes ineradicably entwined with capitalist economics both as a theme and a material means of production. The production of culture necessitates economic procedures and exchanges, and economics itself becomes a conscious, active part of the Singaporean psyche. Hence, a cultural form of materialism or economic determinism is part of the ordinary lives of Singaporeans. For instance, a consumerist culture dominated by the practice of shopping is the classic manifestation of cultural materialism; such a culture has been demonstrated by Chua Beng Huat in his book, *Life is Not Complete without Shopping: Consumption Culture in Singapore* (2003). Another manifestation is the *kiasu* culture. *Kiasu* is a local Chinese Hokkien dialect term indicating a fear of losing out and taking every advantage as soon as possible to ensure that one wins or gets the material object sought after. *Kiasu* is therefore a very typical form of cultural materialism in Singapore.

In Malay cinema, there are specific qualities of cultural materialism in the films of P. Ramlee that I will delineate below. I have already hinted at some of these qualities above. I have noted, for example, that nightclubs are a symbol of cultural materialism in Malay cinema. The emphasis on cultural materialism is a response to the ways through which we may assess the legacy of Malay cinema in its relationship to Singapore. It is my opinion that cultural materialism in Malay cinema is attuned to the social and aesthetic purposes of cinematic expression, more so than other concepts which obviously can apply equally to an assessment of Malay cinema. These other values can include cultural nationalism or spiritualism. For example, against the nightclub, the mosque is, conversely, a symbol of religious spiritualism. It is also seen in the films of P. Ramlee, but the nightclub and its sense of cultural materialism is more resonant to our perception of the way Malay cinema has impacted the development of the cinema in Singapore.

The purpose of this chapter is to evoke the essence of cultural materialism in P. Ramlee's films in more detail. Class is one facet – and it is critiqued in *Antara Dua Darjat* (*Between Two Classes*, 1959), which tells the story of a poor pianist who falls in love with a woman of Malay royalty (her father is against the relationship and plots to separate them by lying to the pianist that she has died). But money in its physical form is probably a key indicator, more so than social class. Money is constantly exchanged in these films and it obsesses their characters as much as the characters of Jack Neo's films in contemporary Singapore cinema. Yet it is important to define the cultural essence of this exchange in order to denote how cultural materialism performs in Malay cinema. In *Bujang Lapok* (1957), P. Ramlee's character, named Ramlee, dates a young woman who cheats him of some money. Later, Ramlee encounters the same woman with another man. He follows her back to her *kampong* and sees her giving money to her children and destitute mother. The mother rejects the money. The daughter gives her a choice, saying, "If we are good and honest, people will step on us; but if we cheat and lie, we are regarded as honourable. Which would you rather be?" "I don't like either option," the mother replies. Watching all this at a distance, Ramlee sighs philosophically, "Such is the theatre of life ("*Inilah sandiwara dunia*"). He turns and walks away. Here, cultural materialism is linked to the concept of *sandiwara dunia* (or the world as stage) implying that it is part of the theatre of life. Money determines this performance of cultural materialism on the world stage.

In another scene, the character of Aziz (Aziz Sattar) gives money to Sapiah, a pitiful young girl to whom he is attracted. The girl immediately recoils from the sight of the cash notes and retreats to her room sobbing. Though Aziz's intentions were honourable, his money triggered a sense of shame and horror in Sapiah. The money reminded Sapiah of her father's action in receiving money from a man so that he could sleep with her. Money and the forms of exchange portrayed in these scenes point to a spiritual backlash of cultural materialism. Perhaps more outstanding is the emphasis on money as a physical sign. When Aziz gives Sapiah money out of pity for her, there is a medium close-up of his hand clutching several bank notes. Money is therefore given prominence as the essential denominator of the cultural materialism that is a theme in this and other films of P. Ramlee.

The cultural materialism that revolves around money encompasses both the good and the bad in a moral sense, exerting an influence even on the young. The film features a precocious brat who is constantly asking for money from everybody he meets, and getting it because he is a conduit for information. The boy bribes his own sister and mother, when either one or the other needs information

10 *Stephen Teo*

or when the sister needs to keep the mother ignorant of her love affair with one of the bachelors in the *kampong* (the character played by S. Shamsuddin). Depending on where one stands, one can either be put off by the boy's materialism or actually praise the boy's industriousness and money consciousness at an early age. In Malay cinema, it is probably a very rare thing to see a boy depicted in such a way, and P. Ramlee is interested in showing that the Malays too can be money-minded and materialistic, thereby breaking the stereotype of the Malay as lazy, unindustrious and non-materialistic. Rightfully then, one might say that the cultural materialism of *Bujang Lapok* is its most outstanding quality.

The films of P. Ramlee can be broadly divided into three groups. The first group, by far the most profuse and most redolent of the principle of cultural materialism, comprises films set in the modern-day period contemporaneous to the filmmakers' lives and which are actually portrayed or reflected in the films. This group of films includes *Penarek Becha* (1956), *Bujang Lapok* (1957), *Antara Dua Darjat* (1959), *Seniman Bujang Lapok* (1961), *Labu dan Labi* (1962), *Ibu Mertuaku* (*My Mother-in-Law*, 1962) and *Madu Tiga* (*Rivals Three*, 1964); and from his Malaysian period (P. Ramlee left Singapore in 1964 to work in Kuala Lumpur's Merdeka Film Studio), *Masam Masam Manis* (*Sourness and Sweetness*, 1965), *Do Re Mi* (1966), *Anak Bapak* (*Papa's Pet*, 1968) and *Putus Sudah Kasih Sayang* (*Love is Lost*, 1971).

The second group comprises period pieces such as *Hang Tuah* (*The Legend of Hang Tuah*, 1956), *Semerah Padi* (*The Village of Semerah Padi*, 1956), *Sumpah Orang Minyak* (*The Curse of the Oily Man*, 1958), *Musang Berjanggut* (*The Bearded Fox*, 1959), *Nujum Pak Belalang* (*The Fortune Teller*, 1959), *Pendekar Bujang Lapok* (*The Three Bachelor Warriors*, 1959), *Ali Baba Bujang Lapok* (1961) and *Kanchan Tirana* (1969). These films are historical epics, period action films or moralistic fables that seem rather abstract from the concept of cultural materialism. After all, cultural materialism relies on being nurtured by the realistic conditions of life (the need to make ends meet for most of the protagonists in the first group) and the impact of Western modernity on traditional cultural values.

A third group of films covers works such as *Tiga Abdul* (*The Three Abduls*, 1964) and *Ahmad Albab* (1968) which are set in imaginary nowhere lands with an abstract link to the modern world, and which also function as moralistic fables. They are satirical and vastly entertaining, and evoke the first group inasmuch as they are parodies of modernity and the obsession with materialism (a work such as *Ali Baba Bujang Lapok* which I categorise in the second group also contains a parody of modernity, showing its characters all dressed up in period costumes using modern implements like bicycles and Vespa scooters). All the films listed here are directed by P. Ramlee, and most, if not all, are also based on screenplays that he has written or co-written.

The first group of realist contemporary films is undoubtedly most relevant to the sense of cultural materialism and all its implications, but the satirical third group alludes to the first group and can therefore be discussed in the same scope. At the same time, the films within the first group may be further varied between those films where a younger P. Ramlee played a young bachelor struggling to

Malay cinema's legacy 11

make a living (*Penarek Becha, Bujang Lapok, Seniman Bujang Lapok, Labu dan Labi*), and those films in which a more mature P. Ramlee has come up in life and settled into the comfortable routine of the upper middle class (*Madu Tiga, Tiga Abdul*). Cultural materialism is even more a fixture of this latter sub-group. For example, in *Madu Tiga*, we see clear signs of a comfortable cultural materialism in the opening sections. Jamil, played by P. Ramlee, is a married business executive. He marries two other women (as is allowed under Islamic law), and has to sort out and manage the petty jealousies of all his wives when they gradually discover they are all married to the same man.

Not long after the film opens, we see the first wife playing mahjong with other affluent housewives on the veranda of her luxurious house. Jamil returns home by car, goes straight to the bedroom to slip out of his Western suit and put on traditional Malay garb, telling his wife that he is attending a friend's wedding. She, however, suspects he is going out to meet another woman. In fact, he is getting dressed for his own wedding, keeping this a secret from his first wife. The wife interrupts her mahjong to find buttons for her husband's traditional shirt. Here, the mahjong and the traditional Malay outfit take on connotations of the cultural materialism that informs the comfortable lifestyle of the upper Malay class.

The Malay costume is a meaningful sign of ethnic and religious identity that assumes significance of cultural materialism, as it is deployed by Jamil. In the context of the plot, the costume validates his marriage to a second wife and his urge to satisfy extensive conjugal desires. In an earlier film (in which he starred but did not direct), *Anak-ku Sazali* (*My Son Sazali*, 1956, directed by Phani Majumdar), we see P. Ramlee's character Hassan, a songwriter and musician, regularly slip in and out of his traditional Malay costume into a Western tuxedo as he goes to work in a nightclub. Here, the Western suit assumes the mantle of the modernity of cultural materialism, and traditional Malay wear becomes a mark of traditional identity. However, this slipping in and out of different costumes aptly illustrates Khairudin's comment that P. Ramlee "intended to highlight [the] need to find a balance between the maintenance of Malay cultural values and the onslaught of modernity" in his films (Khairudin 2006, 120). P. Ramlee was virtually the sole purveyor of a kind of liberalism laced with traditionalism in Malay cinema. He was able to mould a character-personality that was true to his Malay identity, yet simultaneously roguish, carefree, fun-loving, and had very liberal attitudes towards sex and alcohol. Such a persona is all the more startling today when contrasted against the much stricter enforcement of Islamic law governing social behaviour in present-day Malaysia.

Even more startling is the nightclub as a symbol of the kind of liberalism seen in P. Ramlee's films, as we have noted earlier. While P. Ramlee appears besotted with the lifestyle of the nightclub, it is not without cultural and moral implications. In fact, the nightclub lifestyle brings tragic repercussions, as seen in *Ibu Mertuaku* (*My Mother-in-Law*, 1962) and *Putus Sudah Kasih Sayang* (*Love is Lost*, 1971). In the latter film, a nightclub singer-cum-bar hostess Lisdah (Latifah Omar) is the object of affection for P. Ramlee's character (Rostam, a bank manager) and his son, Rosman. This leads, predictably, to a tragic conclusion

12 *Stephen Teo*

that can be attributed to the context of the nightclub lifestyle. *Ibu Mertuaku* is the more definitive work. Here, P. Ramlee plays a popular singer-saxophonist named Kassim Selamat whose programme on Radio Singapore attracts a following of female listeners. He receives a phone call from a young upper class female fan, Sabariah (played by Sarimah). She suggests a meeting in a nightclub. Kassim duly turns up and waits for her. In the background, we see other Malays dancing to the beat of modern band music from that era: the men wearing Western suits and ties, the women clad in *sarong kebaya*. The scene may be unremarkable but from the standpoint of cultural materialism: it shows the Malay middle and professional class at play, partaking of a lifestyle that is not often associated with the more conservative and religious Malays. This social dimension is not without significance. The nightclub therefore takes on the social dimension of a cultural sign, showing the Malays in conformity with all the other races as far as economic aspiration and the capitalistic lifestyle are concerned.

As the plot of *Ibu Mertuaku* unfolds, it becomes clear that the nightclub life, redolent of modern living and aspired to by Malays as much as by other races, is not without its tragic element. The film portrays Kassim Selamat as a tragic figure who, in the course of the film, becomes blind as a result of grief (he marries Sabariah but his mother-in-law, who opposes the union, plots to separate them by deceiving Kassim into believing that Sabariah has died). Though he meets Sabariah again and becomes cured of his blindness, he deliberately chooses to blind himself once more in order to remain loyal to another woman with whom he had fallen in love during his blindness. The film shows Kassim Selamat detrimentally affected by cultural materialism. Here indeed is a wholesale critique of materialism in Malay cinema that is perhaps rare inasmuch as the cultural form of materialism appears as a tolerant pattern of behaviour. Even though Kassim has chosen love at the end, it comes at a certain cost – in this case, self-inflicted blindness. It indicates that Kassim has turned away from the cultural materialist world and has become blind to it.

While this constitutes a critical response to materialism, it could also be argued that it is Kassim's way of accommodating himself to the world ruled by cultural materialism. Earlier, the blind Kassim had shown that he could quite quickly find a foothold in the cultural milieu, rejuvenating his musical career as a blind saxophonist and propelling himself to newfound fame. In returning to blindness, he may only be reclaiming his other status as a famous blind musician. Cultural materialism is thus not necessarily vanquished by his self-sacrifice of blindness. There is more than a touch of self-interest in his decision to return to blindness. In *Ibu Mertuaku*, we see economic materialism as a causal factor of tragedy. Cultural materialism, which may be seen as corruptive and immoral, therefore has its tragic moments.

P. Ramlee's Malaysian period and cultural materialism

It might be argued that P. Ramlee never really belonged to Singapore cinema because of his Malay identity. The sense of Malay nationalism with its implicit cultural nationalism goes against the grain of Singaporean multiculturalism, or is

Malay cinema's legacy 13

rendered somewhat ambiguous in the current development of Singapore cinema where very few Malay feature films are produced. P. Ramlee may have retained a certain iconic status in Singapore's national culture, but it obviously needs constant nurturing and exposure. Meanwhile in Malaysia, P. Ramlee's Malaysian identity is readily acknowledged by the public and the government. He has been appropriated as a national cultural treasure, and his Malay nationalism would no doubt sit well as an integral part of the Malaysian nation. Be that as it may, P. Ramlee remains attached to the themes and concerns of his Singapore phase in his career, and here it is true to say that the concept of cultural materialism, as opposed to cultural nationalism, is indeed crucial to the perception of his status as a cultural icon in both Singapore and Malaysia. On the one hand, it would be awkward to use cultural nationalism to assess P. Ramlee's status in the Singapore context. On the other hand, cultural materialism can actually engage the whole of P. Ramlee's cinema as it relates to both Singapore and Malaysia.

The Malaysian appropriation of P. Ramlee as a national cultural hero does not mean, therefore, a complete break from the Singapore-based era of Malay films. An example of the thematic affinity between the Singaporean and Malaysian periods of P. Ramlee's career is *Anak Bapak* (*Papa's Pet*) a film made for Malaysia's Merdeka Film Studio, released in 1968 (the year of release shows that the film does not belong to P. Ramlee's Singapore period). The film shares the cultural materialist themes expressed in *Ibu Mertuaku*. Both films are remarkably close in tone and material, though *Anak Bapak* is a straightforward farce and is therefore much lighter in mood without the serious overtones of *Ibu Mertuaku*. This makes it substantially different from the earlier film which unfolds with dramatic shifts of mood. Nevertheless, the family-centric premise transforms the two films into companion pieces. One film focussed on the male protagonist's relationship with the matriarch (*Ibu Mertuaku*) and the other on the relationship with the patriarch (*Anak Bapak*). They both share the same anxieties and trepidations of cultural materialism.

The plot of *Anak Bapak* revolves around the easygoing and philandering character of Harun (P. Ramlee) who runs a rubber plantation and lives in a modern country house in Kuala Lumpur, with its downstairs converted into an office. Harun incurs large debts to maintain his easygoing lifestyle, and resorts to getting money on false pretences from his rich father, who lives in Johore, in the South of the country. The father visits his son who now must borrow the wife of his employee Salleh to keep up the pretence that he is married, the excuse that he gave his father on asking him for money. The dominance of money and the role it plays in the film in keeping the characters happy is a transparent theme.

Thus, the film continues the cultural materialist concerns relating to capitalist modernity as the Malay community confronts it. Here, there is basically no difference between the Malay community of Malaysia and Singapore. Both aspire to the same basic kind of lifestyles. Like *Ibu Mertuaku*, *Anak Bapak* shows a very liberal attitude of the Malays towards modernity as expressed through the depictions of nightclubbing, and the singing, dancing and drinking that go with it. In this way, the nightclub in *Anak Bapak* exerts the same kind of symbolic significance of

14 *Stephen Teo*

cultural materialist aspirations that are portrayed in *Ibu Mertuaku*. At the same time, the film shows Harun leading an executive managerial regime which is the economic basis of the cultural materialist lifestyle. Socially, we also see a scene of the family (father and son with their pretended and intended spouses) eating with spoon and fork instead of the traditional method of eating with one's hands. This is a key indicator of modernity.

Harun is an unabashed womaniser. He has an affair with the nightclub singer Normah, who consistently has to demand money from him because his cheques always bounce. Normah is thus portrayed as an out-and-out money-grabber, while Harun rather shamelessly indulges in the cultural nightlife (this naturally provides the background for several numbers by P. Ramlee in the film). He borrows money from an Indian moneylender so that he can partake of the nightlife that is a normal part of his existence. As he carries on the masquerade of marriage, he sets out to seduce his father's nurse, Halimah. Meanwhile, his father Datuk Mahfis (played by A. R. Tompel) is as liberal as his son: the title *Anak Bapak* can be translated to mean "Like Father, Like Son". Mahfis too has an eye for the ladies, and he tries to seduce Normah (his son's ex-lover), proposing that she sleep with him. When Normah asks Mahfis what his son would think, he replies that Harun is very "social and understanding" (using these very same words in English). The figure of the father in this Malaysian production is obviously a departure from the more conservative and reactionary mother figure in *Ibu Mertuaku*, and in this sense, *Anak Bapak* is obviously an advance on the earlier film.

However, in *Ahmad Albab*, released in the same year as *Anak Bapak*, the father figure has become an arrogant, materialistic patriarch with three young daughters whom he wants to marry off to sons of rich families. This is in keeping with his belief that wealth will ensure happiness and prosperity. The film carries on the cultural materialism in *Anak Bapak* and *Ibu Mertuaku* to a more fabulistic level. It plays like a Malay fairytale reworking of King Lear, with Lear transformed into the arrogant Malay patriarch Mashood (played by A. R. Tompel) who wants his three daughters to marry into wealth and power. This premise in itself is the cultural materialist underpinning of the whole story.

Mashood represents the Malay aspiration for wealth and power. His eldest daughter Mastura (Saloma) believes that it is God who will determine happiness and refuses to comply with her father's wish. In retaliation for her disobedience, Mashood marries her off to a poor goat-herder Syawal (P. Ramlee). One day while searching for a lost goat, Syawal goes into a cave and finds a hoard of treasure. A genie appears and tells him that the treasure belongs to one Ahmad Albab. Mastura gives birth to a son but the baby is afflicted with a disability – he is unable to stop crying. The baby is brought to Mashood in the hope that he may be able to stop the crying. He does this by holding the baby to a door and knocking on it, which immediately stops the crying. Upon this, Mashood names the baby Ahmad Albab ("albab" is the Arabic word for door). Syawal then realises that it is his son who now owns the treasure.

Thus, Mastura and Syawal become rich, but in keeping with the fable-like morality of the tale, they remind the patriarch Mashood that wealth does not necessarily bring happiness (as demonstrated by his two sons-in-law who resort to crime to maintain their lifestyles) and that all wealth comes from God. The nightclub in *Ahmad Albab* remains a symbol of cultural materialism as it does in the two other films. It opens with a scene of an imaginary Arabic Nights setting. A rider gets off a camel and greets a street peddler, asking him what the Arabic sign opposite stands for. "That's a nightclub," replies the peddler. Cut to the interior of the nightclub showing a woman dancing on stage. The camera pans and follows a waitress to a table serving drinks to Mashood and two friends. They are discussing how their offspring should get married, with Mashood exclaiming that he has three daughters to marry off.

This is the springboard into the fable-like narrative of the rest of the film. P. Ramlee is obviously having fun playing his character, speaking with an Arabic accent (showing off his prodigious talent in mimicking the accents of various races in the Singapore–Malaysia community). This movie from his Malaysian period reaffirms the Western liberalism of his materialistic worldview from the Singaporean period, with a nod to Islamic didacticism. The climactic moment of the film is when Syawal confronts his father-in-law in the finale. Mashood now realises the folly of his materialistic beliefs and recognises Syawal as the exemplary model of a man who is rich yet humble and god-fearing. Syawal exposes his wealth by stripping off his rustic clothes to show that he is actually dressed in a neat Western-style suit, reminding one again of the changes of clothing in *Madu Tiga*, alluded to earlier.

The Malaysian films of P. Ramlee obviously mirror the Singaporean films in terms of content and theme as well as style and formulae. The standard of Malaysian films was one of even greater austerity than when he was working in the Shaw studio in Singapore, and the general feeling is that the Malaysian films are not as well made as the Singapore ones. The sense of cultural materialism with its theme of miserliness, thrift and hardship could in fact have resulted from the austere production standards of both studios, which came under the management of the Shaw Brothers. The Malay Film Productions studio in Singapore was also famous for its conditions of hardship, which led to a strike by employees in 1957 (Barnard 2008, 162–5). In this way, continuity seems assured; P. Ramlee appears to repeat the same materialistic conditions of shortage and simplicity, trying to overcome perpetual poverty in the Malay community in the business of making films and in society at large.

Do Re Mi (1966) is representative of the way in which P. Ramlee recycled his Singaporean period by carrying over the cultural materialism of his *Bujang Lapok* series into the Malaysian phase of his career. P. Ramlee plays Do, an indebted, unemployed husband who later leaves his wife in the *kampong* in search of gainful employment. He meets up with two other roustabouts, Re and Mi (played respectively by A. R. Tompel and Ibrahim Din), and the trio end up as itinerant snake oil peddlers, chased out of a *kampong* by disgruntled buyers. The cultural materialistic tone of *Do Re Mi* is immediately struck in the first episode of the film devoted to the life of Do. In the very first scene, his wife Mina catches him playing checkers instead of looking for a job. She chases him back to the house where they

16 Stephen Teo

are then hassled by three creditors (a Malay landlord, an Indian *ceti* and a Chinese trader). They hatch a desperate scheme to trick their respective parents out of money to pay the creditors. Mina tells her mother that Do is dead, while Do goes to his father and tells him that Mina has died. They manage to get some money, but the parents turn up at their *kampong* house to pay their last respects, resulting in Do and Mina taking turns pretending to be dead. To add to their predicament, the creditors choose this very moment to turn up to ask for their money. Typically, the respective parents are portrayed as selfish, miserly and utterly hypocritical.

Do Re Mi reprises the formula of cultural materialism, showing that it has hardly changed from the *Bujang Lapok* days (though P. Ramlee's character in *Do Re Mi* is actually married, he resorts to virtual bachelorhood in order to find a job, as if being a bachelor is more conducive to the demands of cultural materialism). As an entertainment formula, it proved so successful that P. Ramlee could carry it over to his Malaysian period without a need for any modification, and it was so successful in *Do Re Mi* that it spawned two other sequels, *Nasib Do Re Mi* (*The Fate of Do Re Mi*, 1966) and *Laksamana Do Re Mi* (*Admirals Do Re Mi*, 1972), which was P. Ramlee's last film. In a sense, cultural materialism shows Malay cinema being fundamentally true to its social roots and representations when the industry shifted away from Singapore.

Cultural materialism takes into account the patterns of social behaviour and the cultural and economic needs of the community. The Malaysian period of P. Ramlee is therefore just as culturally materialistic as the Singapore period, given the similarities of the two societies. Cultural materialism works as a unitary factor, and the talents of P. Ramlee keep the theme humming along in entertaining fashion. The theme provides his characters with the same cinematic identity. There is hardly any sense for P. Ramlee to act or behave any differently in his Malaysian films than his characters in the Singaporean films. Yet, there is probably a lot more scholarship to be done in exploring the ways in which the two phases of P. Ramlee's career (Singapore and Malaysia) actually do differ from each other, aesthetically and socially. This will be a subject for others to conduct.

Even if we do recognise P. Ramlee as a Singapore icon, it is fitting to consider the different circumstances of Singapore as a workplace for Malay artists. It was Singapore's place to be the Mecca of Malay filmmaking, and the cultural materialism that grew out of the golden age was tempered by moral conservative forces and informed by the worldwide struggle against communism. In this background, the films of P. Ramlee were valuable for being able to demonstrate the Malay spirit of liberalism resonating with the capitalistic–materialistic instincts of Singaporeans.

The liberalism of P. Ramlee's cinema is relative to the morally conservative norms implicit in the Malay community. The question to ask is whether such liberalism could have exerted itself without the conditions of the cultural materialism of Singapore and its attendant social circumstances. P. Ramlee died in 1973 in Malaysia, and it is probably true to say that his spirit of liberalism died with him. Today, Malay cinema no longer exists in Singapore; and it is out of the scope of this chapter to examine how Malaysia has appropriated the entire Malay cinema

Malay cinema's legacy 17

and made it more relevant to itself as a nation. However, even Malay films in Malaysia probably could not have continued in the same vein of liberalism found in the cinema of P. Ramlee. In the Singapore context, P. Ramlee remains something of an enigma. A genuinely talented artist, he pointed the way to a form of cinema that I deem to be cultural materialist, probing into the exigencies of economic survival, and trying to maintain a civilised decorum of humanism and spiritualism as an artist and performer.

Conclusion

This chapter has sought to demonstrate the ways in which cultural materialism was exhibited in the films of P. Ramlee, the most memorable of Malay cinema's creative talents. It has sought to be as comprehensive as possible in detailing aspects of cultural materialism in as many of P. Ramlee's prolific output of films from both his Singaporean and Malaysian periods. Cultural materialism is presented here as a theory more pertinent to Malay cinema's historical development in Singapore, and to suggest a continuity between it and the present Singapore cinema. It compels a firmer understanding of the history of the cinema in Singapore, which otherwise may only be perceived to have begun in the 1990s. A scholar approaching Singapore cinema might focus only on the modern period and the new generation of directors who emerged in this period, including such talents as Eric Khoo, Royston Tan, Kelvin Tong and Jack Neo. While it is only fair and right to look further back to the historical era of the film industry that developed in the 1950s, if not earlier, a problem may arise in how to connect the past and the present.

In historical terms, Malay cinema should be regarded as an integral part of the Singapore cinematic narrative, but it is perceived either to be too local, too ethnocentric, or even too nationalistic in the wrong context (the context of Singapore when its political destiny was still interlinked with the Malaysian nation). Given all these limitations, how does one build a case of Malay cinema as a narrative that roughly shows a diachronic continuity between P. Ramlee and a director such as Jack Neo, as the closest modern equivalent to the former? Neo represents new Singapore cinema whose identity is very much related to the late industrialist development of Singapore in the postmodern epoch. Neo has largely demonstrated his talents to become the most typical showman (and spokesperson) of cultural materialism in postmodern Singapore cinema. He conveys the industrial consolidation and strength of the modern Singapore film industry, small-scale though it still is, but he owes it all to P. Ramlee.

It may be a huge jump to link P. Ramlee with Jack Neo, but the jump is a circumstance of the development of the film industry in Singapore which has seen a break from Malay cinema's past to the revival of the industry in the 1990s. From the moment of the huge commercial success of *Money No Enough* in 1997 onwards, Jack Neo's brand of cinema has formed a model for a cinema of national and cultural identity that some scholars have identified as Singaporean. According to Philip Cheah, Singaporeans did not feel they had a film capable of articulating

18 *Stephen Teo*

"their cultural identity" until *Money No Enough* (Cheah 2001, 157–8). This kind of identity is subjected to the multicultural and multiracial national ethos of Singapore, in turn suggesting a kind of inherent ambivalence about that which really constitutes a Singaporean national identity. On the other hand, a concept such as cultural materialism may actually indicate a sense that any identity can be transcended by natural urges for materialistic gain. Cultural identity will become a rather more nebulous form of identity subjected to the trappings of a materialistic identification of culture. Materialism itself is considered a culture, as it seeps into the community and shapes its way of thinking.

The definition of the essence of cultural identity in Neo's films and their import to the concept of cultural materialism is an exercise that I will attempt in another chapter (see Chapter 5 of this volume). Cultural materialism will then become a theoretical process allowing us to deduce a sense of connection between Neo and P. Ramlee. It is P. Ramlee who has guided the process of cultural materialism in this chapter. P. Ramlee's films allow us to recognise his invaluable contributions as a multi-talented artist, but above all, he is the harbinger of the cinematic trend of cultural materialism in Singapore cinema.

References

Alfian, Bin Sa'at. "Hinterland, Heartland, Home: Affective Topography in Singapore Films." In *Southeast Asian Independent Cinema*, edited by Tilman Baumgärtel, 33–50. Hong Kong: Hong Kong University Press, 2012.

Barnard, Timothy P. "Film, Literature and Context in Southeast Asia: P. Ramlee, Malay Cinema, and History." In *Southeast Asian Studies: Debates and New Directions*, edited by Cynthia Chou and Vincent Houben, 162–79. Singapore and Leiden: Institute for Southeast Asian Studies and International Institute for Asian Studies, 2006.

Barnard, Timothy P. "The Shaw Brothers' Malay Films." In *China Forever: The Shaw Brothers and Diasporic Cinema*, edited by Poshek Fu, 154–73. Urbana and Chicago, IL: University of Illinois Press, 2008.

Barnard, Timothy P. "*Filem Melayu*: Nationalism, Modernity and Film in a Pre-World War Two Malay Magazine." *Journal of Southeast Asian Studies* 41, no. 1 (2010): 47–70.

Cheah, Philip. "Film in Singapore from 1972: The Reconstruction of a Film Industry." In *Film in Southeast Asia: Views from the Region. Essays on Film in Ten South East Asia-Pacific Countries*, edited by David Hanan, 146–59. Hanoi: South East Asia-Pacific Audio Visual Archive Association (SEAPAVAA) in association with the Vietnam Film Institute and the National Screen and Sound Archive of Australia, 2001.

Chua, Beng Huat. *Life is Not Complete without Shopping: Consumption Culture in Singapore*. Singapore: NUS Press, 2003.

Harvey, Sophia Siddique. "Nomadic Trajectories: Mapping Short Film Production in Singapore." *Inter-Asia Cultural Studies* 8, no. 2 (2007): 262–76.

Hassan Abd Muthalib. *Malaysian Cinema in a Bottle: A Century (and a Bit More) of Wayang*. Petaling Jaya: Orange Dove, 2013.

Kahn, Joel S. *Modernity and Exclusion*. London: Sage Publications, 2001.

Kahn, Joel S. *Other Malays: Nationalism and Cosmopolitanism in the Modern Malay World*. Singapore: Singapore University Press, 2006.

Khairudin Aljunied, Syed Muhd. "Films as a Source of Social History: P. Ramlee's 'Seniman Bujang Lapok' and Malays in Singapore (1950s–1960s)." In *New Perspectives and Sources on the History of Singapore: A Multi-Disciplinary Approach*, edited by Derek Heng Thiam Soon, 115–24. Singapore: National Library Board, 2006.

Khoo, Gaik Cheng. *Reclaiming Adat: Contemporary Malaysian Film and Literature.* Vancouver and Toronto: UBC Press, 2006.

Mahbubani, Kishore. "Big Idea No. 5: Speak the National Language." *The Straits Times*, 14 June 2014. www.straitstimes.com/news/opinion/invitation/story/big-idea-no-5-speak-the-national-language-20140614 (accessed 28 June 2015).

Uhde, Jan, and Yvonne Ng Uhde. *Latent Images: Film in Singapore.* Singapore: Oxford University Press, 2000.

2 Singapore cinema

Connecting the golden age and the revival

Edna Lim

The history of Singapore's film industry is a fractured one, divided neatly into two distinct periods. The first emerged in the 1950s and matured in the 1960s. Falling under the decade before Singapore's independence, this period has also been considered the golden age of local cinema due to the proliferation of Malay-language films produced by the two dominant studios in Singapore at the time, Shaw Brothers' Malay Film Productions and Cathay-Keris. The second period, from the 1990s to the present, is perceived as a revival or rebirth of film productions after a lull between the 1960s and 1980s, and is best characterised as "post-national" cinema. In contrast to the Malay-language films of the golden age, these films are primarily made in English, Singlish or Mandarin and other Chinese dialects, often with a smattering of other languages to reflect Singapore's multilingual constituency.

Interestingly, the decline in film production and its ensuing period of silence coincided with intense state-driven efforts at nation building and urban development following Singapore's independence in 1965. As rural communities in *kampongs* gave way to skyscrapers and public housing apartment blocks in satellite towns from the late 1960s onwards, these changes in the Singapore landscape have also become visible markers of the second period in the country's film industry. While locally produced films since the 1990s have been unquestionably identified and discussed as Singapore films, Singapore cinema or Singapore national cinema, those from the golden age are often studied as films made in Singapore rather than Singapore films. The decline and eventual disappearance of film production between these two periods has separated and distanced them. They are often discussed as distinct eras, with little or no connection between them. This chapter addresses the discursive fracturing of the two periods by examining the ways in which films from both periods function within the body of work known as Singapore films.

Taking my cue from Richard Bauman (1989, 71), who stated that "all performance involves a consciousness of doubleness, through which the actual execution of an action is placed in mental comparison with a potential, an ideal, or a remembered original model of that action", this chapter argues that the films from both periods collectively constitute a national cinema through different performances of (an)other Singapore, namely, the films from the revival proceed through counter-performance, and the films from the golden age are (re)constituted in performance. The first part on the revival draws heavily on my earlier work on this period where I showed the films' engagement of the national by countering the state's performance of its Singapore (Lim 2007; Lim 2015). This establishes a framework for analysing Singapore cinema's functions as a national cinema, as well as the ways in which it was developed and applied to the films of the golden age. The argument therefore looks at the golden age retrospectively.

Performing (an)other Singapore

Singapore's development from a Third World country to First World one (Lee 2000) has often been characterised as an economic miracle and a model of emulation for other developing nations. According to Rodney King's *The Singapore Miracle: Myth and Reality*, "an impressive mythology, both historical and economic, has arisen to extol the 'Singapore model' and explain its achievements. Tales of spectacular economic success and survival against great odds are regularly told" (King 2008, 4). These tales are reinforced by state-driven narratives and representations of Singapore as a vibrant, accomplished and affluent nation. One example of such a narrative can be seen in the *Visit Singapore* website run by the Singapore Tourism Board, which states:

> In just 150 years, Singapore has grown into a thriving centre of commerce and industry. ... Singapore is the busiest port in the world ... [And o]ne of the world's major oil refining and distribution centres ... It has also become one of the most important financial centres of Asia ... Singapore's strategic location, excellent facilities, fascinating cultural contrasts and tourist attractions contribute to its success as a leading destination for both business and pleasure.
>
> (*Singapore Today*, n.d.)

As I have previously noted, the veracity of these statements is not the issue. These articulations do not express a prior national identity; rather, they "constitute a narrativisation of the country that serves to construct, brand, promote and circulate this particular view of Singapore *as Singapore*" (Lim 2015, 188). Such narrativisation is not unique to Singapore. If the nation is "an 'impossible unity' that must be narrated into being in both time and space" (Anagnost 1997, 2), and "the very impossibility of the nation as a unified subject means that this narrating activity is never final" (Anagnost 1997, 2) then "the nation is not merely constituted by narratives or 'narrated into being' but a process of *being constituted*" (Lim 2015, 188). Therefore, in expanding on Judith Butler's work on gender, I argue that the nation "ought not to be construed as a stable identity or locus of agency from which various acts follow; rather [it] is an identity tenuously constituted in time, instituted in an exterior space through a stylized repetition of acts" (Butler 1993, 179). The statements on the *Visit Singapore* website

22   *Edna Lim*

> are performative gestures perform[ing] *a Singapore*. Each site or citation becomes an act that is stylized and repeatable. These acts occur in a public space, and through their reiteration over time, become conventional ways of performing Singapore. In so doing, these conventional gestures have come to constitute Singapore's identity as a nation.
>
> (Lim 2015, 188–9)

These articulations are essentially state-driven imperatives rooted in the anxiety and fear for Singapore's future after her abrupt separation from Malaysia (*The Straits Times*, 9 August 1965). This fear of failure resulted in an intense period of nation building in the 1970s and 1980s, driving the impetus to first project Singapore as a nation that could be successful to one reinforced by those institutions and discourses normalising the drive for excellence in all areas, such as the education system's emphasis on meritocracy. Therefore, as James Loxley (2007, 122) posits, "our identities ... are the product of these various processes ... to which we are subject". These acts and processes have so effectively produced Singapore as successful, efficient, accomplished and affluent, that to *be* Singaporean, one must also be successful, efficient, accomplished and affluent – i.e. one must perform those gestures to participate in the performance.

However, James Loxley's reading of Butler suggests "there always remains a chance within the performativity of identity for dissonant or disruptive gestures by that which such performativity produces as its outside" because "in producing the normal, it also produces the abnormal" (Loxley 2007, 123). Such performativity is a force that constitutes by exclusion. Thus, the nation state's performance of its Singapore also produces that which it excludes – (an)other Singapore (Lim 2015, 189).

Indeed, (an)other Singapore is consistently depicted in the films from the revival through the setting or choice of locations, and characters that I call "the 'other' Singaporean, the ones who are absent in prevailing official literature and representations of Singapore" (Lim 2007, 1). This is most apparent in early films, like *Bugis Street – The Movie* (Yon Fan 1995) and *Mee Pok Man* (Eric Khoo 1995), which were set in the underbelly space of a red light district in the 1960s showing the grim reality of seedy Singapore, populated by such associated figures as prostitutes, pimps, gangsters and sleazy Western men respectively. The characters inhabiting these spaces, like the transvestites and transsexuals in *Bugis Street*, "are reflected identities of this already marginalized world, this 'other' side of Singapore" (Lim 2007, 2).

Eric Khoo's *Mee Pok Man* was followed by his critically acclaimed *12 Storeys* two years later, and the commercially successful *Money No Enough* by Tay Teck Lock in 1998. These two films are set in the heartland of Singapore. The heartland generally comprises the satellite towns of public housing apartment blocks constructed as part of the state's efforts to provide "adequate public housing for Singaporeans, as well as promote social cohesion and encourage home ownership". Over the years, that which had "started as small, dark two-bedroom apartments in simply designed blocks have since developed into full-grown estates with architectural features, gardens, town councils and facilities like swimming pools and community centres" (Lim 2015, 189). According to the Housing and Development Board (HDB) website, these apartments are "home to over 80% of Singapore's resident population, and with about 90% of these resident households owning their HDB flat, it is one of Singapore's national pride [sic]" (*Public Housing in Singapore* n.d.). Reiterating the point, *Houseword* (2010), an HDB corporate newsletter, notes these apartment blocks, which started as a gleam in the then Prime Minister Lee Kuan Yew's eye have "become the cornerstone[s] of Singapore's progress". The success of Singapore's public housing scheme is not only featured in the HDB's own publications, but also used prominently in the nation state's performance of a successful Singapore.

While officially generated images depict a well-developed, clean, communal heartland filled with happy, smiling families and racially balanced communities, the perspective offered by *12 Storeys* and *Money No Enough* is vastly different. *12 Storeys* "performs the heartland as underbelly" (Lim 2015, 189), and this is apparent from the moment the film begins. The opening sequence comprises a series of relatively long takes and still shots alternating between exterior views of a block of flats to various public spaces within, like the corridor, stairwell and shops that are closed for the day (see Figure 2.1). These are mostly empty spaces devoid of people and activity.

Figure 2.1 Examples of shots from the opening sequence of *12 Storeys*.

24   *Edna Lim*

Together with the low-key, blue lighting and accompanying melancholic music, these images starkly contrast the brightly lit, happy pictures usually used to project the desirability and community of the heartland. The film's style "not only creates a different performance of the heartland but also causes it to perform differently ... the film operates by defamiliarizing images that have become conventional and proceeds by contrasting that image with its performance of a different 'reality'" (Lim 2015, 191–2).

The opening sequence establishes an overall tone of sadness in the film that is reinforced by its overarching narrative of "failure and repression, not success" (Lim 2007, 2). The narrative comprises individual stories of its three main characters, Ah Gu, Meng and San San, all of whom live in the same block of flats, but do not interact with each other. These are disenfranchised characters "who are ultimately trapped by their inability to achieve marital or familial bliss, which are idealized through the family portraits, wedding photos and public message commercials about the joys of marriage and family in the film as markers of success and happiness" (Lim 2015, 191–2). Their stories are told as unconnected fragments that juxtapose, but do not interrelate. Instead of social cohesion and community, *12 Storeys* depicts the heartland as an ironically fragmented space that isolates and separates, and where close proximity enhances loneliness and alienation instead of encouraging interaction. The film therefore offers a cogent counter-performance that "undermines the accuracy of official articulations by performing (an)other Singapore" (Lim 2015, 191), constituted by "other" people who are either left out or have failed to be a part of Singapore's success.

The heartland is a popular setting in Singapore films, not only because the image of these flats has become iconic. The space has also "become shorthand for the local and ordinary in Singapore" (Lim 2007, 2) and used to clearly mark or identify characters as "average" Singaporeans. The people who live in the heartland are called "heartlanders". Former Prime Minister Goh Chok Tong (1999–2004), identified "heartlanders" in his 1999 National Day Rally speech as Singaporeans who:

> make their living within the country. Their orientation and interests are local rather than international. Their skills are not marketable beyond Singapore. They speak Singlish. They include taxi-drivers, stallholders, provision shop owners, production workers and contractors. If they emigrate [sic] to America, they will probably settle in a Chinatown, open a Chinese restaurant and call it an "eating house".

These heartlanders are contrasted with another category of Singaporeans, the "cosmopolitans", whose:

> ... outlook is international. They speak English but are bilingual. They have skills that command good incomes – banking, IT, engineering, science and technology. They produce goods and services for the global market. Many

cosmopolitans use Singapore as a base to operate in the region. They can work and be comfortable anywhere in the world.

(*Prime Minister's National Day Rally Speech*, 1999)

The three main characters in *Money No Enough*, Keong, Ong and Hui, are heartlanders not only because they live in the heartland, but also seem to fit Goh's characterisation of this category of Singaporeans. Although Keong is a relatively successful executive at the start of the film, he quits his job when he is passed over for promotion due to his lack of qualifications, computer illiteracy and poor language skills. Ong, an opportunistic but unsuccessful contractor, is less well-educated. Hui is a coffee shop assistant and the least educated. All three are friends and they all have the same problem: shortage of money. Keong has overextended himself financially to create and maintain the appearance of success. Ong, who seeks a lifestyle he cannot afford, quickly becomes heavily indebted to loan sharks and is forced into hiding. Although Hui is initially happy with his simple life, he becomes more conscious of his disadvantages when he is unable to afford medical care for his ailing mother or a lavish funeral for her when she dies. Hence, it is not merely the shortage of money that the film emphasises, but "the lack of money in consumerist and affluent Singapore" (Lim 2007, 3).

While the film may seem to depict "average" heartlanders, it does not celebrate them. Although the three friends eventually start a successful carwash business together, they still do not have enough money by the film's conclusion. This is because they have squandered away the money they made. While they may have achieved some material success, they are unable to sustain it, and find themselves in the same predicament they were in at the start of the film. The characters learn lessons, but are not essentially transformed by their experiences. The reasons accounting for their lack of money at the beginning of the film are the same reasons for their continued need of money at the end.

Furthermore, the characters' lack of education, qualifications and poor language skill contradicts official narratives about the desirability of Singapore's workforce and the success of its bilingual education system. Tellingly, the film's depiction of heartlanders directly corresponds with Goh's statement as to the different ways in which cosmopolitan and heartlander Singaporeans function in state rhetoric. According to Goh (1999):

Both heartlanders and cosmopolitans are important to Singapore's well being. Heartlanders play a major role in maintaining our core values and our social stability. They are the core of our society. Without them, there will be no safe and stable Singapore, no Singapore system, no Singapore brand name.

Cosmopolitans, on the other hand, are indispensable in generating wealth for Singapore. They extend our economic reach. The world is their market. Without them, Singapore cannot run as an efficient, high performance society.

(*Prime Minister's National Day Rally Speech*, 1999)

26   Edna Lim

As is evident in Goh's statement, heartlanders are important for local identity, and cosmopolitans are crucial to and participants of Singapore's performance of success. As such, Keong, Ong and Hui are not merely average Singaporeans on a collective quest to live the Singapore dream. They are heartlanders, "average Singaporeans who are doomed to being average, and therefore are not part of Singapore's rhetoric of success" (Lim 2007, 3). As the circular narrative of the film implies, these other Singaporeans are forever caught in the perennial cycle of striving but never arriving. Although their eventual success in opening a carwash business may show that one does not need to have a degree or speak English to be successful, their continued lack of money at the film's end also suggests that striving to achieve the Singapore dream is not the same as participating in the state's performance of success. In other words, they may strive for the Singapore dream but remain excluded from the state's performance of success. While *Money No Enough* does not directly challenge the image of the heartland in the same way that *12 Storeys* does, it nonetheless problematises the deployment of the space as shorthand for the local and the ordinary as well as its depiction of heartlanders as average Singaporeans.

As *12 Storeys* and *Money No Enough* have shown, the heartland is also "used as a site through which 'other' voices may be heard" (Lim 2007, 2). The "average" heartlanders in most of these revival films are characters "who fail to rise above their ordinariness to participate in Singapore's performance of success. In some films, this is because they are either too poor or they are juvenile delinquents or gangsters. In other films, they lack either the proper skills or opportunity to do so" (Lim 2007, 2). These films disengage the heartland from the state's performance and redeploy it as a site for counter-performance. If the state's performance projects a successful Singapore inhabited by successful, happy Singaporeans, these films depict (an)other Singapore and (an)other heartland populated by other Singaporeans.

The success of films like *12 Storeys* and *Money No Enough* were vital in raising interest in and reviving film production in Singapore. They are now considered landmark films because of the ways in which they have influenced, and continue to influence subsequent films and filmmakers. Other films that followed either try to mimic *Money No Enough* by emulating its content, use of language and/or comedic style or focus on the silenced and disenfranchised like *12 Storeys*.

For example, Royston Tan's *15* (2003) offers a further overt subversion of the heartland and other recognisable, public spaces in Singapore. The two groups of fifteen-year-old boys, who play themselves in the film, are considered by society to be delinquents. They are rebels, truants and gang members who extort money and indulge in fights, pornography, tattoos and piercings. The film forces us to look beyond the piercings and tattoos, as they encounter and navigate a society that does not (want to) understand them. This is apparent in the stark contrast between public and private spaces in the film.

The public spaces of the heartland are depicted as cold, intimidating and heartless, and where the surrounding structures and blocks of flats dwarf the characters, Melvyn and Vynn, in the first story (see Figure 2.2). Likewise, when they are in a

Singapore cinema 27

heartland playground, the image foregrounds the chain-link fence, creating a stark demarcation between us and the boys in the background who are literally confined within that space and look like they have no way out (see Figure 2.3). The sense of entrapment felt by the boys is reflected in their experience of the space they occupy, transforming the playground from a site of innocence and play into an expression of lost innocence and private pain in a public space.

Figure 2.2 Melvyn and Vynn are dwarfed in the heartland.

Figure 2.3 Melvyn and Vynn in the playground.

28 *Edna Lim*

The second story ventures further afield, challenging and displacing other public and iconic spaces in Singapore. For example, Shaun and Erick flagrantly brandish a blow-up sex doll as they move through Orchard Road, Singapore's famous shopping district, and even go so far as to simulate sex with it at a traffic crossing. The boys also tour various landmarks around the island to help Armani find a perfect building from which to commit suicide (see Figure 2.4).

At once dark and comic, this sequence directly challenges the prominence of these landmarks in official discourses such as tourist literature touting Singapore as successful and "unique". The presence of the three boys in the foreground with the cards pronouncing "I want to die" immediately undermine and displace the iconicity of these places as performative gestures in official discourse, causing them to function instead as potential locations for teen suicide. The deadpan, theatrical cadence of the film's style calls attention to the boys' lack of emotional connection to these iconic sights/sites. Here, they highlight the distance and difference between official performances of Singapore and their own experience of being Singaporean. These sequences, while rebellious, are not attempts to reclaim these spaces but a rejection of them.

In contrast, the boys are more honest, serious and intimate in the private space of the HDB flat, where interior space corresponds to the interiority of the scenes. Here, they have facials, clean each other's wounds and cut each other's hair. This is where we see them cry, comfort and hug each other to sleep. The frequent use of tightly composed shots in these scenes reinforces the sense that we are given a closer, more intimate view of the boys. However, these shots also highlight the restricted space of the flat. While the privacy of the setting enables them to be themselves, that freedom is also ultimately limited and confined. As a result, these interior spaces of the flat are not unlike the entrapment of the fenced playground

Figure 2.4 The boys in front of City Hall.

Singapore cinema 29

and the confines of the fish tank and fish bowl that figure prominently in the mise-en-scène. The fish tank and bowl are recurring motifs in the film reflecting not only the invisible barriers that restrict and entrap the boys, and from which they cannot overcome, but also the way the film makes us gaze at them from beyond the fourth wall ultimately separating us and them. The world of *15* is effectively demarcated as an enclosed, confined and painful universe of (an)other Singapore.

By deliberately enacting a counterposition and a different reality, films like *12 Storeys*, *Money No Enough* and *15* in turn highlight the performativity of the state's representation. Collectively, these films are prime examples of a Singapore cinema exemplifying those dissonant gestures Butler describes, as they disrupt the performativity of the state's own performance of the nation through the creation and repetition of (an)other Singapore. Early revival films like *12 Storeys* established a set of stylised acts that, as a relational force and by virtue of their repetition and consumption through subsequent films like *15*, continue to disrupt the state's performance of successful Singapore as a unified, homogenous national identity.

The past is a foreign country

While Singapore cinema's revival films operate through the counter-performance of (an)other Singapore, where national cinema directly engages and negotiates with state-driven performances, the same cannot be said about films from the golden age. After all, these films were made at a time when the idea of Singapore was not yet developed, much less fully formed. The differences between films from the golden age and the revival are notable. Apart from the fact that golden age films are primarily Malay-language films, these differences are also apparent in the narratives, characters and settings.

Some films, like Hussein Haniff's *Hang Jebat* (1961), tend towards the epic, depicting legendary tales derived from Malay folklore. *Hang Jebat* is based on the story of Hang Tuah during the Sultanate of Malacca in the fifteenth century, which has been chronicled in the *Sejarah Melayu* (the semi-historical Malay Annals) and *Hikayat Hang Tuah* (a rather romantic collection of tales involving Hang Tuah). Hang Tuah is arguably one of the most well-known figures in Malay history and literature, and the film depicts his legendary and tragic quarrel with his best friend, Hang Jebat. However, few audiences today recognise the tale. Indeed, modern viewers of the film need some foreknowledge of the history, the myth, the nuances and gestures as well as the significance of props such as Hang Jebat's legendary keris, the *Taming Sari* (a weapon that makes its owner invincible) in order to properly understand it. The same can be said of the horror films made in that period, which featured such indigenous Malay characters as the *pontianak* (vampire) and the *toyol*, a small child's spirit invoked from a dead human foetus through black magic. These creatures were inspired by local beliefs, legends and superstitions that are much less familiar to audiences today.

Golden age films like *Hang Jebat* also feature musical sequences borrowed from Indian cinema, particularly Tamil films, the Hollywood musical as well as the indigenous Malay theatrical form of the *bangsawan* (White 2002–2003a, 2).

30   Edna Lim

Like the *bangsawan*, these musical performance interludes are often used to delay action or to relieve tension after a dramatic build-up. However, unlike the musical form in Indian cinema, the songs in these Malay films are more motivated by and integrated into the action and story, aligning the function of songs to the convention of the classical Hollywood musical. For example, in *Hang Jebat*, musical sequences occur in two ways: as formal performances in the palace performed by court dancers for its audience of courtiers and the sultan, or when particular characters sing about their emotions and thoughts. In the former, the musical sequences are conducted like Hollywood's backstage musicals whereas the latter is reminiscent of Hollywood's integrated musicals. Such musical performance interludes are typical of Malay films at the time. However, unlike the Hollywood model, where musicals are a specific genre or type of film, song and dance sequences are included, and in fact often required, in almost all films from the period (White ibid.). As such, these films were not musicals per se but comedies, drama, horror or crime films with musical numbers, a convention that has since disappeared from Singapore films after the decline of the golden age. With the exception of films like Royston Tan's *881* (2007) and *12 Lotus* (2008), there are hardly any musicals produced by the industry.

Period films like *Hang Jebat* or horror films like *Orang Minyak* (*The Oily Man*; L. Krishnan, 1958) also tend to be situated within a village or *kampong* milieu that has disappeared from the landscape of contemporary Singapore as a result of the industrialisation and urbanisation of the nation which began in the 1960s. The state's urban redevelopment programmes escalated and massively increased in the 1970s and 1980s, as *kampongs* were progressively cleared to make way for housing developments and commercial projects. According to the Urban Redevelopment Authority of Singapore's website, "[b]etween 1976 and 1989, a total of 184 hectares of land were cleared ... [And], Singapore's Central Area was transformed from an area of slums and squatters into a modern financial and business hub" (*Our History*, n.d.). In addition, these films tend to use a more formal Malay language, which, while consistent with the period quality of their narratives, also enhances the foreignness of these films. These epic and horror films are so far removed from present-day Singapore and the kind of films we recognise today as Singapore films, that the experience of watching them is akin to watching a foreign film.

In contrast to films by Hussein Haniff, those made by P. Ramlee, perhaps the most prolific filmmaker of that period, are more personal and concerned with the daily lives of ordinary characters. The setting of his more "modern" films like *Bujang Lapok* (1957), *Seniman Bujang Lapok* (1961) and *Labu dan Labi* (1962) offer us glimpses of a Singapore that is more recognisable, even though it is a recognisably older Singapore. Since these films were made before the nation's independence in 1965, the Singapore they captured is, as it were, a pre-national one, marked by the *kampongs* and low-rise buildings characterising the city before it underwent massive urban renewal.

Although these images of Singapore's cityscape seem more recognisable, they are also fleeting. The primary locale and milieu of these films is not the city, but the more rural landscape of the *kampong*. In fact, as Timothy R. White has noted, one of the recurring themes in Ramlee's films is the difference between the city and the *kampong* (White 2002–2003a, 6–7). For example, in *Bujang Lapok*, there is a clear disparity between the formal, transactional, functional nature of the city and the idyll and community spirit (*gotong royong*) associated with the *kampong*. The film revolves around Ramlee, Sudin and Ajiz, three friends who share a room in the *kampong* while working in the city as a perfume salesman, an office worker and a lorry driver respectively. We first encounter the characters when they are in the city as Ramlee attempts to sell perfume to Sudin's boss. However, based on this opening sequence of Ramlee in Sudin's office, one would not have known that these two characters are good friends, as they do not acknowledge each other at all. It is only after they meet Ajiz in his lorry outside Sudin's office that we realise they are friends. In comparison, the film emphasises the *kampong*'s spirit of community almost immediately after the three friends leave the city. Upon arriving in the *kampong*, they decide to buy a chicken for dinner. They happily split the cost equally, a neighbour helps them clean the chicken, and they cook and eat it together. These scenes, occurring very early in the film, immediately establish the formality of the city in relation to the informality of the *kampong*, which is underscored by the film's focus on costume. After they return to the *kampong*, the three friends deliberately strip off the layers of their "formal" work attire to reveal their tattered underwear beneath. This is a rather extended sequence that serves as both comedy (because they make fun of each other) and a means of highlighting the difference between the city and *kampong* through costume (see Figure 2.5).

The formality of the city is further reinforced when Ramlee dresses up in a formal suit to go on dates in a coffee shop in the city. The women he dates in the city repeatedly cheat him. As White observed, "[i]n each [date], the urban coffee shop is a site in which Ramlee, seeking a romantic relationship, is cheated of both companionship and money" (White 2002–2003b, 6). In contrast, he eventually falls in love with his *kampong* landlady, Cik Normah, who does not care about the disparity in their social standing and class. The community also rallies to help Sudin in his quest to marry Zaiton, a neighbour and daughter of a rich widow. Zaiton's

Figure 2.5 Tattered clothing in the *kampong* vs. formal wear in the city in *Bujang Lapok*.

32   Edna Lim

mother insists on a high dowry, which Sudin cannot afford. So, under the coconut trees in the night, the three friends, together with Zaiton and several villagers, concoct a plan for Zaiton to steal her mother's ring, which they will pawn in the city to raise money. In fact, almost the entire *kampong* follows the three friends to the city to visit the pawnshop where they discover that the ring is fake. In the end, Cik Normah intercedes on the couple's behalf and appeals to Zaiton's mother, who finally allows the lovers to marry. Much of the story is located in the *kampong*, which as noted by White, are highly stylised sets with obvious painted backgrounds unlike the visually realistic outdoor location shots of the city (White 2002–2003b, 4). The marked difference between the depiction of the *kampong* and city emphasise the film's treatment and deployment of both spaces. The *kampong* is seen as an idyllic space, marked by coconut trees, free roaming chickens and communal living. In contrast, the city is depicted as a noisy space, characterised by traffic, blaring horns and concrete (low-rise) buildings. Based on the logic of the film, the city is a cold, formal place associated with crime and driven by monetary concerns, whereas the *kampong* is a simpler place where community resides and the characters can be themselves in their tattered underwear.

While films like *Bujang Lapok* and *Hang Jebat* may have social and even political resonances at the time they were made, these narratives, like their settings, seem less imperative in, and far removed from, urban Singapore today. This is not to say that these films are no longer relevant; rather, they resonate differently today. At stake in this argument is not the meaning of the films at the time they were made, but the meaning we assign to them when we watch them today. The experience of watching these films today is of more interest than the particular significances and meanings conveyed by these films and their narratives.

How then should we consider films from the golden age of Singapore cinema? How are they consistent with Singapore films from the revival? The problem of claiming these films from the golden age is complicated by Singapore's shared history with Malaysia (Malaya). The lack of familiarity experienced when watching these films, especially among younger local audiences, reflects the historical distance and identifiable difference between contemporary Singapore and the Singapore that was once part of Malaya, and later, Malaysia. The apparent differences in narrative, thematic concerns, language, style, and even the images of Singapore, between the films from the golden age and the revival recalls L.P. Hartley's statement that "the past is a foreign country, they do things differently there" (Hartley 1953; Lowenthal 1985, xvi). So, do we merely consider these golden age films as films from a bygone era in Singapore's cinematic history that is long gone?

Several accounts of Singapore cinema have charted the golden age within a chronological, developmental trajectory of the industry (Uhde and Uhde 2000). Others have considered these films as reflections of a particular culture such as Malay films (Aljunied 2005), within the body of work of particular filmmakers (Barnard 2002) or studios (Lim 1991). Attempts have also been made to locate them within the context of that past – as colonial and/or post-colonial films (Hashim and Hanan 2007), for example. While these studies are valuable to our understanding of Malay films, the golden age or the development of Singapore cinema as a whole, to only do so runs the risk of containing these films in, and designating them to, either the past or a particular culture. The consequence is that there exists a kind of discursive fissure in the historiography of Singapore cinema, between the golden age and the revival, as two distinct cinemas distinguished by difference with little or no connection between them.

This chapter contends that connections to Singapore cinema as we know it today could be made precisely because "the past is a foreign country". Films from both periods constitute a Singapore cinema that functions as a national cinema by depicting (an)other Singapore. The difference, however, lies in their performance strategies. While films from the revival depict (an)other Singapore via counter-performance strategies staged in the texts themselves, golden age films do so much more literally. While films like *Hang Jebat* are considered historical films at the time they were made because they are period films, the same cannot be said of the more contemporary films. These productions of the golden age cannot be considered historical films, as they were neither made for the sole purpose of recording or documenting history, nor were they made as period films to enact, capture or recapture that past. Instead, these films are viewed as historical today because, quite simply, they show us something of the past as we watch them now. As Susan Sontag, writing about cinema, says:

> this youngest of the arts is also the one most heavily burdened with memory. Cinema is a time machine. Movies preserve the past ... [They] resurrect the beautiful dead; present intact vanished or ruined environments; employ, without irony, styles and fashions that seem funny today; solemnly ponder irrelevant or naïve problems.
>
> (Sontag 1992, 370)

While this may be so, one also remembers that which Vivian Sobchack calls "the once arcane lesson of [Hayden] White's *Metahistory* – that historiography is about arranging and telling stories, not about delivering objective truth" (Sobchack 1996, 4). Although these films allow us to travel back in time, they should not be taken as factual documents or accurate accounts of past reality. As Pierre Sorlin notes in his paper, "Endgame?", Hugo Müsterberg had already voiced the reservation that films were artefacts distorting reality as early as the 1910s (Sorlin 1999, 3). They are biased, fraught and incomplete. But as Sorlin (1999), citing Siegfried Kracauer, also points out:

> in spite of these distortions, it is still possible to deduce from the pictures evidence about the environment, the life-styles ... of past periods. This record has the advantage of being permanent, it could be endlessly rescreened and, ... it could be a means of resisting the passage of time.

Although the analogy of cinema as time machine is a tempting one, it is not entirely accurate. Entering a time machine suggests that we can travel back in time through these narratives, but we are ultimately not present in that past time. According to

34 *Edna Lim*

Thomas Elsaesser and Malte Hagener, "[f]ilms … presuppose a cinematic space that is both physical and discursive, one where film and spectator, cinema and body encounter one another" (Elsaesser and Hagener 2010, 4). So, "spectators … inhabit two worlds (the cinematic universe, the diegesis, and their own physical environment and ambient space), suspending one in favour of the other, or shuttling between them …" (Elsaesser and Hagener 2010, 4). Therefore, Elsaesser and Hagener posit that "it is the lived body encountering the window/frame [of a film] as 'container' in which dimensions of time and space are held, that allows one to distinguish a 'here' and an 'I' from a 'there' and a 'you'" (Elsaesser and Hagener 2010, 179). This is akin to Nataša Ďurovičová's observation of film's propensity for creating "perceptual mismatches" that are "[b]uilt as [cinema] … on the paired desires to bring the distant closer and to make the proximate strange enough to be worth seeing" (Ďurovičová 2010, 90). According to her (Ďurovičová 2010, 91),

> [t]he complementary attraction of the moving image was that it also rendered one's own place strange, foreign even … What in literary application of modernism was known as irony, that is, double vision, found its equivalent in cinema's capacity to get a spectator to see his or her self as an Other even while seeing the other as a variant of one's self.

When applied to space, and more specifically to the Singapore captured in these films from the golden age, this double vision lies in the spectator's understanding that the scene perceived is a variant of and different from present-day Singapore. Furthermore, the distance between the screen and the viewer makes conscious the act of watching, of something being performed, much like a theatrical performance would, highlighting the "specter of comparison" (Ďurovičová 2010, 91) in the encounter with such films. Therefore, in watching these films from the golden age now, we are aware of the time difference, and the differences between the space of a Singapore captured in the film and the Singapore of the spectator's present. The past becomes part of the present experience, not the other way around. This experience reflects that which Thomas Elsaesser says of history, whereby the past "now appears to exist in suspended animation, neither exactly 'behind' us, nor part of our present, but shadowing us rather like a parallel world which is un-real, hyper-real and virtual, all at the same time" in each viewing of these films (Elsaesser 1999, 1).

When we watch these films from the golden age now, "the consciousness of doubling" described by Bauman occurs between the Singapore we see in these films and the Singapore that is materially present today, where we simultaneously acknowledge the Singapore we see and recognise this Singapore (or much of it) to be no longer existent. Hence, we see a Singapore cinema that has distinctly different conventions and narrative concerns, and is performed in a different language from the films made today. In effect, we are seeing (an)other Singapore.

As the films from the revival mark their characters and spaces as outside of the state's performance of Singapore, watching these films from the golden age today places the viewer as outsiders to the past. Indeed, the Singapore of golden age films looks like a foreign country and we visit it like tourists, seeing (an)other Singapore in performance at each viewing. In short, the films of the golden age may be very different from those of the revival period, but they collectively function as a national cinema constituted by performances of (an)other Singapore.

References

Aljunied, Syed Muhd Khairudin. "Films as Social History – P. Ramlee's 'Seniman Bujang Lapok' and Malays in Singapore (1950s–60s)." *The Heritage Journal* 2, no. 1 (2005): 1–21.

Anagnost, Ann. *National Past-Times: Narrative, Representation and Power in Modern China*. Durham: Duke University Press, 1997.

"A Pledge by Lee: We Want to Co-operate with Central Government." *The Straits Times*, 9 August 1965.

"A Stake in the Nation." Houseword, 2010. http://houseword.sg/newsletter/201001/article.php?aid=31#A%20Stake%20in%20the%20Nation (accessed 17 February 2010).

Barnard, Timothy. "The Ambivalence of P. Ramlee: *Penarek Beca* and *Bujang Lapok* in Perspective." *Asian Cinema* 13, no. 2 (2002): 9–23.

Bauman, Richard. *International Encyclopedia of Communications*, edited by Erik Barnouw. New York: Oxford University Press, 1989.

Butler, Judith. *Bodies That Matter: On the Discursive Limits of Sex*. London: Routledge, 1993.

Ďurovičová, Nataša. "Vector, Flow, Zone: Towards a History of Cinematic *Translatio*." In *World Cinemas, Transnational Perspectives*, edited by Nataša Ďurovičová and Kathleen Newman, 90–120. New York: Routledge, 2010.

Elsaesser, Thomas. "'One Train May Be Hiding Another': Private History, Memory and National Identity." *Screening the Past* 6. Last modified 16 April 1999. http://tlweb.latrobe.edu.au/humanities/screeningthepast/reruns/rr0499/terr6b.htm (accessed 24 June 2015).

Elsaesser, Thomas, and Malte Hagener. *Film Theory: An Introduction through the Senses*. New York: Routledge, 2010.

Goh, Chok Tong. *Prime Minister's National Day Rally Speech 1999: First-World Economy, World-Class Home*. www.nas.gov.sg/archivesonline/speeches/view-html?filename=1999082202.htm (accessed 24 June 2015).

Hartley, Lesley Poles. *The Go-Between*. London: Hamish Hamilton, 1953.

Hashim, Rohani, and David Hanan. *Malay Comedy in the Colonial and Post-colonial Context: The Singapore Comedy Films of P. Ramlee, 1957–1964*. Melbourne: Monash University, 2007.

"Housing and Development Board. A Brief Background – HDB's Beginnings." Housing and Development Board, n.d. www.hdb.gov.sg/fi10/fi10296p.nsf/WPDis/About%20UsA%20Brief%20Background%20-%20HDB's%20Beginnings?OpenDocument&SubMenu=A_Brief_Background (accessed 12 April 2008).

King, Rodney. *The Singapore Miracle: Myth and Reality*. 2nd edition. Australia: Inglewood Press, 2008.

Lee, Kwan Yew. *From Third to First World: The Singapore Story – 1965–2000*. Singapore: Singapore Press Holdings, 2000.

Lim, Edna. "Coming Up For Air: Film and the Other Singaporean." *Kinema*, no. 28. Fall 2007. www.kinema.uwaterloo.ca/article.php?id=384&feature (accessed 24 June 2015).

Lim, Edna. "Counterperformance: The Heartland and Other Spaces in Eating Air and 15." In *Asian Cinema and the Use of Space: Interdisciplinary Perspectives*, edited by Lilian Chee and Edna Lim, 187–203. New York: Routledge, 2015.

Lim, Kay Tong. *Cathay: 55 Years of Cinema*. Singapore: Landmark Books, 1991.

36   *Edna Lim*

Lowenthal, David. *The Past is a Foreign Country*. Cambridge: Cambridge University Press, 1985.

Loxley, James. *Performativity*. London: Routledge, 2007.

"Our History: Development." http://app.www.sg/who/40/Development.aspx (accessed 17 February 2010).

"Our History." Urban Redevelopment Authority of Singapore, n.d. www.ura.gov.sg/about/ura-history.htm (accessed 10 March 2012).

"Public Housing in Singapore." Housing and Development Board, n.d. www.hdb.gov.sg/fi10/fi10320p.nsf/w/AboutUsPublicHousing?OpenDocument (accessed 17 February 2010).

"Singapore Today." VisitSingapore.com, n.d. www.visitsingapore.com/publish/stbportal/en/home/about_singapore/singapore_today.html (accessed 17 February 2010).

Sobchack, Vivian. "Introduction: History Happens." In *The Persistence of History: Cinema, Television and the Modern Event*, edited by Vivian Sobchack, 1–16. New York: Routledge, 1996.

Sontag, Susan. "Film and Theatre." In *Film Theory and Criticism: Introductory Readings*, edited by Gerald Mast, Marshall Cohen and Leo Braudy, 362–74. 4th edition. Oxford: Oxford University Press, 1992.

Sorlin, Pierre. "Endgame." *Screening the Past* 6. Last modified 16 April 1999. http://tlweb.latrobe.edu.au/humanities/screeningthepast/firstrelease/fr0499/psfr6a.htm (accessed 24 June 2015).

Uhde, Jan, and Yvonne Ng Uhde. *Latent Images: Film in Singapore*. Singapore: Oxford University Press, 2000.

White, Timothy R. "Exactly The Same But Completely Different: Product Differentiation in the Singaporean Films of Shaw Brothers' Malay Film Productions and Cathay-Keris." In *Screen Histories and Historiography*, Course outline, Department of English Language and Literature, National University of Singapore. Semester One, 2002–2003a. http://courses.nus.edu.sg/course/elltrw/Film/history.html (accessed 10 March 2012).

White, Timothy R. "P. Ramlee's Cinema of the Kampong." In *Screen Histories and Historiography*, Course outline, Department of English Language and Literature, National University of Singapore. Semester One, 2002–2003b. http://courses.nus.edu.sg/course/elltrw/Film/history.html (accessed 10 March 2012).

3 Convergence and slippage between film and history

Reviewing *Invisible City*, *Zahari's 17 Years* and *Sandcastle*

Loh Kah Seng and Kenneth Paul Tan

Contentious history and a new generation of filmmakers

A modest but growing literature has noted a discontinuity in Singapore's cinematic history, wedging a period of the "dark ages" between a "golden age" of mostly Malay-language studio films that entertained large numbers of Asian cine-magoers from 1947 to 1972 and a "revival" of the film industry since the late 1980s, driven by economic policy considerations and consisting mostly of Chinese and English-language films aimed at an international audience (Millet 2006; Uhde and Uhde 2000). Uncannily, this depiction of the middle period as culturally deficient reflected the virtual absence of politics in the 1970s, following the historic defeat of political alternatives that had animated the post-colonial consciousness in the preceding decades. The victors emerged to form a hegemonic People's Action Party (PAP) state, armed with broad-ranging apparatuses of social control and driven to achieve high economic growth. This "administrative state" was conducive to the depoliticisation of citizens chiefly into producer–consumer subjects and model workers, willing to enter into a simple social contract with a paternalistic state that decides and provides (Chan 1975).

The re-emergence of parliamentary opposition and civil society from the 1980s heralded a gradual "return" of politics, with the state finding greater difficulty in maintaining hegemonic dominance over an increasingly variegated citizenry with more incompatible demands (Tan 2012c). More diverse understandings of history, particularly of the political events of the 1950s and 1960s, have slowly destabilised the dominant state-sanctioned narrative of Singapore's history, usually called "The Singapore Story" (Loh 1998).

Naturally, the arts have also – since the 1980s – seen a return to more daring and explicitly political engagement following the harshly repressive state practices of detention and censorship in the 1970s (which continued, albeit in a less bluntly applied way, into the 1980s and 1990s). A new generation of filmmakers seized the expanded artistic opportunities in a seemingly more culturally liberal Singapore to advance social and political criticism, while building careers that were also valued by a state now speaking the neoliberal language of creative economies. Jack Neo's films – still the most commercially viable among all Singapore films to date – made fun of politicians and their policies, but refrained

38   Loh Kah Seng and Kenneth Paul Tan

from providing a systematic and radical critique. Eric Khoo's and Royston Tan's films – still among the most critically acclaimed – developed themes like alienation and loss as a result of soul-destroying practices of rapid modernisation, but they often came close to indulging in nostalgia, beautified by an arthouse aesthetic (Tan 2008).

In more recent years, some young and independent filmmakers have started to pay more attention to matters of history, producing films that went beyond nostalgic excursions, valorised marginalised voices of history and challenged establishment accounts. This chapter discusses three such films: Martyn See's *Zahari's 17 Years* (2007), Tan Pin Pin's *Invisible City* (2007) and Boo Junfeng's *Sandcastle* (2010). While *Zahari's 17 Years* and *Invisible City* were independently made documentary films and *Sandcastle* was a higher-budget fictional feature film, all three employed socially engaged approaches to Singapore's contentious political past.

These films are remarkable in that they were made within a dominant-party state, not in the aftermath of regime change. Since Lee Hsien Loong became Singapore's Prime Minister in 2004, there has been gradual political liberalisation, which has afforded greater contestation of the past by both elderly ex-leftists and younger Singaporeans. The films can be seen as the combined outcome of a more liberal state, the efforts of socially engaged filmmakers and the agency of ex-leftists in ending their silence. This is quite unlike the shape of historical memory elsewhere in Southeast Asia. In Thailand, as Thongchai Winichakul (2002) explains, the military's suppression of the student movement in October 1976 remains "politically unspeakable" for the notion of state crime transgresses the national culture of harmony. On the other hand, following Suharto's fall in 1998, many Indonesians have reacted with disappointment to the new historical films, which have failed to adequately acknowledge the widespread suffering inflicted by his regime (Schreiner 2005). The Singapore films stand somewhere in between their Thai and Indonesian counterparts: they were able to address controversial histories while, with the exception of *Zahari's 17 Years*, enjoying relative tolerance and even funding support from the government. That this government has been in power since 1959 means there remains in Singapore a continuing, though diminishing, fear of the repercussions of speaking about sensitive pasts, particularly among the older generation. This is borne out in two of the films.

Zahari's 17 Years, currently banned in Singapore under the Films Act but available online, is essentially an extended interview with Said Zahari, who in the 1950s and 1960s was a journalist and later editor-in-chief of *Utusan Melayu*, a Jawi-script Malay newspaper, and President of Partai Rakyat Singapura, a left-wing Malay nationalist party. The film featured Said's experiences of political detention without trial for 17 years, following his arrest in 1963 by the Singapore, Malayan and British colonial governments in a joint security operation known as "Operation Coldstore". Accused of engaging in subversive activities, more than 100 people were arrested and detained during the crackdown. In the film, surrounded by shelves of books in the corner of his office in his home in Kuala Lumpur, Said responded eloquently (occasionally in fluent Mandarin) to See's interview questions. The questions and answers faithfully reflected the contents of a book (2001) that Said had written to document his detention. Vividly highlighting the injustice of his incarceration, Said characterised former Prime Minister Lee Kuan Yew in unflattering terms, accusing him of using internal security laws to put away legitimate opposition politicians. By making history's defeated his protagonist, See sought to present an account of history that challenges the PAP state's hegemonic version.

Invisible City depicted different people's attempts to discover, uncover, remember and assert their own versions of Singapore's pasts through at least six intercutting interviews: an archaeologist digging for tangible fragments of the past, an ageing documentarian struggling to remember the years immediately after the Second World War and his extensive collection of 16mm footage, a bedridden British lady reminiscing about the photographs she had taken of colonial buildings that were being demolished, a Japanese reporter investigating the horrors of the Japanese Occupation in Malaya but packaging it as a "beautiful story" that her people can more easily accept. Finally, there was former political detainee and Chinese middle school student activist, Han Tan Juan, struggling as much with himself as with his interviewer over the public use of his historical memories and photographs. Like See, Tan Pin Pin gave Han a public voice through her film. But as a filmmaker exploring historical memory, she was also mirrored in the people she interviewed (Tan 2012a).

Like Tan, Boo dealt with the memory of Chinese student activism in *Sandcastle*. He maintained that his film was about history and did not have any political agenda (Ng 2010). In the film, teenager En pursued fragments of this past from brief dialogues with his grandfather, mother, even his friends, and from photographs and an old handwritten note. The film attempted to show how people coped with the trauma of their pasts. Detained for his activism as a student, En's father went into self-imposed exile in Malaysia. En's mother had also been a student activist, but had chosen to remain in Singapore to raise her family, in effect disavowing her youthful idealism and embracing the values of the PAP state. She, and her son, could thus enjoy a fairly comfortable material life in Singapore. However, En's investigation of the past led him to greater knowledge of and respect for his father and the Chinese student movement.

History and film: different spaces and interfaces

We seek to explore the spaces and gaps between history and film. In the three films, the ex-leftists and young filmmakers partially converged in exploring Singapore's political history, possessing similar though ultimately distinct motivations and viewpoints of the past. Both groups pursued different objectives: the ex-leftists rejected the state's labelling of them as subversive "pro-communists" and affirmed their contributions to Singapore's independence through young filmmakers by urging the public towards greater historical reflexivity. In the films, the relation between the two groups can be likened to an oral history interview rendered public, with the testimony being a joint product of the interviewer and interviewee. This was the case when Martyn See interviewed Said Zahari, or

40 *Loh Kah Seng and Kenneth Paul Tan*

when Tan Pin Pin questioned Han Tan Juan about the past, or indirectly in a film script, where En conversed with his grandfather or where En's father recalled the past in a monologue voiceover.

However, the relationship between interviewer and interviewee is not necessarily an equal one. Only Tan appears to have thematised this problematic relationship in *Invisible City*. In *Zahari's 17 Years* and *Sandcastle*, filmmakers and former leftists seemed to have found common ground in a critical examination of authoritarian rule in Singapore, particularly of detention without trial under the Internal Security Act (ISA). Thus, in See's and Boo's films, the distinct voices of the interviewer and interviewee had partially converged.

We also approach the films from the vantage points of public, oral and academic history, each of which has its own standards in deciding that which constitutes good practice. Public history is frequently a counter-hegemonic endeavour aiming to empower the narrators and expose social injustice (Westerman 2006). This does converge with oral history's intent to return history to the people who made it. However, there is an important difference between the two. Oral history was in the main intended to focus on ordinary people or social groups that did not write their history and were ignored in the historical record. This distinction appears to have been lost in Singapore, where oral history remains largely preoccupied with political and economic elites, including ex-leftists, who are able to write and articulate their views of the past, as can be seen in the three films (Tan *et al.* 2011, Tan and Jomo 2001).

Academic history, while characterised by multiple approaches, differs from public and oral history in one important aspect: in its rigorous examination of sources (often archival) and its use of a "scientific method" of inquiry to produce impartial accounts. We do not suggest that all historians subscribe to the scientific method; indeed, some historians use oral history in their research and others move between academia and society to make their work socially relevant. Nonetheless, academic history also contains an important criticality in discerning gaps, silences and the selection of facts in historical accounts. Arguably then, academic historians, in their social roles, can support a public or oral history project, including one presented through film, but also maintain a critical posture towards it as they would towards state-sanctioned narratives.

Unlike academic history, films – including historical documentaries – have a less restrictive standard of historical truth. Filmmakers, after all, also work within different sets of logic that relate to the aesthetic sphere and to commercial purposes, as much as they may seek to tell historical "truth". Historical truth, one might conclude, is quite different from filmic truth, even when the films are ostensibly about actual people, places or events. The academic historian, much more than the filmmaker, is typically engaged in a detective-like pursuit of scholarship that is driven by a scientific preoccupation with rigorous research, the interpretation of facts, and debate among peers. The filmmaker, however, regards history fundamentally as source material for creative work that obeys primarily the logic and rules of aesthetic practice. The filmmaker is attentive to such formal concerns as narrative and plot, characterisation, dramatic development, symbolism, visual composition, sound design, and other elements and techniques of filmmaking.

As a way of investigating and presenting the past, academic history is not necessarily superior to film for at least three reasons. First, the neoliberal globalised research university has transformed the professional demands made on academics. Funding has increasingly favoured large-scale research that is deemed to have applied value. Discovering the historical truth may thus have to compete with other more pressing goals that have insinuated themselves into the careers of university-based historians. Second, academic history writing may not be capable of reflecting the fullness of the past, which is only partially communicable through prose. Academic history is further limited by the material dimensions and editorial restrictions of the book, journal article or opinion-editorial piece. Third, many academic historians have come to terms with the impossibility of being "objective". Such a claim is difficult to sustain as a result of both the reflexivity of historians and critiques by non-historians. At one level, one might argue that the past is fluid, elusive, or perhaps even unknowable. At a second level, no matter how determined the historian might be, it is quite impossible to eliminate personal and cultural biases. At a third level, history is often written as a didactic or teleological text, directed towards some moral or political purpose. Finally, at a fourth level, as some postmodernists will argue, one can usually identify an underlying structure in history texts that corresponds to literary tropes such as the romance or tragedy (White 1986).

Likewise, we should not dismiss films as works of fiction, unsuited to the pursuit of historical truth (Rosenstone 2006). In documentary filmmaking, there is often very rigorous research involved, not unlike academic research. We take heed of Marcia Landy's concerns about how the "insistence on the part of traditional historians and film critics for 'accuracy' is a major obstacle inhibiting a proper assessment of the uses of the past in cinema" (Landy 2001, 12) Documentary filmmakers may certainly take artistic and dramatic licence, and sometimes at the expense of historical accuracy, but the larger truth and meaningfulness of their subject matter may be better expressed this way. Hayden White's notion of "historiophoty" highlights the significance of giving due attention to the visual images and filmic discourse in which history is represented (White 1988).

In the spaces between film and history also lies the "fragment". As Gayatri Spivak (1988) explains, fragments are the incomplete bits of stories of ordinary people or marginalised groups that may destabilise the dominant narrative, but which do not in themselves amount to an alternative account. An example of a fragment is the oral history testimony of the defeated side in history, unrelenting in its criticism of the victors. Although it challenges the dominant narrative, the fragment is not necessarily the historical truth. Furthermore, the seemingly oppositional fragment may in fact turn out to be derivative. The public and oral history of the Singapore left has not been fully assessed, particularly in the aims and methods of nation building and development that the left shared with other political groups in post-war Singapore, including the PAP itself. As Partha Chatterjee (1986) argued, nationalism in the non-Western world

42 *Loh Kah Seng and Kenneth Paul Tan*

was a derivative discourse, tied to the scientific–rationalist modernity of post-Enlightenment Europe. This perspective may be applied to the various nationalist groups of post-war Singapore. Like the PAP government, but using different ideas and methods, the Singapore left expressed a modernist outlook in seeking to establish a new society in Malaya and to engineer its people into citizens. For this reason, the public and oral history of ex-leftists are not really counter-publics: they challenge the dominant PAP story, but are also, in their optimism about organising the political future of Singapore and Malaya, tangled with it. Arguably, it was not the left, but the workers, school students, rural residents and other marginal groups who were the true subalterns and remain largely under-studied (Loh 2013).

Zahari's 17 Years

While all three films focussed on the political history of Singapore, the political element is most overtly expressed in *Zahari's 17 Years*, a film that See made after his *Singapore Rebel*, a 2005 documentary on opposition politician Chee Soon Juan. See was investigated by the police and *Singapore Rebel* was banned by the state censors as a political film. In 1998, the Singapore Parliament had revised the Films Act to make it an offence to import, make, distribute or exhibit "party political films" which include films "directed towards any political end in Singapore". Offenders could be fined a maximum of S$100,000 or imprisoned for a maximum term of two years. Whilst under investigation for *Singapore Rebel*, as See explained his making of *Zahari's 17 Years*, "I felt it was also incumbent upon me to push the boundaries even further, so that the Films Act can be relaxed and eventually abolished" (See and Tan 2010, 274).

When See interviewed him for the film, Said Zahari had written two auto-biographies and, being based in Kuala Lumpur, was part of a small group of Singaporeans willing to speak openly about being detained without trial (Said 2001, 2007). It was thus unsurprising that *Zahari's 17 Years* emerged as overtly critical of the PAP and particularly Lee Kuan Yew. In seeking to further explore the authoritarian nature of the PAP government, See framed his interview around Operation Coldstore. The interview questions See presented to Said, which were based on his books, resulted in an interview that was framed by and in turn drew heavily upon his reflections. Out of the twenty interview questions, only one was specifically on Lee Kuan Yew, namely, "Are you afraid that the Singapore government, in particular Lee Kuan Yew, will sue you for your comments?" However, See believed that Lee became the focal point in the interview and that Said Zahari's pointed critiques of Lee were the reason the film was subsequently banned (See and Tan 2010, 279).

See's film began and ended with the following captions,

> February 2, 1963. Security police in Singapore launched Operation Coldstore – the mass arrests and detention of over a hundred activists for alleged involvement in "leftist" or "communist" activities…

Singapore released its longest serving political detainee, Chia Thye Poh, on November 27, 1998. There are currently no political prisoners in Singapore. The Internal Security Act remains in force in Singapore and Malaysia. There are currently 36 detainees held under the ISA in Singapore – for alleged involvement in terrorist-linked activities.

Zahari's 17 Years provided an account of the event immediately preceding Said's arrest – his attendance of a meeting on 1 February 1963 of Partai Rakyat Singapura leaders, during which he was appointed the party chairman. Surprisingly, Said had little to say about the psychological and emotional impact of detention, beyond brief phrases such as the Internal Security Department (ISD) interrogation being "very intense, very oppressive". On his political ideals and the political climate of the times, Said's most substantive statements were on the 1961 strike by employees of Utusan Melayu, an independent newspaper, against editorial interference from Malayan politicians, and his distinction between the "independence politics" of the left and the "colonial politics" of the PAP. Said emphasised the left's efforts to establish "a united, democratic Malaya", including Singapore, while asserting that the separation of the two territories was "man-made". Said did not tell us why merger was such an article of faith among the leftists, neither did he acknowledge that the PAP also subscribed to the ideal of reunification, as did most politicians of post-war Singapore.

Said instead concentrated on the issue of political detention. He adopted a dual role, combining that of the ex-detainee and the historian. He referred to the "bundles" of declassified British files he had read which, he asserted, established Lee Kuan Yew's complicity as a collaborator with the British government. Said was referring to colonial documents that British historians had used to throw light on the politics involved in the making of Malaysia. The documents revealed that Operation Coldstore was a political concession made to Singaporean and Malaysian leaders by Whitehall, over the objections of local British officials who believed that the Singapore left was a constitutional, not subversive, opposition and who had resisted the call for arrests until they were overridden by their superiors (Ball 1999). For Said, however, the detention issue held a deeper and more personal significance: it was proof of Lee's "cunningness", "personality" and "politics". It was, he said, testament to Lee's vindictiveness towards his political opponents. "That's the sad thing about Lee Kuan Yew: he's supposed to be brilliant," Said surmised, adding that Lee proscribing his opponents was "a very sad thing for Singapore".

The Coldstore issue has since become a major controversy in Singapore, with the government accusing ex-leftists and revisionist historians of trying to distort history and undermine its political legitimacy (Lee 2014). However, these allegations aside, the debate is really about sources: as long as the Singapore and Malaysian archives remain closed to independent researchers, ex-leftists and historians are forced to rely on British documents, which contain the perspectives of two colonial officials in Singapore, British Commissioner George Selkirk and his deputy Philip Moore, as well as their records of meetings with Lee and

44   Loh Kah Seng and Kenneth Paul Tan

other Singapore and Malayan leaders. In these records, also used by Said Zahari and other ex-leftists to support their accounts, the evidence for the argument that Operation Coldstore was politically motivated is very strong.

As public history, See's film spoke to the elderly generation of former leftists and political detainees. It would resonate better with Singaporeans opposed to the ruling government, for whom it served as affirmation. The critic of the establishment would have found empathy with Said's claims about the authoritarian rule of the PAP, the political thinking and methods of Lee Kuan Yew, and the abuse of the ISA. It was not surprising that the most outspoken opposition party in Singapore, the Singapore Democratic Party, has claimed to inherit the legacy of the Singapore left, even though the former seems to stand for Western liberal democracy rather than leftwing socialism (Singapore Democratic Party 2011).

The film, however, provided few new insights into history for the uninitiated. From its contents, younger Singaporeans growing up in a prosperous post-separation Singapore would probably have found out little about the popular ideal of a united Malaya, much less the socialist one. Being taught about the "communist threat" in schools, they would not have realised that the term "socialism" was rich, fluid and deeply contested: for example, it could refer to socialisms of the Fabian or Marxian varieties. Different political groups of various ideological leanings, including the PAP, Barisan Sosialis and two university student organisations – the University Socialist Club and Democratic Socialist Club – used the term but ascribed divergent meanings to it. The term was given the burden of encapsulating these varied meanings, while also expressing the commonly held aim among politicians and activists of the post-war period to replace colonial society with a new order where the state could redistribute wealth in favour of the low-income population (Loh *et al.* 2012).

Thus, the film was less successful in triggering a process of self-reflection among those wishing to explore new sides of history and new possibilities for the future, as this would require a more reflexive and multidimensional account of the past. See, however, was satisfied with recovering the marginalised voice of Said Zahari. Viewers, he explained, could examine the different accounts and arrive at their own conclusions (See and Tan 2010, 285–7).

Invisible City

Unlike See's film, the work of Tan Pin Pin and Boo Junfeng are examinations of historical memory more than history. In *Invisible City*, Han Tan Juan is one of several protagonists struggling to remember the past. This is not to say that memory films are less contentious than historical films. As Tan explained, to question the memory on which our claims about the past are based was "more insidious" than a straightforward presentation of one side of history, for this encouraged the viewer to think critically about the present and to find out more (See and Tan 2010, 275).

Far more than Said Zahari and although also a former political detainee, Han moved beyond the theme of political suppression to discuss the politics of Chinese school student activists. He recalled the crackdown on the student movement by Chief Minister Lim Yew Hock in October 1956, when police fired tear gas into the school compounds where students had gathered to protest the closure of two Chinese middle schools. But Han's larger aim was to challenge the state's demonising of the student movement as communist-controlled, emphasising instead its non-violent and non-communist nature. Even his account of the 1956 crackdown leaned towards the theme of the students' collective resistance, rather than the crackdown per se.

Han showed his old photographs: at the beginning of his segment, we see some of the images close-up, such as students being manhandled by the police. Han asked whether the students were being violent and who really were being violent. The photograph was complemented by the song: in another segment, Han broke spontaneously into a rendition of "Unity is Strength", a song commonly sung by Chinese school students in the 1950s in opposing colonial rule. Han's reminiscences revealed an important theme in the political history of post-war Singapore: the idealism. The passion of the youthful Chinese students, he related, was logical in the context of the day. He did not, however, elaborate on the roots and influences of the idealism, which was inspired by the international anti-colonial and communist movements, such as the communist victory in China, the independence of India and Indonesia, and the struggles of Algerian and Latin American nationalists.

There was another tangible difference between Han and Said. Where the latter was fearless in his critique of Lee Kuan Yew, Han, as a resident in Singapore, shifted back and forth between remembering the past and avoiding it. On the one hand, Han wanted to correct the state's portrayal of the Chinese students and affirm their contributions to Singapore history. In a talk at the National Library captured in the film, he insisted, "history is made by both the victors and losers/ defeated" (The Tangent 2007). At the same time, however, Han struggled with the imagined consequences of his speaking out. At one point, he cautioned himself, strikingly, with a Chinese saying, "When you have been bitten by a snake, you are frightened when you see a rope." He warned that the handwritten captions behind the photographs were emotive and critical of the state. He also mused that the ISD might soon invite him for "a cup of tea" and that his citizenship has been revoked before. At the beginning of the interview, he thought that his interviews would have to be censored. Indeed, Han's eventual decision to retain his segments in the film turned out to be the more effective in dissipating the fear than Said's fearless exposition.

It also became clear that Han's memory of the past shifted over the years. In the National Library talk, he opened with the statement, "[I was] born in the 1940s, grew up in the 1950s, struggled in the 1960s, lost in the 1970s, became reflective in the 1980s, and started anew in the 1990s." An attempt to make use of oral history as a counter-hegemonic source needs to take heed of the malleable nature of memory, which is shaped by the social context.

Sandcastle

Photographs were integral to oral history and memory in *Sandcastle* as they were in *Invisible City*. In Boo's film, En's efforts to find out about his father turned into a mission to investigate the history of the Chinese student movement, of which his

46 *Loh Kah Seng and Kenneth Paul Tan*

father was a member. In using negatives rather than actual prints, Boo drew upon Han's statement that many activists had destroyed their photographs of student politics due to the closed political climate.

Due to the dramatic considerations of a feature film, the presence of the past was most diluted in *Sandcastle*: it was distilled through En's conversations with his family and a classmate. The latter was involved in a casual (and thoroughly unconvincing) exposition on the history of Chinese student activism, in a club no less! "That was a contentious issue also," the friend said, "whether those arrested were really communists." Among his family members, only En's grandfather offered a sympathetic account. He introduced En to the negatives and posed a rejoinder, "How do you actually brainwash someone?" to the allegation that En's father had been duped by the communists. Echoing Han to some extent, the grandfather argued that the students acted out of their convictions. Again, however, the students' motivations were not fully explained, with the notion of youthful idealism at risk of becoming a convenient catchphrase. In fact, much of the Chinese student activism was pragmatically grounded, since the students were anxious over a likely bleak economic future in a society that privileged English-educated graduates. But En's conversation with his grandfather was interrupted by the present – he took a call on his mobile – and his grandfather passed away that night.

Avowed ignorance and avoidance of the past dominated the responses of the rest of the family. En's grandmother responded with, "Don't talk about the past anymore", before closing her eyes and ignoring further questions. Likewise, En's mother replied that she only knew his father had been involved in a student union. She claimed to know nothing about the student protests of 1956, or of 1961, when Chinese middle school students organised an examination boycott protesting the PAP government's reform of Chinese-stream education. "I think they brainwashed him," she explained. En's determination to uncover the hidden past was thus more than matched by his mother's pragmatic but nonetheless painful acceptance of the state narrative, in which naïve students were brainwashed by the communists. It was En's girlfriend, his neighbour from China and a foreigner, who helped him make a breakthrough. She translated his father's handwritten note to his mother, which had been placed together with the negatives and written in the traditional Chinese script (although a teenager from China would also only know the simplified script used by Singaporeans). The girlfriend also identified En's mother in the old photographs. Both the photographs and the note established that his mother, like his father, had been a committed student activist, although she had since rejected her past. While En's father documented their youthful dreams in words, she had expressed them in plays.

As the note stated, En's father was arrested and detained for his political activities. Unlike Said and Han, En's father chose self-imposed exile. In the note, he told the story of a man who returned from a utopia under the sea, but was unable to convince the people on land of its existence. He gave up the utopia in order to remain with his family. One day, near death, he returned to the water's edge and realised that he had no more courage to go into the water. In closing, he accepted that his dreams and struggles would be forgotten; his only wishes were that his son

Convergence and slippage 47

would know the sacrifices his mother had made in raising him, and that she would live a full life and be true to herself.

Lim Cheng Tju and Hong Lysa had criticised the film for privileging the perspectives and concerns of young Singaporeans. On several occasions, it was the present that unveiled the past – the scanning and digitisation of the negatives, and the recourse to sources and resources outside the family. In an interview, Boo acknowledged that, unlike Tan Pin Pin, he did not persist in reaching out to former Chinese school student activists after they turned down his request for an interview. In response to Lim and Hong's critique, we argue against similarly privileging the ex-leftists' perspectives. By mainstream reckoning, En's mother lived a full and meaningful life, and was true to her role as a single mother, bringing up her son in PAP-controlled Singapore. Her "sacrifices" ought to be understood in the historical context and recognised (Lim and Hong 2010). Her refusal to acknowledge her and her husband's involvement in Chinese student activism, and her use of the official explanation of "brainwashing" should be seen as important ways of protecting individual and family interests, as most Singaporeans did after the 1960s. The relationship between her memory and the state narrative was one of accommodation to the official account. *Sandcastle* deserves credit for contextualising the agency undertaken by Singaporeans like En's mother under the circumstances. They, rather than the ex-leftists, are the silent subalterns of Singapore's history.

Conclusion

Even in Singapore's more open political climate, there remained limits to which controversial films are acceptable to the establishment. In 2014, Tan Pin Pin's latest documentary film, *To Singapore, with Love*, was effectively banned after its public screening was prohibited. In explaining the ban, Prime Minister Lee Hsien Loong stated that the film, which featured interviews of Singaporean exiles forced to leave the city-state in the 1960s and 1970s, mostly on charges of communist subversion, was a self-serving account of history; the film, shot in the format of a documentary, was more likely to mislead Singaporeans than a book, he added (Nur 2014). However, the proscription of *To Singapore, with Love*, which shared with *Invisible City* Tan's interest in memories of Singapore's fraught political history, highlighted the arbitrary nature of the decision. Compared to *Zahari's 17 Years*, the film was mildly critical of the PAP government, with Tan focussing on the exiles' experiences of living away from Singapore. More useful for understanding the ban was the context: 2015 would be the 50th year of Singapore's independence, effectively an occasion to celebrate the achievements of the party- state, and an election year. The ban coincided with the government's move to reject claims of wrongful detention in Operation Coldstore by ex-leftists and revisionist historians (Gafoor 2014).

All this goes to show how history and film texts are ideologically positioned. Historians and filmmakers engage in – or are at least an unwitting part of – ideological struggle to maintain or destabilise consensus. History and film texts are sometimes explicitly and sometimes implicitly partisan: they may advance

48 *Loh Kah Seng and Kenneth Paul Tan*

elite interests and viewpoints, which often privilege the voice of history's winners, but also that of the elite losers. When the winners' voices dominate, we get hegemonic texts. When the losers' voices become audible, we get counter-hegemonic texts, which may be part of an emergent or residual politics challenging the status quo. While the voices of losers are important for a more complete understanding of history, they are still elitist in nature, especially within the confined circles of formal politics. Non-elite texts may feature the experiences of ordinary people, presented through a quotidian point of view. Yet other texts will attempt to give voice to marginalised social groups, who, on their own, may not be able to speak or speak up for themselves. The problem with using texts of this kind is that well-intentioned historians and filmmakers have at times imposed their own values onto the people they purport to represent.

It is important to critically investigate the history of detention without trial, and the injustices and sufferings afflicted onto detained activists and their family members. In this, oral history, and filmmaking that utilises it, plays an important social role. As Robert Rosenstone (2006, 16) observes, film "does more than want to teach the lesson that history hurts; it wants you, the viewer, to experience the hurt (and pleasures) of the past". When speaking directly to the public, oral history avoids the pitfalls of many formal truth and reconciliation commissions, which often sacrifice truth for reconciliation (Lundy and McGovern 2006). Acknowledging the silenced past is vital to the maturity of any society. At the least, Singaporeans should acknowledge the contributions and experienced hardships of wrongfully detained ex-leftists, and say to them, "thank you" and "sorry".

At the same time, a greater historical task awaits filmmakers and historians. It is crucial not to lose sight of the historical fact that, in the struggle between the PAP and its leftist foe, one modernist project of nation building had triumphed over another. Since Operation Coldstore, most Singaporeans had progressively been integrated into the fabric of the PAP state and accepted their new roles as model citizen-workers in an industrial nation state based on foreign capital investment. The Marxist utopia under the sea, which never came to be as a result, was in fact a mirage: it was a visionary form of modernisation, development and social engineering organised along the Marxist model. This model was different from but parallel to the PAP's Fabian socialist programme.

Our reflection on the relationship between academic history and historical films underlines a crucial convergence between the two: in their own ways, they encourage mediation on the meaning and significance of the past. As Rosenstone (2006, 163) argues, "The details of the past are necessary, interesting, even fascinating but what we really want to know is how to think about them, what they mean. The printed page and film are both ready to tell us." Both films and academic history are "metaphorical" in seeking to convey the inscrutability of the past through the familiar images and codes of the present. Like high-quality academic histories, well-made documentaries, historical films, experimental films, or simply films that treat historical matter in a sensitive way, are all capable of presenting and contesting narratives of the past, but with the advantage of providing a multi-sensory restaging of history. This is all the more compelling in a post-literate society dominated by visual culture.

References

Ball, Simon J. "Selkirk in Singapore." *Twentieth Century British History* 10, no. 2 (1999): 162–91.

Chan, Heng Chee. "Politics in an Administrative State: Where has the Politics Gone?" In *Trends in Singapore: Proceedings and Background Paper*, edited by Seah Chee Meow, 51–68. Singapore: Singapore University Press, 1975.

Chatterjee, Partha. *Nationalist Thought and the Colonial World: A Derivative Discourse.* Minneapolis: University of Minnesota Press, 1986.

Gafoor, Burhan (Singapore High Commissioner to Australia). "Response to Poh Soo Kai's Allegations." *New Mandala*, 18 December 2014. http://asiapacific.anu.edu.au/newmandala/2014/12/18/reponse-to-poh-soo-kais-allegations (accessed 26 December 2014).

Landy, Marcia. "Introduction." In *The Historical Film: History and Memory in Media*, edited by Marcia Landy, 1–24. London: Athlone Press, 2001.

Lee, Hsien Loong (Prime Minister of Singapore). "Facebook Status Update" (no URL available), 20 December 2014. https://www.facebook.com/leehsienloong (accessed 24 March 2015).

Lim, Cheng Tju, and Hong Lysa. "The Shifting Sands of Time: Boo Junfeng's *Sandcastle* as Filmic History." *S/PORES*, No. 8 (December 2010). http://s-pores.com/2010/12/sandcastle/ (accessed 27 June 2011).

Loh, Kah Seng. "Within the Singapore Story: The Use and Narrative of History in Singapore." *Crossroads: An Interdisciplinary Journal of Southeast Asian Studies* 12, no. 2 (1998): 1–21.

Loh, Kah Seng. *Squatters into Citizens: The 1961 Bukit Ho Swee Fire and the Making of Modern Singapore.* Singapore: NUS Press and Asian Studies of Australia Association Southeast Asia Series, 2013.

Loh, Kah Seng, Edgar Liao, Lim Cheng Tju, and Seng Guo-Quan. *The University Socialist Club and the Contest for Malaya: Tangled Strands of Modernity.* Amsterdam: Amsterdam University Press, 2012.

Lundy, Patricia, and Mark McGovern. "'You Understand Again': Testimony and Post-Conflict Transition in the North of Ireland." In *The Oral History Reader*, edited by Robert Perks and Alistair Thomson, 531–7. 2nd edition. London; New York: Routledge, 2006.

Millet, Raphaël. *Singapore Cinema.* Singapore: Editions Didier Millet, 2006.

Ng, Yi-Sheng. "Interview with Boo Junfeng on *Sandcastle*." *CivicLife.sg*, 5 August 2010. www.civiclife.sg/blog/?p=1563 (accessed 28 June 2011).

Nur Asyiqin Mohamad Salleh. "Exiles in 'To Singapore, with Love' Shouldn't Get Chance to Air 'Self-serving' Accounts: PM." *The Straits Times*, 3 October 2014. www.straitstimes.com/news/singapore/more-singapore-stories/story/exiles-singapore-love-shouldnt-get-chance-air-self-servi#sthash.SlAWxL0Z.dpuf (accessed 5 February 2015).

Rosenstone, Robert A. *History on Film/Film on History.* New York: Pearson, 2006.

Said, Zahari. *Dark Clouds at Dawn: A Political Memoir.* Kuala Lumpur: INSAN, 2001.

Said, Zahari. *The Long Nightmare: My 17 Years as a Political Prisoner.* Kuala Lumpur: Utusan Publications, 2007.

Schreiner, Klaus H. "*Lubang Buaya*: Histories of Trauma and Sites of Memory." In *Beginning to Remember: The Past in the Indonesian Present*, edited by Mary S. Zurbuchen, 261–77. Seattle: University of Washington Press, 2005.

See, Martyn, and Tan Pin Pin. "Film and the Making and Keeping of Singapore History and Memory: A Dialogue with Martyn See and Tan Pin Pin." In *The Makers and Keepers of Singapore History*, edited by Loh Kah Seng and Liew Kai Khiun, 272–87. Singapore: Ethos Books and Singapore Heritage Society, 2010.

Singapore Democratic Party website. 2011. http://yoursdp.org/index.php/perspective/booksreviews (accessed 27 June 2011).

Spivak, Gayatri Chakravorty. "Can the Subaltern Speak?" In *Marxism and the Interpretation of Culture*, edited by Cary Nelson and Lawrence Grossberg, 271–313. Urbana and Chicago: University of Illinois Press, 1988.

Tan, Jing Quee, and Jomo K.S., eds. *Comet in Our Sky: Lim Chin Siong in History*. Kuala Lumpur: INSAN, 2001.

Tan, Jing Quee, Tan Kok Chiang, and Hong Lysa., eds. *The May 13 Generation: The Chinese Middle Schools Student Movement and Singapore Politics in the 1950s*. Petaling Jaya: SIRD, 2011.

Tan, Kenneth Paul. *Cinema and Television in Singapore: Resistance in One Dimension*. Leiden: Brill, 2008.

Tan, Kenneth Paul. "Alternative Vision in Neoliberal Singapore: Memories, Places, and Voices in the Films of Tan Pin Pin." In *Film in Contemporary Southeast Asia*, edited by David C.L. Lim and Hiroyuki Yamamoto, 147–67. Oxford: Routledge, 2012a.

Tan, Kenneth Paul. "Cinema as a Language of History: Explorations into Two Related Worlds." Keynote speech at ASEAN Museum Directors' Symposium 2012, National Museum of Singapore, 13–14 January 2012b.

Tan, Kenneth Paul. "The Ideology of Pragmatism: Neo-liberal Globalisation and Political Authoritarianism in Singapore." *Journal of Contemporary Asia* 42, no. 1 (2012c): 67–92.

The Tangent. "Forum on *Education at Large: Student Life and Activities in Singapore, 1945–1965*." 3 February 2007.

Thongchai Winichakul. "Remembering/Silencing the Traumatic Past: The Ambivalent Memories of the October 1976 Massacre in Bangkok." In *Cultural Crisis and Social Memory: Modernity and Identity in Thailand and Laos*, edited by Shigeharu Tanabe and Charles F. Keyes, 243–83. Honolulu: University of Hawaii Press, 2002.

Uhde, Jan, and Yvonne Ng Uhde. *Latent Images: Film in Singapore*. Singapore: Oxford University Press, 2000.

Westerman, William. "Central American Refugee Testimonies and Performed Life Histories in the Sanctuary Movement." In *The Oral History Reader*, edited by Robert Perks and Alistair Thomson, 495–505. 2nd edition. London; New York: Routledge, 2006.

White, Hayden. *Topics of Discourse: Essays in Cultural Criticism*. Baltimore, MD and London: Johns Hopkins University Press, 1986.

White, Hayden. "Historiography and Historiophoty." *The American Historical Review* 95, no. 5 (December 1988): 1193–9.

4 Independent digital filmmaking and its impact on film archiving in Singapore

Karen Chan and Chew Tee Pao

Introduction

The first film archives were established in the 1930s, as a reaction to the threat of silent films vanishing with the emergence of sound films. The way film preservation is conducted today is, to an extent, the reaction of film archives towards the emergence of new formats brought about by technological development. The paradox though, is that while film archives were born to preserve a dying format, new digital formats could now be the death knell of the very institutions that are attempting to preserve them.

This chapter tracks the expansion of digital technology within Singapore's independent film industry and provides perspectives from the practice of film archiving vis-à-vis Singapore digital filmmaking. Film preservation plays an important role in film history and culture, but it is a topic that is not widely understood by the public. Our discussion aims to highlight the characteristics of digital media that concern archivists, and increase awareness of the mechanics of the digital film preservation process and the challenges involved. Using actual archival case scenarios encountered within the Asian Film Archive (AFA), the practices of local independent filmmakers in managing their digital materials and the problematic dilemmas in preserving such films will be illustrated. The archiving approaches outlined are in no way prescriptive, but instead exemplify the ways in which archives have to be adaptable in adopting practices to situations that may be unique to them.

Singapore's independent filmmaking can be traced to the 1970s, after the end of the studio era of the Shaw Brothers and Cathay-Keris. Fewer than ten Singaporean films were made in the decade, and these included Tony Yeow's *Ring of Fury*, the Chongay company's *Two Sides of the Bridge*, *The Hypocrite* and *Crime Does Not Pay*, the late George Richardson's *They Call Her ... Cleopatra Wong*, *Dynamite Johnson* and Peter Bogdanovich's *Saint Jack*. With the revival of feature filmmaking in the 1990s, a more experimental approach was adopted towards the art form among independent filmmakers. The absence of a major studio presence saw an industry that welcomed various independent filmmakers and film production companies, bringing about films like *Money No Enough*, *Forever Fever*, *12 Storeys*, *The Road Less Travelled* and *Eating Air*. This

52   Karen Chan and Chew Tee Pao

period also witnessed the birth of a pioneering movie company, Raintree Pictures, the film production arm of MediaCorp Pte Ltd that has since made over thirty feature films (See MediaCorp Raintree's Corporate Profile 2010). The staggering number of Singapore films made from the revival of feature filmmaking in the 1990s to the present has been compiled by the Media Development Authority of Singapore in its *List of Singapore Movies 1991–2014* (MDA 2015).

The term "independent film" can be subjective in definition, but it has generally been accepted that an independent film is made outside a traditional studio system on a small budget with the filmmaker's original vision kept intact from corporate corruption, and has an original, strong and/or controversial storyline that is character driven ("What exactly is an independent film?" 2012). The difficulty in defining an independent film is partly because independent filmmaking is motivated by highly personal convictions. The filmmakers are aware their works may never enjoy a wide theatrical release, but are content to play for specific niche audiences. Such a mindset has seen independent Singapore filmmakers evolve their approaches, as seen in the collaboration of seven Singaporean filmmakers in the creation of omnibuses *Lucky 7* (2008), *7 Letters* (2015) and the collaborative work of the film collective, 13 Little Pictures. This cooperative filmmaking style is reminiscent of other Southeast Asian independent filmmakers, including Malaysia's Da Huang Pictures and Filmless Films of the Philippines, where filmmakers take on different roles in each other's films.

As digital filmmaking equipment developed in sophistication and appeared not to have compromised film quality, it did not take much to sway Singapore filmmakers towards utilising the more economical and easily available digital or tapeless formats in place of expensive 35mm film stock. Independent and television productions were replacing the use of costly professional camcorders with affordable, yet highly proficient digital single-lens reflex cameras (DSLR) such as Canon's 5D Mark II, the first DSLR camera that could shoot full HD videos (Digital Photography Review Staff 2008), the EOS C300, as well as the Blackmagic Cinema Camera (See Blackmagic Design's Cinema Camera product page). The wide range of inexpensive editing software like Adobe Premiere Pro and Final Cut Pro allowed independent filmmakers to create quality films at a fraction of the cost. Given the alternatives that digital technology provided, filmmakers could, in the years prior to 2011, opt to make their films digitally before producing 35mm prints for commercial theatres. Examples of such films included *The Carrot Cake Conversations* (2008), *Gone Shopping* (2007), *Pleasure Factory* (2007), *The Days* (2008) and *Truth Be Told* (2007).

As digital cinema technology advanced, many commercial cinema theatres around the world, including Singapore, have gradually converted wholesale to digital cinematic projection (Lui 2013). Cinema chains like the Cathay Cineplexes and Shaw cinemas screen films through a file known as the Digital Cinema Package (DCP), the current output format now required for cinematic exhibition. Digital files are uploaded onto a computer system in order to be projected on-screen. An independent cinema operator, The Projector, opened in January 2015, and is equipped to exhibit films through DCP (Duggal 2014; see also The Projector website). Similarly, the National Museum Cinémathèque also procured a system to play DCPs since late 2014 to meet the needs of programming and screening digitally made, and digitally restored films from the legacy formats (Lui 2013). These alternative venues provide independent filmmakers with greater showcase opportunities. However, there is no publicly available information as to whether the theatres have a digital preservation plan in place, are merely keeping the digital content of films, or like most commercial cinemas, delete the content after their screen run.

Digital filmmaking is further boosted with web platforms showcasing films such as YouTube, Vimeo and Viddsee, an online short film portal that allows viewers to view a growing collection of Southeast Asian short films on web or through an iOS mobile application (See Viddsee website). While Viddsee accepts film submissions from filmmakers in a variety of digital formats, it functions as an easily accessible film-watching portal for Internet audiences rather than as a digital repository. If filmmakers are willing to take the risks and conditions that come with the internet platforms, these platforms provide digital filmmakers the option of gaining audiences once their works are uploaded. Singapore filmmakers such as Tan Pin Pin have utilised the online platform to make her films available for rent via Vimeo On Demand (Tan 2015). Even preservation can be done virtually, though use of it comes with conditions, the Internet Archive offers storage and access to collections of digitised materials over the World Wide Web. According to its website, the Internet Archive's Moving Image Collection consists of a range of materials including advertisements, educational and industrial films, home movies, as well as films that are in the public domain like D. W Griffith's *The Birth of a Nation* (1915). Many of the movies and collections are licensed with Creative Commons (CC) Licenses that allow the distribution of copyrighted works. Users are able to download many of these films in high-resolution with liberal use restrictions (Internet Archive n.d.).

There are obvious benefits for filmmakers to embrace the digital medium, and film researchers are similarly excited at the level of accessibility that digital material present. However, the verdict on the impact of digital filmmaking on film archives is yet to be determined, as archives race to keep up with the archiving changes that the digital formats have brought at various operational levels. For the purposes of this chapter, four case scenarios from the AFA's encounters with digital materials of Singapore independent filmmakers will be used to analyse the changes that digital technology have brought to the archiving operations of asset management, preservation, documentation, rights management and access provision.

Archives, by definition, are places in which public records or historical documents are preserved. Film archiving thus refers to a process of maintaining a coherent and secure film repository. A collection of films and videos on a shelf does not constitute a film archive. Central to the entire concept of archiving is the act of preserving and making the materials within the care of the archive available to users. It is recognised that the best attention invested in caring for these films would be pointless without providing access to them. This fundamental idea and the basic archiving tasks of selection, preservation (documentation and technical), access provision, and all the incumbent considerations of these tasks are applicable to both analogue and digital materials. However, implementation of a digital repository would undoubtedly impact existing archiving practices. The functionality of digital technology, as G.K. Sampath Kumar puts it, "comes with complexity" (Kumar 2011, 71). Janna Jones's succinct observations about a moving image archive further capture the complexity of the organisational practices involved in film archiving, as there is a certain "dialectic of creation and destruction, control and chaos … logic and ingenuity, order and disruption" that define the "discovery, interpretation, re-presentation, and accessing" of the visual experience of cinema (Jones 2012, 9).

This complexity is multiplied for a young archive like AFA that was founded in 2005 to preserve the rich film heritage of Asian cinema. With support from the National Archives of Singapore, AFA is able to archive its materials in a climate-controlled environment. However, AFA has to negotiate the complexity of an Asian rather than a national collection, and the number of digitally borne Asian independent works made is phenomenally high. Selection, appraisal and access rights management of an Asian digital film collection are areas that require particular attention and sensitivity.

To further illustrate the areas requiring attention and sensitivity in the archival process, the following four archival case scenarios are provided:

Scenario A

The Archive approaches the filmmaker to preserve a feature film. The film is available only in the form of an 80-gigabyte QuickTime file (1920x1080, 25p) rendered from Final Cut Pro with Apple ProRes Compression. Chinese and English subtitles are burnt onto the image.

Scenario B

The Archive approaches a filmmaker to preserve a feature film. The film is available as a digital file that is kept on an external hard disk of an independent theatre. The filmmaker, who travels frequently, suggested that the Archive retrieve the file from the theatre to duplicate a copy onto a physical tape like Digital Betacam.

Scenario C

The Archive is presented with a 500-gigabyte external hard disk by a third party. The external hard disk contains several file versions of an eighty-minute Asian independent film, the working Final Cut Pro Project File and the rushes. The disk is only readable using a Macintosh. The rights to the film are unclear.

Scenario D

A distribution company sends the Archive an encrypted copy of a film on DCP for a screening. During a test, it was discovered that the film could not play because the Key Delivery Message (KDM) provided by the company to decrypt the digital file was configured wrongly.

Selection and appraisal

To help in prioritising the materials acquired for preservation, every archive develops a set of selection criteria to guide them along. Given the finite resources and the huge quantity of materials churned out, especially in this digital era, the selection guidelines are vital to deciding the materials acquired for preservation. AFA adheres to a selection guideline as well, and these guidelines (which are available for reference online on the AFA website) are periodically reviewed to ensure they remain relevant (AFA n.d.). Additionally, AFA operates on a broad acquisition principle of prioritising works from Southeast Asia, followed by East Asia and South Asia. Exceptional works from Central Asia, Southwest Asia and North Asia would be considered if they articulated strongly with works from the priority regions, and particularly if they are not already preserved by any other archive in the world (AFA n.d.).

In preserving analogue materials, the format of the content is a serious consideration and several questions arise – is there playback equipment, does the physical condition require migration or restoration, is the original copy or a pristine version of the film available? The AFA's experience is that many filmmakers are reluctant to deposit their original material or sole master copy until they have no further use for it, by which time, the technical quality of the material may have deteriorated. Such considerations are presumed to be easily resolved with the digital format. Given the ease of making copies with the digital formats, filmmakers can be persuaded to deposit their materials in the archive as backup sources. Assuming that an archive has the funding to purchase or increase its digital storage capacity, the selection criteria could be less stringent; and it could even be argued that the guidelines on format become pointless, since the digital materials could all be contained in a single hard drive and saved in a variety of file formats. However, as Scenario D illustrates, the digital format such as an encrypted DCP can fail without a correctly configured KDM, which makes it an unsuitable digital preservation format.

Ross Harvey noted in *Digital Curation*, the selection criteria and curation of digital content differ from that of traditional film medium and should be based on the reality of exponential growth in data. Without being carefully selective, there would be too much content to be handled appropriately; and the expense of the organisational capacity and skilled personnel needed to maintain the burgeoning digital repository would skyrocket (Harvey 2010, 136). Harvey put forth that the selection policy of digital materials should cover the following: future users (the designated community); both economic and technical preservation feasibility; legal and intellectual property rights; mission critical data; and associated data such as metadata, description and representational information (Harvey 2010, 138).

In practical terms, many obvious problems can be gleaned from the case scenarios and provide some justification for Harvey's points above. Scenarios A through C illustrate the huge amount of data that may be comprised in a single digital feature film. While the digital realm technically offers limitless space once physical carriers are eliminated, and storage space is freed up, the amount of investment in virtual space and infrastructure required to house the digital files of

56 Karen Chan and Chew Tee Pao

films are so large that it would make the cost savings from physical space negligible. To further illustrate the enormity of the size of the digital files, the Academy of Motion Picture Arts and Sciences provided an example: The digital files required to match the visual quality of a film made on 35mm and presented on a 4K digital cinema would entail more than 50 megabytes per frame (twenty-four frames are produced every second), more than 8 terabytes per master version of a two-hour film, more than 2 petabytes for an entire movie production (Maltz and Shefter 2008). The estimated cost of preserving film archival master material per title annually in 2007 was USD 1,059, while the digital preservation of the same material was estimated at USD 12,514 (Malt and Shefter 2008, 1–2). Factor in inflation and the growing numbers of digital films produced every year, and it can be extrapolated from these figures that any long-term digital preservation of film would be exponentially costly.

Preservation

Digital technologies offer filmmakers and audiences some distinct benefits, from higher sound and theatrical presentation quality, visual effects and animation once thought impossible, to immediately viewable images for directors and cinematographers. On the preservation front, digital files appear to be the solution to the problem of deteriorating film stock, analogue and digital tapes. Even with optimum storage conditions, deterioration from time and climate-related decay like mould, fungus and vinegar syndrome can only slow down but not eradicate the corrosion, as most of these conditions are irreversible.

However, there are situations in which digitally created materials can be unsuitable for preservation. This is where selection based on feasibility of preservation, as suggested by Harvey, comes into play. Scenario A is an example of this situation. The filmmaker had saved his film on a file with subtitles burnt into the image, thus leaving no room for future editing or duplication of the film or its subtitles. This means the file is not ideal as a preservation file. If however, this is the only copy of the film, there is little choice but to keep the file. In Scenario C, the cluster of data files of different versions of the film makes it difficult to identify the critical data. Without the filmmaker classifying the files, there would be no way of ascertaining which files are important and relevant to the film. This brings to point the importance of categorising and documenting digital data accurately at the moment of creation to prevent future problems of confusion.

The AFA collection has digital videos in formats from miniDV to HDcam, but the Archive has been cautious in acquiring tapeless digital films until it has the necessary funding and infrastructure to properly preserve such materials. These filmmakers are encouraged to archive a copy of their film on tape as a backup to the data files. This means Singapore digital filmmakers need to learn the proper methods of keeping their materials in a manner that would ensure the longevity of their data until they are able to deposit the digital materials with an archive able to care for it. This is one of the reasons behind AFA's series of film preservation talks

Independent digital filmmaking 57

for film students, as it raises awareness on the necessity of filmmakers' initiative in preserving their films, regardless of formats.

Archives in the region are handling the digital revolution cautiously with some taking larger steps than others. The National Archives of Malaysia is researching the different available preservation methodologies in an effort to devise digital preservation plans, while the Hong Kong Film Archive is keeping a watchful eye on developments to determine its next course of action. The National Archives of Singapore has begun to migrate old analogue formats into digital file formats. Some of the more established archives in the Asia-Pacific, the National Film and Sound Archive (NFSA) in Australia, and Ngā Taonga Sound & Vision (New Zealand Archive of Film, Television and Sound Ngā Taonga Whitiāhua Me Ngā Taonga Kōrero) have embarked on digital preservation programmes to varying extents.

Currently, NFSA is exploring the technology of creating preservation backup and reference copies of digitally borne materials as they are received. However, NFSA also noted that the "current digital assumptions further highlight the importance of retaining original components, which remains one of the key archival principles underlying the NFSA's Collection Policy and curatorial values" (NFSA 2010, 4). To guide its archivists, the NFSA has developed "A Preservation Strategy for the NFSA" that has been implemented since late 2010. This strategy has been compiled into a document, and is used by NFSA staff in combination with the NFSA's Collection Policy and Statement of Curatorial Values to guide their preservation endeavours. Some of the key points in the NFSA preservation strategy to digitise its video collection are worth closer examination (NSFA 2010):

- Storing multiple copies of each digital object in different physical locations (three initially) and utilising backups and integrity checking to ensure that no data is lost owing to media decay or catastrophe.
- Characterising and validating each digital object to determine the requirements for its preservation.
- Recording metadata about each digital object and allocating unique persistent identifiers to ensure that no object will be lost.
- Creating and evolving representation information over time.
- Implementing a comprehensive technology watch mechanism to provide warning of the need to take preservation action.
- Developing or acquiring tools to perform preservation actions on digital objects to ensure that they can continue to be used and understood.
- Investigating the development of a set of preferred digital standards for digital acquisition.
- Applying a set of digitisation standards to all activities.
- Factors such as historical, aesthetic, scientific, cultural, provenance, representativeness, rarity, condition and interpretive potential to determine collection digitisation queue.

Ngā Taonga Sound & Vision (New Zealand Archive of Film, Television and Sound Ngā Taonga Whitiāhua Me Ngā Taonga Kōrero) has similarly implemented

58   *Karen Chan and Chew Tee Pao*

digitisation projects for materials within its collection, but is limiting projects to obsolete formats and on materials requested by users or screening requests. Ngā Taonga Sound & Vision does acquire large numbers of digitally borne titles such as television programmes off-air recorded in a digital format, files from broadcast producers and digital features from emerging filmmakers (Callanan 2011).

The digitisation strategies of NFSA and Ngā Taonga Sound & Vision demonstrate that there is a major concern on the loss of materials through data corruption and obsolescence of technologies within the digital environment. This explains the emphasis on detailed backup systems, technological verification and standards development. Since digitally borne media can be manipulated, converted and easily duplicated, transferring material into different storage media can be achieved with no loss in quality. There is no "distance" within the digital environment, and files can be transmitted and shared easily through networks. Complete information on a film, from the originals to out-takes, scripts, stills and audio files can be archived as seen in the case scenarios. These characteristics of the digital format, which are prized by independent filmmakers, are advantageous to archivists in easing preservation work processes and economising resources such as physical space. However, these same characteristics create a different set of problems for archives.

Digital media storage such as external hard disks have a much more unstable and shorter life span (Anthony 2013) than those of the film medium and tape formats, whose longevity have been proven if cared for under the right conditions. The ever-increasing pace of change in digital technology means digital content requires migration from one hardware or software configuration to another, or from one generation of computer technology to the next. There is also an issue of compatibility between the content and hardware/software features. For instance, in Scenario C, Final Cut Pro version 4.5 would not have been able to open any of the project files on the hard disk if they were created on Final Cut Pro version 5.1. Even if it were possible, there may be a loss in integrity within the content. Additionally, the external hard disk had been formatted to be readable and writable specifically through a Macintosh and would not be accessible through a PC.

Another potential issue with preserving digital content is the lack of standardisation on data formats. Digital content can be produced in varying degrees of dependence on particular hardware and software. The films from Scenarios A through C were all QuickTime data files, although they could potentially be encoded differently, or have varying resolutions depending on the original format in which the filmmaker(s) created them. QuickTime is also a propriety multi-media framework developed by Apple Inc., which present compatibility issues with a different propriety multi-media application like Microsoft's Windows Media Player. In order to enhance interoperability, it is then necessary for archives to carry out transcoding, or conversion of the data files onto open formats, which can be a costly and time-consuming process. It is also commonly a lossy process with generation loss. Open file formats are specifications that can be accessed using proprietary, free and open source software. An example of an open source format is Motion JPEG 2000, an ISO standard that provides both lossless and lossy compression, and is now

Independent digital filmmaking 59

considered a digital archive format by audiovisual archives including the Library of Congress ("Motion JPEG 2000 File Format" 2014).

The risk management strategies of traditional and digital archiving differ greatly and require different professional skill sets within the archive. While monitoring the physical storage and environmental conditions surrounding the repository is part of the risk management strategy for archiving analogue materials, archives need to employ good management and surveillance practices within the networked environment that can be prone to viruses, power breakdowns and loss of digital information due to human errors and other factors. It is therefore important to have metadata to manage encryption and security mechanisms that can be remotely controlled in the face of format and media changes where the digital item is stored.

Metadata, the elements that define and describe a digital asset, is an important component of digital archiving as it makes the digital assets accessible and searchable. Archived digital film, video and audio files would be rendered non-viable without useable metadata. As with all archived materials, providing access to archived digital content to future generations of users and audiences is a key purpose of preservation. Depending on the particular technologies and user communities (who created the content), practitioners estimate the cycle of hardware/software migration to be between two to ten years (Kumar 2011, 66). Should the digital content become inaccessible, Cheryl McKinnon aptly points out that it would truly be the "Dark Ages 2.0" for many (McKinnon 2010).

Cataloguing and documentation

All archives strive to generate detailed catalogue contents of their collections, as the catalogues provide permanent and accurate records of both published and unpublished materials. AFA maintains an inventory of every physical item, listings of technical characteristics, conservation work performed and other relevant information about the items. Detailed catalogue information of each film include the item's accession number, title of film, cast/crew listing, year of production and release, country of production, language, runtime, synopsis, search keywords, technical notes, budget, shooting and master formats, as well as information on the film and music copyrights owners. The manual creation of this metadata is time-consuming and relies heavily on the human element – cataloguers who view the films in order to prepare intellectual descriptions. All of this requires training and understanding of the collection, while archive staff monitoring movements of physical carriers and carrying out condition assessment reports require consistency in documentation. The accuracy of information is also dependent on the diligence of the filmmakers who create the pen and ink metadata, such as annotations on scripts, writings on tape labels, still photographs, etc., which are all pieces of information forming part of the documentation.

While cataloguing and documentation information are essential even for digital materials, the manner of creating metadata on analogue materials may not be feasible for digital materials due to the possibility of having too much data to

60 Karen Chan and Chew Tee Pao

organise, access and curate. The "…automatic generation of metadata" (Kumar 2011, 63), in which metadata standards and content rules, may provide a unique key for finding any digital object and linking that object to other related objects. NFSA, for instance, uses the standard of the Material eXchange Format (MXF), a container format that could support the interchange of audiovisual material with associated data and metadata, with the aim of achieving interoperability between mixed and propriety file formats, while wrapping all elements (audio, video and metadata) of a project for continued production or archiving. The proper functioning of the MXF file also serves as a tool for media management as well as improving the content-creation workflows by eliminating repetitive data re-entry, and easing the sharing and distribution of the digital content (Devlin 2002).

Access provision and legalities

For a film archive, providing access to materials from its collection is just as important as preserving them. The support of the National Library Board (NLB) has enabled AFA to achieve this by allowing the library@esplanade to house films for public reference. The collection at the library consists of both published and unpublished Singapore and Asian independent short films as well as features that can be viewed within the library premises in DVD format. One of the reasons for not providing loanable copies is to protect the rights of filmmakers whose works have yet to be published. Due to the complicated nature of copyright of films, AFA, like all archives, sign archival agreements that delineate rights between the owners and the archive.

Film archives are constantly at pains to explain to filmmakers and distributors who deposit materials that archives should not be treated as convenient warehouses. As non-commercial entities, archives provide a public service to their stakeholders (filmmakers and rights owners) and to the general public. In exchange for the time, effort and resources invested in preserving and storing the films within their collections, archives usually ask for the right to copy material for preservation, access, and for the non-commercial use in exhibitions and publications that aid in outreach and education.

With digital materials, access provision technically becomes easier and more inexpensive. The original can be kept unutilised, while multiple copies can be created in open, well-supported formats for different purposes. Usage can be simultaneous with users accessing the material from home or the office. However, some filmmakers and archivists alike have raised concerns that once data files are made available for access, regardless of resolution, the materials can be downloaded and manipulated without detection. Anyone and everyone can own a part of a film. Referring once again to the case Scenarios of B and C, the issue of rights come into question. In Scenario B, depending on the agreement between the filmmaker and the theatre, does the theatre have the right to reserve the use of that specific file for its own purposes or hold any rights to reproduce the file? In Scenario C, given the uncertainty of the origins of the hard disk, the archive is bound by all the legal considerations to determine its ownership before anything can be done to the contents. The issue of rights management of digital materials must include providing or restricting access as appropriate, and changing the access rights where necessary (Kumar 2011, 70).

The question of the legal rights of the independent theatre versus the filmmaker is of concern in Scenario B, as the use of the data file would be tied to the agreement between the theatre and the filmmaker. The cluster of data files in Scenario C poses the issue of identifying the critical data by differentiating the versions of the film.

Independent digital filmmaking in Singapore has undoubtedly created a wealth of material that should be preserved as part of Singapore's popular and cultural heritage. The digital media has opened up opportunities and avenues for filmmakers to experiment and push boundaries that were previously restricted by non-digital formats. These digital materials have made archivists rethink the preservation methodologies adopted on the new technological formats and tapeless materials that have come into archives. While the responses of the archives in the region indicate that going digital is an inevitability, the approach is still one of cautiousness and a preference for the traditional formats that have withstood the test of time.

Apart from concerns of coping with formats and usage, the impact of digital technology on the archiving profession has had an effect on the philosophy of the archiving profession, and the role of audiovisual and film archivists. Once perceived to be the person maintaining the integrity and provenance of the materials under his or her charge, would the role of the archivist have to be changed to that of an IT manager instead?

Film and audiovisual archives are not the only institutions deliberating on the prospect of digital preservation. Museums, cinematheques, libraries and exhibitors have all evolved to include a facet of preserving the different media types that have come to define aspects of our heritage. In Singapore, apart from the National Archives of Singapore and the AFA, the National Museum Cinémathèque has been involved "… in film preservation, especially the heritage of Asian cinema, and has worked with regional film archives to subtitle and archive important film classics" (NMS 2011) The NLB of Singapore enforces the NLB Act on legal deposit, which requires "Singapore publishers to deposit two copies of every publication, such as documents stored or published in physical or handheld devices such as CDs and DVDs. The purpose of legal deposit is to ensure that the nation's published heritage is systematically collected and preserved" (NLB 2015a and 2015b).

The impact of digital media may currently be felt most keenly by film and audiovisual archives, but its effect would eventually come to bear on other institutions that are preserving film as part of their collections. In order to preserve the data and information generated in digital form and which represents our cultural heritage, there has to be a technical, legal, economic and organisational commitment to this monumental task (Kumar 2011, 72). Even as film archives ponder the relevance of their existence and their ability to manage the preservation of digital film materials, it may require all the resources and expertise of different institutions to take on the role of preserving future digital films and their related materials before they are lost forever.

References

Anthony, Sebastian. "How Long Do Hard Drives Actually Live For?" *ExtremeTech*, 12 November 2013. http://www.extremetech.com/computing/170748-how-long-do-hard-drives-actually-live-for (accessed 6 September 2015).

Asian Film Archive (AFA). "Collection Guidelines." Singapore: AFA website, n.d. http://asianfilmarchive.org/Collection/CollectionGuidelines.aspx (accessed 5 September).

Blackmagic Design. "Blackmagic Design: Cinema Cameras." https://www.blackmagicdesign.com/products/cinemacameras (accessed 5 September 2015).

Devlin, Bruce. "MXF – The Material eXchange Format." *EBU Technical Review* (July 2002): 1–7. http://www.fpdigital.com/Resource/Files/MXF.pdf (accessed 4 September 2015).

Digital Photography Review Staff. "Canon EOS 5D Mark II: 21 MP and HD Movies." *Digital Photography Review*, 17 September 2008. http://www.dpreview.com/articles/3491252931/canon-5dmarkii (accessed 5 September 2015).

Duggal, Uday. "New Indie Cinema The Projector Woos Hipsters with Original, Retro Seats and Specially Curated Indie Films." *Mothership.sg*, 13 December 2014. http://the-projector.sg/wp-content/uploads/2015/01/The_Mothership.pdf and http://mothership.sg/2014/12/new-indie-cinema-the-projector-woos-hipsters-with-original-retro-seats-and-specially-curated-indie-films (accessed 5 September 2015).

Internet Archive. "Frequently Asked Questions." *The Internet Archive*, n.d. www.archive.org/about/faqs.php (accessed 5 September 2015).

Jones, Janna. *The Past is a Moving Picture: Preserving the Twentieth Century on Film.* Gainesville: University Press of Florida, 2012.

Kumar, Sampath G.K. *Practices of Digital Archiving.* New Delhi: Adhyayan Publishers & Distributors, 2011.

Lui, John. "Film-Makers and Cinema Exhibitors Going Digital." *The Straits Times*, 6 September 2013. http://stcommunities.straitstimes.com/entertainment/movies/st-review/film-makers-and-cinema-exhibitors-going-digital (accessed 4 September 2015).

Maltz, Andy, and Milt Shefter. *The Digital Dilemma: Strategic Issues in Archiving and Accessing Digital Motion Pictures Materials.* 2nd edition. Los Angeles: Science & Technology Council, Academy of Motion Picture Arts and Sciences, 2008. www.cosmo-digital.com/cd2015/digital_dilemma.pdf (accessed 6 September 2015).

McKinnon, Cheryl. "From information overload to Dark Ages 2.0?" *OpenSource.com*, 2010. http://opensource.com/life/10/10/information-overload-dark-ages-20 (accessed 4 September 2015).

Media Development Authority of Singapore (MDA). "List of Singapore Movies (1991–2014)." Singapore: MDA, last modified March 2015. www.mda.gov.sg/IndustryDevelopment/IndustrySectors/Film/Documents/1%20-%20Box%20Office%20Information%20for%20Singapore%20Films%20from%201991.pdf (accessed 5 September 2015).

Mediacorp Raintree Pictures. "Corporate Profile." *MediaCorp Raintree Pictures*, last modified 2010. www1.mediacorp.sg/raintree/about_us/abt_us.htm (accessed 5 September 2015).

"Motion JPEG 2000 FILE FORMAT." *Sustainability of Digital Formats: Planning for Library of Congress Collections.* US Library of Congress Digital Preservation, last modified 21 October 2014. www.digitalpreservation.gov/formats/fdd/fdd000127.shtml#sustainability (accessed 6 September 2015).

National Film and Sound Archives (NFSA). "A Preservation Strategy for the NFSA 2010–2012." Acton, Australia: NFSA, April 2010. www.nfsa.gov.au/site_media/uploads/file/2011/05/13/Preservation-Strategy-2010-2012.pdf (accessed 4 September 2015).

National Library Board (NLB). "Digital Deposit." Singapore: NLB, last modified 2015a. www.nlb.gov.sg/deposit/faces/voluntaryDeposit.jsp;jsessionid=5237B08FF10EC-89D21AD2F503FA74AC4 (accessed 6 September).

National Library Board (NLB). "Legal Deposit." Singapore: NLB, last modified 2015b. www.nlb.gov.sg/deposit/faces/knowld.jsp;jsessionid=5237B08FF10EC89D21AD2F-503FA74AC4 (accessed 6 September).

National Museum of Singapore (NMS). *In His Time: The Films of Edward Yang Media Release*. Singapore: NMS, 2 February 2011. https://web.archive.org/web/20111211035605/http://nationalmuseum.sg/PressRoomDetail.aspx?id=67 (accessed 6 September 2015).

Ross, Harvey. *Digital Curation: A How-To-Do-It Manual*. London: Facet, 2010.

Singapore Film Commission. "Films." Singapore: Media Development Authority of Singapore (MDA), 2014. www.mda.gov.sg/IndustryDevelopment/IndustrySectors/Film/Pages/Film.aspx (accessed 6 September).

Tan, Pin Pin. "Make A Demand." *Notes From Serangoon Road* (blog), 21 January 2015. www.tanpinpin.com/wordpress/?p=935 (accessed 5 September 2015).

The Projector website. http://theprojector.sg/.

Viddsee website. www.viddsee.com/.

"What Exactly is an Independent Film?" *Make Independent Films: A Resource for Information about Independent Film Production and Film Festivals*, last modified 2012. www.makeindependentfilms.com/definition.htm (accessed 4 September 2015).

Personal communications

Virginia Callanan, Director of Systems Development at Ngā Taonga Sound & Vision. Response to an Asian Film Archive questionnaire when Ngā Taonga Sound & Vision was still known as New Zealand Film Archive, September 2011.

Part II
Cine-citizenry

5 Jack Neo, conformity and cultural materialism in Singapore film

Stephen Teo

The cultural materialism of Jack Neo

In contemporary Singapore cinema, Jack Neo is by far the most commercially successful talent as an actor and director. A large measure of Neo's success lies in his true-to-life portrayals of everyman characters, and their responses to the material conditions and needs of survival in Singapore, which is seen as a competitive, self-seeking society. In this way, Neo presents materialism as a culture that motivates and consumes all the characters on the screen. In fact, it might be said that Singaporeans are basically driven by a culture of materialism and Neo is the one Singapore filmmaker who has proven to be the most empathetic of this culture. Because of this empathy, I hold that Neo is the most materialistic filmmaker in Singapore cinema. I will expand on Neo's materialism when I address the concept of cultural materialism as it relates to Neo's films. But one could say that Neo is also materialist inasmuch as he steadfastly avoids intellectual themes or a consciously artistic style (this is very much in keeping with the culture of materialism among Singaporeans who basically do not pursue artistic careers; the refrain one usually hears is that one cannot make a living through art).

Neo's films, which are mostly comedies (or comedic melodramas), are deemed to be more local. They are dependent on that which Olivia Khoo has called "the self-consciousness of slang images" (Khoo 2006, 88), as they do not translate easily to an international audience. This localism (or perhaps one should say, slangism) puts Neo in the company of another local artist who also shares his materialist obsessions, but who worked in the bygone era of the Malay cinema based in Singapore, P. Ramlee. In my other chapter in this volume, I have proposed a theory of cultural materialism to understand the historical connection between P. Ramlee and Jack Neo. Both talents exude a materialistic worldview, but their distinctiveness lies in the cultural trimmings through which they perform this materialism. Both are perceptive observers as well as insiders of the Singapore society they depict, albeit in different times. Localism, which is perhaps (mis)understood as a disadvantage, is thus understood as a historicist process in which filmmakers like P. Ramlee and Jack Neo demonstrate their receptiveness to the Singaporean condition of materialism. Thus, localism is intrinsic to the development of cinema in Singapore.

68   *Stephen Teo*

Like P. Ramlee, Neo's materialist instincts are responsible for the perception of his films as populist products. Neo appeals to the masses like a politician playing to the gallery and deliberately calculates his films to play up the hopes and fears of the audience. This populism is the core of the problem of how Neo should be critically perceived. While his films obviously do not lack social content, do they contain serious critiques, or is Neo too much of a conformist? Through his films, Neo has been critical about many aspects of policy, including education, language, taxes and fines (pet hates being Electronic Road Pricing and parking fines), health care and national service. At the same time, Neo is careful not to overstep the boundaries; on occasion, he is fervently patriotic. What is the best approach in appraising Neo? His work, in fact, has not been entirely neglected by local scholars (Chua and Yeo 2003; Tan 2008). This chapter marks another attempt to demonstrate his importance to Singapore cinema, taking the position that Neo is part of a process of development based on historical precedents. Underpinning this development is the concept of cultural materialism. With cultural materialism, it is possible to consider Singapore cinema as a materialist conception of history in which the cinema has developed. Essentially, the cinema in Singapore has developed in a major way over two periods: the Malay cinema in the 1950s and 1960s, and the contemporary epoch of the new Singapore cinema from the 1990s to the present.

Historians have recorded the importance of the Malay cinema to the cultural heritage of Singapore. From the perspective of film history, it is imperative to connect Malay cinema to contemporary Singapore film, but there are problems of historical baggage that are not entirely offloaded, not least due to political sensitivities over the nationalist loyalties of Malay cinema. Historical materialism suggests that political sensitivities can be overcome through objective analysis, while at the same time, the notion of cultural materialism intimates a causal connection between P. Ramlee and Jack Neo. The similarities inherent in both artists will be discussed later, but cultural materialism binds both artists together as kindred spirits, revealing their capabilities to comment on and critique the facets of materialism in Singaporean society as it has progressed through time. Thus far, local scholars have regarded Neo as something of a critic of Singaporean life. His films are more "attentive to the subjectivities in the archetypal Singaporean struggle to make it into the world of wealth and status *apropos* the nation's economic success" (Chua and Yeo 2003, 120). This is a view that is more sympathetic to the kind of historical materialism that I am proposing. However, the view leaves us room to explore the "subjectivities in the archetypal Singaporean struggle" which is where cultural materialism is applied to consider Neo's attentiveness to these subjectivities.

Like P. Ramlee, Neo has also been regarded as an ethnic filmmaker, which is the first sign of localism. Neo, however, has been described as "an organic intellectual" instead of a local one, speaking on behalf of Chinese-speaking Singaporeans "whose 'authentic' culture has been not only disorganized to eliminate their political clout, but also reorganized for economic purposes" (Tan 2008, 153). In this ethnocentric view, Neo acts as a cinematic spokesperson of "marginalized"

Chinese alienated by a Singapore society "blindly embracing modern Western values and lifestyle choices" and who then struggle to find their niches "within a basically Westernised English-speaking society" (Tan 2008, 150). Such a view of Neo's ethnic role is similar to the role played by P. Ramlee, who was, of course, concerned with Malay alienation and "refuted the backwardness of the Malays" (Hassan 2013, 59).

While Neo's Chinese roots are certainly a deeply entrenched part of his persona, our concern here lies in examining Neo as a prototype of cultural materialism. The notion of cultural materialism rectifies the ethnocentrism perceived to be at the heart of the films of both P. Ramlee and Jack Neo. In P. Ramlee's films, we often see Malay, Chinese and Indian characters in stereotypical money-grabbing poses. Cultural materialism imposes its values on ethnic communities who behave in materialistic ways that transcend ethnocentrism. Even though Neo may be ethnocentric in essence, his characters are guided more by the morals and standards of cultural materialism. A cinema of cultural materialism reflects mainstream values that are the sum total of ideological and social engineering attuning Singaporeans towards a highly pragmatic or materialist acceptance of economic determinism as the lead factor in their lives.

Cultural materialism can thus be defined as a process in which culture becomes ineradicably entwined with capitalist economics. The production of culture necessitates economic procedures and exchanges. Economics is a conscious, active part of the Singaporean psyche and determines the lifestyle of Singaporeans. A culture of materialism therefore arises, including such facets as gambling, loan sharking, consumerism, or a more social culture of *kiasu* (a local Hokkien dialect terminology indicating a fear of losing out and therefore taking every advantage as soon as possible to ensure that one wins or gets the material object sought after), or a culture of *geng* (to take advantages of the system through malingering). Great material importance is attached to the possession of objects such as money, cars, condominiums and other things. In Singapore cinema, cultural materialism is a cinematographic vision of the physical, material world of Singapore wherein citizens fully partake of such culture. It is the filmmaker's own cultural translation or transformation of economic determinism. This cultural reworking is the key to understanding the concept of materialism in Neo's films.

Though the words "materialism" or "materialistic" are often used to describe Neo's work, his brand of cinema has generally not been theorised in depth, and certainly not so much for its resonance on the subject of cultural materialism. Neo's films remain largely underappreciated because of their perceived materialism. It is therefore the purpose of this chapter to provide an evaluative assessment of Neo's films as the exemplary expression of cultural materialism in present-day Singapore cinema. Cultural materialism should also be understood as a critique of Singaporeans' tendency to conform to mainstream society. Hence, it embeds critique in conformity to materialism. This is not to say that Neo is less than genuine in his critiques. The content of Neo's films may spin around materialism but they do not necessarily exude a triumphalism of materialism. They are thus typically *cultural materialist* in the fashion of Jack Neo in that they mirror a

70   *Stephen Teo*

culture of materialism in Singapore and critique this culture. For our purposes, the films that can be classed as Neo's most representatively cultural materialist works are *Money No Enough* (1997), *I Not Stupid* (2002), and its sequels *Money No Enough 2* (2008) and *I Not Stupid Too* (2006). These films form a loose tetralogy portraying cultural materialism as both an infusive philosophy and a lifestyle in Singapore.

Other Neo films that can also be considered in the same cultural materialist vein are *The Best Bet* (2004), *Ah Long Pte. Ltd.* (2008), *Where Got Ghost?* (2009) and *Being Human* (2010). In all these films, materialism is manifested as a culture or a way of life. Characters are habitually struggling to make a living through shady or illegal businesses. They are often naïve and not well-educated but they possess a streetwise sense of making money, and they gamble (*The Best Bet* is the most representative of this obsession). The characters are working class or lower middle class who climb up the economic ladder and enter the ranks of the *nouveau riche*. Their material and social standing makes them more relatable to audiences. They are also prone to suffer setbacks in their careers and must resort to desperate measures to ensure that money keeps coming in so as to maintain their social class status. Making money (whether legally or illegally) is the main theme of cultural materialism, which gets in the way of more spiritual and family-ethical concerns.

Cultural materialism is so pervasive that it marks the style of the films themselves. Kenneth Paul Tan has commented on the commercialism of Neo's films as "evidenced by Neo's flagrant resort to product placements and endorsements" (Tan 2008, 149). This is a manifestation of cultural materialism as a business that makes use of the film's structure; this cultural materialism is ingrained in the style and structure of Neo's films. Generally speaking, Neo's style is one of broad comedy marked by occasional vulgarity. However, currents of raw drama also seep through when his characters give vent to tearful and grasping pleading between themselves or in supplication before the gods. These are the kind of effects induced by cultural materialism. Significantly, when Neo's characters are driven to spiritual discourse with the gods, it is often to pray for materialistic success, or for selfish purposes to satisfy biological needs (as in *That One Not Enough* where Neo's character prays to the goddess Guanyin to keep his extra-marital affair secret from his wife).

Furthermore, Neo's narratives are often free-flowing, episodic and loosely structured. While this may be an influence of television, a medium in which Neo first found his fame, it is also a style that fits the cultural materialism implicit in his stories. Cultural materialism seems to demand the loose, episodic structures of his narratives. His characters are driven by materialism and therefore a culture of excess. The concept of cinematic excess can be applied to Neo's narrative structures in the way that they do not seem to cohere. According to Kristin Thompson, a film depends on materiality for its existence, and excess is created in the sense of flabbiness in the narrative if there is matter that cannot fit neatly into the unified relationships in the work (Thompson 1977). In Neo's films, the material conditions of life (as well as the loss of these material conditions) are the cause of his narrative excess and lead his characters to behave excessively so that gaps appear in the structure of the narrative. Alternatively, Neo's protagonists dart in and out of their material conditions of excess sometimes quite literally. *Being Human*, for example, shows Max, the protagonist, being constantly harassed by his own conscience figure who represents a non-materialist, and indeed, spiritual form. Max shifts between the two realms of being: material and non-material. But the protagonists of Neo's films ultimately find some accommodation within the materialism of Singaporean life.

In his effort to please the audience, Neo's style of comedy is often crude and sometimes slapstick, but his films connote a sharp, critical discourse towards Singapore society and its government. It has been said that the element of critique in Neo's films is an outgrowth of the authoritarianism and control of Singapore's ruling party, the People's Action Party (PAP), which has ruled the city-state ever since independence in 1965. Where governments are generally repressive, artists have a tendency to embed critiques within their work rather than be openly critical. This argument has been forwarded by Chua and Yeo (2003). They analyse Eric Khoo and Jack Neo as the two local directors who have most fervently targeted the government for criticism in their films. Khoo does so from the margins and Neo from the mainstream. The former portrays the marginalised in Singapore society "with a cold and objective, perhaps analytic lens, distant and unsympathetic to those who have fallen out of the 'success net'" while the latter provides "an insider's view with heart, eliciting sympathies from the audience for the obstacles the characters have to overcome in their struggles to join the economically successful" (Chua and Yeo 2003, 123). Chua and Yeo suggest Khoo is too much in the margins for his criticism to really hit home, while Neo's populist method is more effective and obviously carries a lot more weight as critique.

Though the argument of artists functioning as critics in an authoritarian system is well taken, this chapter takes the view that cultural materialism really formulates the critical stance of a director like Jack Neo. The government of Singapore has a role in shaping the cultural materialism that appears both as a theme and a process in Neo's films. His films then may be seen, as Kenneth Paul Tan has suggested, "as sites of ideological negotiations and struggle where both resistance and complicity might be observed to exist in complex and shifting tension" (Tan 2008, xx). Both resistance and complicity imply levels of consciousness. Cultural materialism is the methodology of deciphering the implicit consciousness behind cultural materials. In film studies, the auteur is the artist most responsible for the total outcome of a film. Neo's own role in the fashioning of his films, as director, screenwriter and star, engenders his approach as social critic, and which should by right concern us here. However, Neo's status as auteur is contingent on his *ideological negotiations* with the system and is compelled by the cultural materialism overseen by the state.

Cultural materialism as process implies that Neo has taken a critical approach towards his narrative materials in the form of a social analysis of his city-state and its citizens. Neo then offers a critique of the system as an insider, since he himself really is a beneficiary of the system, conforming to its values and reaping rewards from it. *Ah Boys to Men* (released in two parts in 2012), Neo's biggest box office

72   *Stephen Teo*

success to date, is a good example of the way he appears to critique the system of national service, while being very positive about the whole institution. In fact Neo takes pains to show that he is positively patriotic even when he is critical. On the more negative side, Neo shows a culture whereby national servicemen can take petty advantages of the system through the method of malingering or *geng* (in Hokkien slang). At one point, his young serviceman, Ken Chow, is mistakenly called 'Chow Geng' (meaning to perform a *geng*), a far from subtle pun on the name to suggest the extent to which the culture of malingering is ingrained in the army among new recruits who must do national service. "National service is as much a part of Singaporean culture as Singaporean food" Neo has been quoted to say (Wahyuni Hadi 2013, 107). Basically, by culture, Neo is pointing to the cultural materialism of the whole phenomenon of national service, including the practice of *geng* and the ways that some families resort to in order to gainsay the system as a means of protecting their children.

Neo may be said to be more of a harmless social critic as a result of the "complicity" between the citizen and the state that appears embedded in the process. However, Neo's social criticism can work on its own intensity as a counterbalance against more radical and divisive criticism of the political kind. In *Homerun* (2003), Neo's stance on politics is quite clear. The film tells the story of a poor family trying to meet basic economic needs and hoping to do so with dignity. Cultural materialism manifests as a singular obsession with a pair of worn out shoes that was earlier lost, but which the child protagonists, a brother and his younger sister, search for and eventually find in a junkyard. At that point, they become inadvertently entangled in a violent conflict between workers and police. The children watch in horror as a worker and a policeman grab one shoe to fight each other, and tear it to shreds. The message is crystal clear: politics is destructive. Cultural materialism, symbolised by the shoe, is a philosophy of need, and politics destroys this need. The shoes as a symbol of cultural materialism function as a social driver of the film's characters to struggle and compete, and ultimately, to progress and press ahead.

According to Chua Beng Huat and Yeo Wei-Wei, Neo's criticism of the system is tempered by his tendency of happy endings that ultimately "let the system off the hook" (Chua and Yeo 2003, 124). This is not only in keeping with Neo's disgust with politics, as he showed in *Homerun*, but is also in line with the commercialism inherent in the kind of genre in which Neo's films operate, namely the Chinese New Year movie. Many of Neo's films are made to be released in time for the Chinese New Year holidays and to sustain the holiday mood of the audience. The Lunar New Year is traditionally a time that accentuates prosperity and happiness rather than charity or religiosity. Thus, the content of the films exactly mirrors the cultural materialism surrounding Chinese New Year (a time of year that in fact celebrates the culture of materialism): the giving of red packets of money (*hongbao*), the exchanges of greetings stressing prosperity (*gongxi facai*), the playing of mahjong and cards in which to gamble for a run of luck in the new year, and gorging on special dishes of food prepared precisely for their affinity with luck and fortune (raw fish to signify surplus, black moss to signify prosperity, and so on).

As far as "letting the system off the hook" is concerned, Neo's characters constantly seek to find some accommodation within the cultural materialist framework of the system. In *The Best Bet*, for instance, the characters played by Mark Lee and Christopher Lee are sent to prison for illegal dealings, but they show no bitterness towards the system because the system itself is so attuned towards their cultural materialist aspirations that they accept failure and setbacks only to go forward. Prison is par for the course in a cultural materialist system. If they were to take it out on the system, it would end their reason for existence. Neo's critique of the system is, in this way, basically positivist, an attitude conforming to the populism of cultural materialism. The tendency towards happy endings might also be put down to Neo's populism as an inherent factor in his work.

Populism as a factor in Neo's work should be acknowledged at the outset as a vital condition of Neo's enduring popularity. It shows how much he is in touch with the populace. His stories and protagonists are representative of Singaporean citizens, and their aspirations and problems. Because of this representativeness, Neo's films have been discussed by politicians in Parliament, and in 2005, he was awarded the Cultural Medallion, the highest art and cultural award in the country. The award was given not without some controversy (Chew 2005; Tan 2008, 145–6). Generally, such awards are given to practitioners in the more highbrow art forms such as theatre, literature, sculpture, dance and music, but Neo has remained distinctively lowbrow and populist in his film work. In addition to his populism, Neo's personal behaviour as a celebrity has also attracted scandal and gossip (as in his extramarital affair with an actress–model that was exposed to the press in 2010). His populism, perceived as a lowbrow element of his art, makes it imperative that we understand the nature of Neo's contribution to culture and cinema in Singapore, as well as the nature of his films.

Jack Neo and the political economy of cultural materialism

To begin with, it is important to position Neo in the context of a Singapore film industry that has practically emerged from ground zero in the early 1990s to its present state of a small but thriving industry. David Birch's article "Film and Cinema in Singapore", published in 1996 (when Singapore cinema was still a nascent thought), analysed the conditions of the cinema and filmmaking scene in Singapore where the government was censorious but actively promoting an environment for the creation of a film industry. From the late 1980s onwards, the Singapore International Film Festival became active in the promotion of a local film culture through exhibitions of short films. The government got on board to support this burgeoning film culture, but Birch recounts the problems arising from the fact that Singaporeans, as avid filmgoers, watched films posing "a number of potential threats to a social fabric which has been carefully constructed by a government anxious to develop a loyal citizenry driven by a culture of self-sacrificing nation building" (Birch 1996, 189). These were "not the values … of most of the films screened in Singapore or likely to be made in Singapore in the future" (Birch, ibid.). In examining the films that were actually made in Singapore

74   *Stephen Teo*

since Birch wrote these remarks, those of Jack Neo have put the lie to Birch's comments. Neo's films, as a whole, represent a value system that appears to refute the assertion that Singaporeans would not likely make films consonant with the values the government aimed to develop.

It is of course necessary to evaluate the values present in Neo's films, which I have broadly interpreted as cultural materialism, and to ascertain the ways in which they fitted into the government's vision of "a loyal citizenry driven by a culture of *self-sacrificing* nation building" (Birch 1996, 189, emphasis mine). The principle of cultural materialism in the films of Jack Neo shows that nation builders need not be self-sacrificing. While they should in fact look out for their own interests, this does not mean that they are not contributing to nation building. It is also arguable of course that Neo's protagonists are not self-sacrificing in their own way. Cultural materialism does not preclude the necessity for self-sacrifice. Neo's success in the cinema has been achieved within a political and cultural context of a government that has moved away from Birch's somewhat simplistic notion of self-sacrificing nation building to one where the government was "desperately trying to engender 'creativity'" in an economic environment made up of "knowledge-based economies of high-technology, high-finance and biosciences" (Chua and Yeo 2003, 124). These were the necessary enterprises "to achieve the next phase of national economic growth" in Singapore as the country entered the new millennium (Chua and Yeo 2003, 124).

Neo's achievement has resulted in him becoming "the national icon of creativity and success" (Chua and Yeo 2003, 124). However, Neo's success and iconic status must be put in local perspective and within the more specific context of the film industry. From the beginning of his career, Neo had been tagged as a local filmmaker. Olivia Khoo states that Neo's films are regarded as "local content films" in relation to the Singapore film industry's desire to internationalise its cinema as it moved into a more mature phase of industrial consolidation (Khoo 2006, 86). Neo's local identity means that his films have "little or no success in foreign markets (with the exception of Malaysia): they are too localized, too colloquial, to be exportable or consumable further afield..." (Khoo 2006, 87). Thus Neo's importance as a cultural figure rests on his local nativism as an artist, immediately apparent through the Singlish-sounding titles of most of his films (e.g. *Money No Enough, I Not Stupid, Just Follow Law, Ah Boys to Men*), and on his success in portraying the social environment created by the government's cultural–industrial policies. The scholarship thus far on Neo has neglected the historical materialism behind his development, and which might, in fact, drive the films. Neo's localism lies in his ability to work within the framework of an economically deterministic historicism. In order to re-envision Singapore cinema from the standpoint of cultural materialism, we should see Neo as a new historicist figure whose work is invariably shaped by the socio-economic themes emerging from Singapore's obsession with economic growth and creativity.

Of course, Neo's films simply cannot be dismissed or ignored critically because they are local. The films can actually serve as cultural study objects, which I take them to be, utilising the notion of cultural materialism as a critical method to

Jack Neo 75

understand Singaporean culture as reflections of the social life of Singaporeans in all its materialist aspects. The focus could be on the culture of "make money" (a local expression) as the end of social life. Incidentally, money links Neo to P. Ramlee, who understood the culture of making money in *Bujang Lapok* back in 1957 (for references to this film, see my chapter on P. Ramlee). With money as a motif, we clearly see Neo's films as expressions of cultural materialism in the social lives of Singaporeans rather in the same way as P. Ramlee had portrayed it in *Bujang Lapok*. As with P. Ramlee's films, Neo's films can function on a metatheoretical level whereby they are critical of cultural materialism that has money at its heart. The aphorism, "Money is the root of all evil" is rephrased by Neo in his own inimitable Singaporean manner as "Money no enough is the root of all evil". Neo shows the material conditions of life in Singapore and exposes the pressures faced by Singaporean families and individuals. The obsession with money (and gambling) comes at the cost of sacrificing human values and virtues. In presenting this theme, Neo is indeed critical of Singaporean society and its government.

Chua and Yeo have already made the point that Neo "presents a direct critique of the government" in that his films such as *Money No Enough* and *I Not Stupid* show "the resonance of his representations with the Singapore audience who see their lives played out and their grouses voiced on screen" (Chua and Yeo 2003, 120). This critique takes place amidst the context of "the Singapore Success Story" – Neo's characters being archetypal Singaporeans who struggle "to make it into the world of wealth and status *apropos* the nation's economic success" (Chua and Yeo, ibid.). Singapore has experienced economic downturns, but Neo's films have remained relevant in good times as well as bad times, and can still be seen as valid critiques of cultural materialism even in the context of the global financial tsunami of 2008–2009 that had affected many Singaporeans. In a sense, the cultural materialism of Neo's films is a universal and timeless force that Neo has captured in his own manner to be manifested as content in his films.

Neo's brand of cultural materialism is therefore prescient, but less because Neo is a prophet, and more because of the historical materialism of capital and its cycle of boom and bust. We might also see cultural materialism as an inherent process of cinema where the filmmaker treats his material critically, as a form of social analysis. Thus, Neo's brand of cultural materialism is tied to the condition of critiquing. If they were mere entertainments, the element of cultural materialism is of lesser value since they would demonstrate another aspect of the economic determinism of Singaporean social and cultural policy. This is where economics would depoliticise Singaporeans and "divert (them) away from all things *political*" (Leo and Lee 2004, 208; emphasis theirs), reflecting the strategy of the government in the 1990s. Ironically, the creativity of an artist such as Neo emerged from the government's strategy of depoliticising the populace through an emphasis on economic growth to ensure "the smooth and efficient running of the economic machinery as Singapore aggressively industrialized to expand its entrepot economy into one that is based on manufacturing" (Leo and Lee 2004, 208).

Neo's growth as an artist has also taken place against the backdrop of the government's attempts to forge a state-sponsored national culture from the economy

76 Stephen Teo

itself, or rather from global capitalism, as C. J. W.-L. Wee has noted (2000). Wee speaks of a resultant "national culturalism" that is "able to mobilize the country towards the economic goal of becoming a first-world society under the conditions of a burgeoning international economy" (Wee 2000, 130). As Singapore progressed from its stages of growth, passing through cycles of boom and bust (or rather boom and downturn), its form of national culturalism produced at least some significant models of cultural materialism. In other words, Singapore's national culture, derived from the materialistic aspects of production, has up to now produced a handful of classic cultural materialist works in Jack Neo's films. Under the conditions of economic rationality, the government emphasised creativity, particularly in the media. In 2003, it set up the Media Development Authority (MDA) to oversee the media, including cinema. Innovation and creativity became the standards of Singapore's economy, as it moved into the age of information and the rise of new media. In the new economy, Neo became an icon of creativity. In essence, this meant that Neo had become a paradigm of cultural materialism where *creativity* involved exercises of social analysis and criticism. As Petrina Leo and Terence Lee have remarked:

> "Creativity," at a critical level suggests the need for one to operate with a questioning disposition: that creativity ventures into the realms of conventions and status quos for the purpose of challenging them to discover alternatives. Upsetting the preferred states of power relations thus seems to be a prerequisite of creativity.
>
> (Leo and Lee 2004, 209)

Leo and Lee go on to say that such a position of "creativity" is "highly problematic in the context of a government-made Singapore" but as Singapore "gravitates towards a culture of creativity, there are signs that a new humanist perception of creativity as the economics of productivity will conform to the requisites of the Singaporean authorities" (Leo and Lee 2004, 210). So far, the signs of conformity appear to be spot on, and this has by and large become a standard among filmmakers, with some exceptions that resulted in the banning of a few films in recent years. However, conformity rules because creativity operates in such a way as to offer criticism within the system, where materialism is still the bedrock of national culture. Neo's films are vehicles of national culture based on economic materialism. They are critical without being overly offensive to the government. Although Neo's films are shaped as comedies, they become more like satires when they exert a critique on government and society.

Neo is by no means alone in showing the cultural materialism of Singapore and exposing that which is critical about living in Singapore. Cultural materialism works as an exposé of the material conditions of life in the Marxist sense of an economic analysis, and as an artistic treatment of the culture of most Singaporeans who are compelled by economic necessity to work hard and "make money". Culture is understood in Chinese-speaking societies as that which revolves around money – this being the culture that has been firmly rooted in the immigrant

Chinese population of Singapore, the Chinese migrants elsewhere in the region, and perhaps now also in China itself. Cultural materialism also imposes a sense of matter-of-factness in one's approach to life. Chinese everywhere are fond of saying that they are very "realistic" (*xianshi*) about life, meaning they are pragmatic – and Chinese Singaporeans are no exception. This pragmatic nature of the Chinese can be translated in cinematic terms into a sort of realist cinema that is essentially the veneer of cultural materialism in Singaporean film. "By reality," Chua and Yeo wrote, "Neo means the problematic aspects of Singaporean social reality" (Chua and Yeo 2003, 121). One might call it Jack-Neo-realism, which should be recognised as a unique product of Singaporean cinema, a form of realism determined by the circumstances and conditions of Singaporean cultural materialism.

This tendency of Jack-Neo-realist cultural materialism in Singapore cinema is evident in the films of other directors, most outstandingly in Woo Yen Yen and Colin Goh's *Singapore Dreaming* (2006) and in Wee Li Lin's *Gone Shopping* (2007). These are essentially melodramas in the realist style, but they also contain satirical edges in their critiques of Singaporean materialism. *Singapore Dreaming* describes the average Singaporean dream of owning the "5 Cs" (cash, car, credit card, condominium and country club membership). Before making the film, the co-director Woo Yen Yen conducted research among Singaporean youths, which showed that the young people were overwhelmingly into the "pursuit of credentialist and materialist goals"; the film was then conceived as a "critical reflection" on these "ways of being" (Woo 2008, 322). *Gone Shopping* is about the average Singaporean habit of shopping as a form of therapeutical behaviour, or rather the excesses of such a habit that has captured the attention of scholars who study it practically as a unique Singaporean lifestyle without which, life is not complete (Chua 2003).

Hence, both films exhibit the same tendency as seen in Neo's brand of comedy with an emphasis on realism, since its intention is to poke fun at and criticise the cultural materialism of middle class Singaporeans (this, I call Jack-Neo-realism). Here, the essence of cultural materialism implies that Singaporeans are by and large unable to look beyond the realist/pragmatist, materialistic tendency of treating life's travails and challenges. In other words, Singaporeans are unable to love each other and be tolerant of failure, or aspire to more idealistic notions of charity and serving society selflessly as responsible citizens. Neo's comedies, and films like *Singapore Dreaming* and *Gone Shopping*, remind Singaporeans that there are other values besides those engendered by making money and getting rich. This greater tendency of satire and critique of the materialist lifestyle shows that Singaporean culture, or more specifically, Singaporean film culture, is to a great extent deeply rooted in cultural materialism.

Cultural materialism as historical force in Singaporean film

Historically, Singapore's film production industry and its film distribution industry has focussed on aligning its disparate audience base, composed of Chinese, Malays and Indians, with separate cinemas specifically catering to each ethnic

78   *Stephen Teo*

group. In fact, the respective communities are practically segregated from the cinematic point of view, and each ethnic group is not expected to patronise the films of the other groups. In terms of production, only the Malay film industry was actually based in Singapore. Its heyday was the 1950s and 1960s, a time when Singapore and its close neighbours, Thailand, Malaysia and Indonesia, were facing a threat from communist parties supported by China. In that same period, Chinese films were produced in Hong Kong, which became the base of production for both the Cathay Organisation and the Shaw Brothers Organisation – the two competing studios dominating the film market in Singapore and Malaysia.

Strong traces of cultural materialism can be seen in both the Malay films and Chinese films produced in this period, corresponding with the Cold War against the communist threat. I have already explored the cultural materialism of P. Ramlee's cinema in my other chapter in this anthology. Cultural materialism in Malay cinema is succoured by the same symbols seen in the Chinese films that came out of Hong Kong as an attempt to infuse capitalist middle class lifestyle values into the community as a counterweight against the cultural propaganda of socialist China (the nightclub, for example, is a perennial site of cultural materialism in both Malay and Chinese films). The classic examples of cultural materialist works in the Hong Kong-produced Chinese-language films are the Cathay studio's musicals such as *Mambo Girl* (1957), *Air Hostess* (1959) and *Wild, Wild Rose* (1960), which offer sprightly, modernist visions of materialistic lifestyles set to dance and music, often dialectically contrasted with more traditionalist outlooks that seem to jar with the aspirational capitalistic desires of the lead female protagonists (played in all these titles by the actress–singer Grace Chang). These films were made to appeal to Chinese in the Diaspora, then including Hong Kong and Taiwan as well as Singapore and Malaysia, all capitalist states or mini-states that were fervently anti-communist and therefore had a vested interest in promoting capitalist–materialistic lifestyles.

In the Malay cinema, P. Ramlee created that which may well be the earliest prototype of a cultural materialist personality in Singapore culture. This cinematic persona of P. Ramlee is entirely compatible with the Jack Neo persona in his comedies produced in present-day Singapore. It is tempting to say that Neo might have been influenced by P. Ramlee. As an ethnic Chinese, Neo has probably drawn more influences from Hong Kong comedy actors such as Michael Hui and Stephen Chow, but there are distinctive similarities between P. Ramlee and Jack Neo to show that their cultural connections are rooted in the same source, namely the local cinema of Singapore. Both worked in the cultural milieus (or ethnic ghettos) of Singapore, and both are multi-talented artists who could perform, write and direct. Indeed, Neo has been called a "Chinese version" of P. Ramlee (Millet 2006, 88). Their similarities extend to the ways in which both artists tell stories in similar fashion and in the same genres. The stories are based on the social interchanges of everyman characters, and these characters are shown to be immersed in the materialist circumstances of their homes and communities.

Both men share some storytelling devices such as having their screen characters occasionally break the fourth wall by turning directly to address the audience. They are fond of featuring male protagonists in threesomes, as in the *Money No*

Enough films that strongly echo the *Bujang Lapok* films. Both are essentially concerned with male obsessions of materialist culture, prime of which is a mania for excess or surplus of possession. Such materialism of surplus extends to matters of sex or marital relations, reflecting essentially male attitudes, as seen in Neo's very first film as director, *That One Not Enough* (1999), which deals with conjugal problems and extramarital affairs. This film is mostly forgotten today, but it gains some resonance in view of Neo's own real life extramarital affair that was exposed by the press in 2010. Neo's film actually recalls *Madu Tiga* (1964), in which P. Ramlee plays a married man who goes on to marry two other women, keeping it a secret among all the wives to hilarious effect.

As I have indicated above, the thematic links between P. Ramlee and Neo are considerable such as the money obsession of their characters, and the ethnic identification and bonding. In Neo's films, there is more a kind of clan bonding in that many of his characters are Hokkien or speak the dialect. It is useful to retread a few other key links here in further detail in order to pinpoint the mutual connections between P. Ramlee and Neo. First, the theme of survival in a tough economic environment is certainly present in the most memorable works of both directors. In this respect, *Homerun* is a key film in Neo's oeuvre. The adverse circumstances of *Homerun* recall those of *Penarek Becha* (1956), *Bujang Lapok* (1957) and *Seniman Bujang Lapok* (1961). *Homerun* consciously evokes the *kampong* (rustic village) environment, the home environment of the Malays in P. Ramlee's films. In *Homerun*, the *kampong* is where the protagonists live, and its rustic nature automatically connotes poverty and misery that augments the theme of survival. Neo sets his narrative in the year 1965, when Singapore was still a part of Malaysia before separation and independence, and when Singapore was still a poor, Third World country.

Hence, the social environment and the characters we see in *Homerun* are not all that much different from the *kampong* setting and characters of P. Ramlee's *Bujang Lapok* films. From an economic point of view, they are practically the same. The *kampong* setting is a sort of tribute to Singapore's brief Malaysian era as well as a nostalgic sensibility outstretched towards the cinema of P. Ramlee. It assumes more consequence when we realise that Neo is effectively looking back to an antecedent period, as if searching for something, from his perspective of a modern Singaporean. In fact, Neo can fit the description of a postmodern figure in Singapore cinema. His sense of conformity to the neoliberal, late-capitalist development principles puts him in good stead to be a kind of sceptic–historian of the economic materialism of Singapore. In his previous films such as *Money No Enough* and *I Not Stupid*, he was essentially commenting on and reacting against the economic conditions of Singaporeans as citizens of a First World state. In *Homerun*, he depicted a period of want and abjectness. The theme of survival therefore persists as a cultural materialist theme through cinema, even if the films of P. Ramlee and those of Jack Neo contain different complexities and timelines.

A second thematic link between P. Ramlee and Jack Neo is that of realism which has to be qualified further. I have earlier referred to "Jack-Neo-realism" as a unique expression of cultural materialism in Neo's films. This kind of realism

80 *Stephen Teo*

is exceptional to Singapore cinema, but it does have a generic application to the social realism explicit in P. Ramlee's films. Realism then implies a causal connection between P. Ramlee and Jack Neo through the adherence to a realistic, materialistic manner of depicting society and characters. This manner of realism in P. Ramlee's films contains levels of wish fulfilment (or fantasy), as, for example, in *Seniman Bujang Lapok* and *Labu dan Labi*. Despite this element of wish fulfilment, the films are basically realistic in their intent to show the ways through which the Malays tried to overcome poverty and backwardness, and to integrate themselves into the modern practices of city living. There are similar scenes of wish fulfilment in Neo's otherwise realistic films (as in *Money No Enough 2*, *The Best Bet* and *Ah Boys to Men*). The special kind of realism portrayed in the films is driven by and in turn drives the cultural materialism of the characters.

Realism in these films is defined through the pragmatic efforts of the characters to overcome their material conditions of poverty, or any kind of social disadvantages perceived to be inhibiting their progress through life. Thus, in the films of Jack Neo and P. Ramlee, cultural materialism is a form of realism distinctive from other forms such as neo-realism or social realism or magical realism (although it could incorporate all these forms). It justifies materialism as a morality of economic behaviour that can deliver social justice, if not equality. It justifies the lifestyle of material acquisition and consumption. Above all, it allows P. Ramlee and Jack Neo to depict the ways in which Singaporeans or Malaysians address their own natures when confronted with materialism. The realism associating Neo with P. Ramlee is a kind of home-brand realism that has historical connections. In *Homerun*, Neo draws on the realism of the past, showing that Singapore had a Third World kind of realism. This was an evocation of an era recalling P. Ramlee's films. Conversely, P. Ramlee's realism was actually a reflection of the modern times of the era. He was in his own way, a modernist. Neo, of course, is also a modernist commenting on the realism of the present. The realism of Neo's films reveals the materialistic behaviour of the moderns: this becomes the Jack-Neo-realism of contemporary life with characters consumed by materialistic obsessions, which is really no different from the realism of P. Ramlee.

Finally, a third thematic link may be that of the implicit clash between modernity and tradition in the films of both P. Ramlee and Jack Neo. They are thus similar in their approaches towards this theme because both men are essentially conformists, complicit in their acceptance of modernity and eager to demonstrate the ways in which the Malays (in the case of P. Ramlee) and the Chinese (in Neo's case) are pragmatically engaged with the business of modern life. Tradition nevertheless exerts itself, when, in getting on with modern living, one's rootedness in culture interrupts the flow of modernity. Neo's *The Lion Men* (2014) exemplifies this theme in its story of a young lion dancer at odds with his master and breaking away to form his own troupe, merging traditional moves with modern hip hop. Like Neo, P. Ramlee is attentive to Malay traditional values and an unabashed modernist at the same time.

Thus, P. Ramlee and Neo have it both ways in conforming to modern values and tradition. However, it seems necessary to investigate the essence of the clash

Jack Neo   81

of tradition and modernity as giving rise to a contradiction. I would like to discern this contradiction in terms of a structural sense of narrative more than anything else. The contradiction can be interpreted as a farce or satire in the way P. Ramlee has constructed some of his films such as *Ali Baba Bujang Lapok* (1960) and *Ahmad Albab* (1968), but it can also work out as a shifting of moods in the narrative. A definitive work of this kind is P. Ramlee's *Ibu Mertuaku* (1962). The film is quite neatly split down the middle with a very light first half that plays like a justification of cultural materialist modernity in the Malay cultural milieu, and a very serious second half that is all about the power of love or tradition acting as restraint against the excesses of materialism.

Thence, in the first half, cultural materialism is signified not only by P. Ramlee's carefree personality, but also by the rich mother-in-law of the title who demands that her daughter Sabariah marry a doctor and is aghast when Sabariah defies her by declaring that she is in love with a musician. The mother then forces Sabariah to marry Kassim and sends the couple into exile where they leave Singapore to live in Penang. In the tragic second half, cultural materialism is manifested as evil, signified by the manipulations of the mother-in-law who schemes to get her daughter back and tricks Kassim into believing that she is dead. As a result, Kassim becomes blind from grief but meets a benefactress by chance and he then falls in love with the benefactress's daughter. Meanwhile, Sabariah has given birth to Kassim's child but has remarried.

Cultural materialism has given rise to tragic moments in the films of Jack Neo too, an example being *Money No Enough 2*, which also revolves around a mother. In those moments, we see economic materialism as a causal factor of human tragedy. This is of course the central theme of *Ibu Mertuaku*, but the film is otherwise notable for its shifts of mood, from light to dark and serious, and from comedy to melodrama. Neo's films develop in similar veins, although none of them are as neatly split down the middle as *Ibu Mertuaku*. In Neo's films such as *Money No Enough 2* (which is Neo's equivalent of a mother movie like *Ibu Mertuaku*), the shifts of moods are spontaneous or synchronic, interruptive of the narrative flow rather than smoothly executed. Such shifts can be perceived or understood in terms of historicism in cultural materialism, which develops according to economic and material conditions of boom and bust. Both P. Ramlee and Jack Neo share the nature of storytelling according to material conditions of boom and bust in human affairs and emotions. There are moments of joy and moments of high drama in the films of both artists, explaining the transparently uneven nature of their narratives, and that is because they are united essentially by the force of cultural materialism in Singapore cinema.

Cultural materialism allows us to see that Singapore cinema encapsulates both tradition and modernity. Historically, P. Ramlee has provided Singapore with its first real taste of a national film culture, if we predicate this film culture on the notion of cultural materialism. Given the materialist underpinnings of this film culture, it is relevant for us to acknowledge that Malay cinema was supported by the capital of modernity and sustained by the tradition of Malay performances. The cultural materialism present in P. Ramlee's films can be seen as an expression

82 *Stephen Teo*

of Malay cultural aspiration, consistent with the general materialistic tone of modernity driving all other races. In this way, P. Ramlee demonstrates that he is the historical equivalent of Jack Neo. In turn, Jack Neo has sought to evoke strains of cultural materialism that can only resonate with the antecedence of P. Ramlee's examples.

Conclusion

The above has been an attempt to define the essence of cultural materialism in Neo's films and their import to the historical development of Singapore cinema, including the historical growth of Malay cinema, which we have seen through the representative lens of P. Ramlee. Cultural materialism is a process that allows us to deduce the cultural similarity between Neo and P. Ramlee. It allows us to recognise Neo as a crucial contributor to cinematic trends in Singapore cinema. The wider task ahead is to examine the ways in which cultural materialism is a more generic force of performance and conduct in Singapore cinema. Limited space has compelled me to focus on Jack Neo and to conclude that his social satire of the economic determinism of Singapore society is quintessential to the discovery of the larger trend of cultural materialism in Singapore cinema.

I have alluded also to other Singaporean films addressing the concept more generically, such as Colin Goh and Woo Yen Yen's *Singapore Dreaming* (2006) and Wee Li Lin's *Gone Shopping* (2007). These films are perhaps more obvious examples of the expression and manifestation of cultural materialism in works other than Jack Neo's. There are other films which are less typical, and which are regarded more as art films, such as those directed by Eric Khoo, Royston Tan, Kelvin Tong and others. The films of these latter directors are also marked by strong symptoms of cultural materialism as a historicist manner of development in Singapore cinema. It is beyond the scope of this chapter to analyse and ascertain the strains of cultural materialism evident in some of the films of the aforementioned directors such as Khoo's *My Magic* (2008), Tan's *15* (2003) or *881* (2007), and Tong's *It's a Great, Great World* (2011). I will leave it to other scholars to pursue this research.

Neo's work may serve as the classic examples of plainspoken, candid cultural materialism in contemporary Singapore cinema. They are funny and caustic, but run the risk of political incorrectness and therefore of being marginalised. Indeed, the rationale for this chapter has been that Neo's work has been critically neglected because he is mainstream and populist, and that his *cultural* status is therefore more controversial. Neo's films are customarily deemed to be lesser cinematic vehicles and are routinely neglected by international film festivals. In contrast, the works of Khoo, Tan, Tong, and most recently, Anthony Chen (*Ilo Ilo*, 2013), have more international currency and they do get picked up by film festivals around the world. Their films may be seen as more *cultural* than materialistic, but this does not signify that cultural materialism is less of a driving force in their work. However, this chapter contends that the concept of cultural materialism has found its niche in Jack Neo and it has elevated Neo to paradigmatic prominence in the Singapore cinema, making him somewhat more of a cultural figure than he is perceived to be.

The films of Jack Neo acknowledge the materialism of Singaporeans, while critiquing this same materialism. Neo's trademark satirical comedy incorporates the critique of materialism. It is therefore constitutive of a cultural expression of materialism that comments on and enriches the materialistic aspects of his content. Neo's work is both cultural *and* materialistic, offering treatises about the culture of materialism and the materialism of culture. They seek to explain the material conditions of life in Singapore and show its culture of materialism. Thus, cultural materialism denotes that Neo's films are culturally and materially specific to Singapore society and its film industry. Neo's films have, without any shadow of a doubt, left an indelible mark on the standards of the production of Singaporean film and its cinematic culture.

References

Birch, David. "Film and Cinema in Singapore: Cultural Policy as Control." In *Film Policy: International, National and Regional Perspectives*, edited by Albert Moran, 185–211. London and New York: Routledge, 1996.

Chew, David. "Jack of All Trades." *Weekend Today*, 22–23 October 2005, 40–1.

Chua, Beng Huat. *Life is Not Complete Without Shopping: Consumption Culture in Singapore*. Singapore: NUS Press, 2003.

Chua, Beng Huat, and Wei-Wei Yeo. "Singapore Cinema: Eric Khoo and Jack Neo – Critique from the Margins and the Mainstream." *Inter-Asia Cultural Studies* 4, no. 1 (2003): 117–25.

Hassan Abd Muthalib. *Malaysian Cinema in a Bottle: A Century (and a Bit More) of Wayang*. Petaling Jaya: Orange Dove, 2013.

Khoo, Olivia. "Slang Images: On the 'Foreignness' of Contemporary Singaporean Films." *Inter-Asia Cultural Studies* 7, no. 1 (2006): 81–98.

Leo, Petrina, and Terence Lee. "The 'New' Singapore: Mediating Culture and Creativity." *Continuum: Journal of Media and Cultural Studies* 18, no. 2 (2004): 205–18.

Millet, Raphaël. *Singapore Cinema*. Singapore: Editions Didier Millet, 2006.

Tan, Kenneth Paul. *Cinema and Television in Singapore: Resistance in One Dimension*. Leiden and Boston: Brill, 2008.

Thompson, Kristin. "The Concept of Cinematic Excess." *Cine-Tracts* 1, no. 2 (1977): 54–63.

Wahyuni A. Hadi, ed. *Behind the Camera: Personal Recollections of Contemporary Singapore Cinema*. Singapore: Objectifs Pte Ltd, 2013.

Wee, C. J. W.-L. "Capitalism and Ethnicity: Creating 'Local' Culture in Singapore." *Inter-Asia Cultural Studies* 1, no. 1 (2000): 129–43.

Woo, Yen Yen Joyceln. "Engaging New Audiences: Translating Research into Popular Media." *Educational Researcher* 37, no. 6 (2008): 321–29.

6 Sensuous citizenship in contemporary Singapore cinema

A case study of *Singapore GaGa* (Tan Pin Pin, 2005)

Sophia Siddique Harvey

Introduction

This chapter seeks to articulate the ways through which films like *Singapore GaGa* (Tan Pin Pin, 2005) engage with the contemporary filmic fabric of Singapore's urban imagination. I am particularly interested in the ways in which Singaporean filmmakers image and imagine life, vitality and living in the city-state of Singapore. As evocative cultural texts, films like *Singapore GaGa* deploy a sensuous vernacular that speaks to Singapore's shifting, transient urban landscape and its complex socio-cultural and ethno-racial fabric. Singaporean films that I examine in my book, *Screening Singapore: Sensuous Citizenship Formations and the National*, engage with the complexity and multiplicity of the senses. Rather than privileging the ocular, where sight and vision predominate, their films make sense and embody the haptic, the tactile, the odorific, the optic and the sonorous.

These texts produce a textured and rich tapestry of emotional depth and resonance. They bristle and resonate with an intensity of affect. In these engagements with the senses, no one sense organ claims authority over perception; instead, the senses of smell, hearing, touch, taste and sight engage in a dialogical interplay with each other. By expanding cinema's sensorial capabilities, these films ask the audience to feel the frame, touch the shot, hear the cut and taste the images. They manage to challenge our attachment and attunement to our various senses. This sensuous vernacular works to destabilise the centrality of vision and deprivilege the ocular as the grounding sense of perception and subjectivity through a diverse array of formal and narrative strategies.

In the context of this chapter, I argue that *Singapore GaGa* employs an evocative sound design and an experimental narrative to reconfigure our ways of perceiving the world around us. These multiple perspectives layer Singapore's city-space with an emotional architecture that engages with Singapore's complex cultural milieu. Our circuits of sensation are rewired, and through this re-conceptualisation of our sensory systems, we, perhaps, walk away with a transformed sense of Singapore as a place and nation. In essence, films like *Singapore GaGa* offer the tantalising prospects of alternative conceptualisations of power, individual agency and political subjectivity in twenty-first century Singapore.

Sensuous citizenship

In *The Political Life of Sensation*, Davide Panagia takes the provocative position that "...political life is fundamentally a perceptual enterprise" (Panagia 2009, 5) and interrogates the complexity of vision and visuality in the process of political and democratic sense-making. Panagia (2009, 12) writes:

> Narratocracy, or the rule of narrative, is the organization of a perceptual field according to the imperative of rendering things readable. Narratocracy refers both to the governance of narrative as a standard for the expression of ideas and to the rules that parse the perceptual field according to what is and is not valuable action, speech, or thought. That an event may be rendered readable thus gives it a value and enables its mediatic circulation and access to the conditions that constitute its political legitimacy.

It is my contention that the People's Action Party (PAP) government, in power since Singapore's independence in 1965, exercises its disciplinary power within and through such a practice of narratocracy. In this narratocratic mode, the state produces and regulates citizen-subjects scripted according to its narrational narratives of progress, competitiveness, pragmatism and survival. Theorists of Singapore culture, politics and the media like Chua Beng Huat, Kenneth Paul Tan, C.J.W.-L. Wee and Terence Lee articulate these engagements with state power, and negotiations of resistance and opposition in a number of methodologically and theoretically compelling ways (Lee 2010; Tan 2008; Wee 2007; Chua 1995). It is the state, in the context of Singaporean political and public life, that positions itself as the dominant force imagining and outlining what is sensible, what makes sense and therefore what is readable.

This disciplinary power finds its reach and expression in many spheres of Singaporean life. Out-of-bound (OB) markers, for example, straddle the spectrum of the readable. What speech utterances are rendered visible and therefore hearable? These markers serve to regulate and discipline what utterances are permissible and therefore governable. Such OB markers are, at times, difficult to recognise as changing policies of the state and the pulse of the political climate determine their readability (Tan 2008, 5). When, for example, does an utterance become hearable as noise or protest? I argue that the senses of touch, sight, taste, hearing, and sensory organs like the eye and the ear are strategically deployed by the state to serve the imperatives of its narratocracy.

The pursuit of progress, national cohesion, pragmatism and survival depend upon the state's ability to capture the *Singapore heartbeat* and program the *Singapore heartware* (phrases that are often used by national leaders to present policies and plans). This state's hyperbolic anatomical rhetoric homogenises the heterogeneity of each citizen-subject's interior bodily processes and subjectivity. The heart as a biological entity and a vessel for a range and intensity of emotions becomes a mere cog in the machine of nation building. The success of state-orchestrated public campaigns calling for Singaporeans to share a common goal

86   Sophia Siddique Harvey

in this knowledge-based economy rests on the ability of the state to implement this anatomical rhetoric along readable lines that resonate with the population. The sense of sight predominates where vision, gaze and image reconfigure an organ that embodies touch, sound (beat) and emotion (passion). Homi Bhabha acknowledges, "...the position of narrative control is neither monocular nor monologic..." (Bhabha 1990, 301).

Homi Bhabha further argues that the citizen-subject is split in a "double time" in which citizen-subjects function as "pedagogical objects of the State" and as "performative" subjects (Bhabha 1990, 297–300). His insight suggests citizenship is not only subject to regulatory and disciplinary practices, but is also steeped in an embodied subjectivity that is lived, practiced and felt. Citizenship is performed and enacted through the body and its senses. These performances constitute acts, expressions and iterations of sensuous citizenship. The sensuous dimensions of citizenship ask us to consider what it *feels* to be Singaporean. Sensuous citizenship opens a space within which to explore these senses of belonging. It is rooted in perception, as a way of moving and being in the shifting material and psychogeographical urban landscapes of Singapore.

I turn to the film scholarship of Vivian Sobchack, Jennifer M. Barker and Laura U. Marks to inform my analysis of sensuous citizenship in contemporary Singapore films like *Singapore GaGa*. These scholars synthesise existential phenomenology with film theory. In her seminal work, *The Address of the Eye: A Phenomenology of Film Experience*, Vivian Sobchack draws upon the figure of Merleau-Ponty to "interrogate vision", "cinematic signification" and "cinematic intelligibility" (Sobchack 1992, xvii). For Sobchack, vision is framed as an "embodied vision" (Sobchack 1992, xvii). Laura U. Marks and Jennifer M. Barker build upon Sobchack's legacy as they rupture the primacy of vision to reveal that which has been occluded, namely, the tactile properties of vision. These authors challenge the conventions of film theory that remain deeply rooted in the primacy of vision as the dominant sense of perception in cinema. Their arguments concerning *haptic visuality* (Marks 1999) and *cinematic tactility* (Barker 2009) take the reader into the folds of the film form. From the surface of touch (haptic visuality) to the surface of skin, and the depths of musculature and viscera (cinematic tactility) within the filmic apparatus and the embodied spectator, Marks and Barker articulate a vision of cinema's capacity for connection.

I position *Singapore GaGa* as a cultural text that offers a sonic-vision into Singapore as nation. The documentary decentres the ocular as the dominant mode of perception and dislocates the eye as the primary sensory organ. It refuses to be seduced by the comforts of a linear narrative and closure; it celebrates the polysemy of Singaporean cultural and national life with its ambiguity, vitality and ambivalence. Composed of a diverse array of voices, some previously rendered inaudible, others, silenced, *Singapore GaGa* revels in polyphony. Its experimental narrative structured according to a series of vignettes invites the audience to participate in the process of making sense. In light of Davide Panagia's proposal that, "...heterology is the ontological condition of democratic politics" (Panagia 2009, 3), what might this sonic-vision indicate about the state of political subjectivity and political life in twenty-first century Singapore?

Singapore GaGa: polysemy and polyphony

Tan Pin Pin best describes the essence of *Singapore GaGa* in her contribution to online journal *Criticine* (2006):

> It consists of vignettes of Singaporeans performing for the camera; while these musical numbers seem unrelated, when seen cumulatively, they give audiences a sense of life in Singapore as well as and its history. It was my attempt to communicate a view of Singapore with other Singaporeans by tapping into our communal aural memory … Our primary target audience were people who cared deeply about Singapore. Their patriotism is tempered by worries about Singapore's political process's inability to accept different and discordant voices (*Singapore GaGa* is after all about sounds and music that are ignored or forgotten). This audience had a healthy skepticism about the Singapore presented to them by the mass media and would go out of their way to seek an alternative, independent and more truthful representation of Singapore and of our life here.

These sonic practices underscore, for example, the tension and interplay of sounds and silences, singing and speaking, listening and hearing. The strength of *Singapore GaGa* speaks to its polyphonic musicality in which instruments and sounds of daily living are foregrounded. I argue that *Singapore GaGa* enacts the production of a sensuous citizenship through its sonic tactics of interruptions, circumlocutions, interventions and revelations. For de Certeau (1984, xix), a tactic:

> …insinuates itself into the other's place, fragmentarily, without taking it over in its entirety, without being able to keep it at a distance … a tactic depends on time – it is always on the watch for opportunities that must be seized "on the wing." Whatever it wins, it does not keep. It must constantly manipulate events in order to run them into "opportunities."

De Certeau's description of a tactic illustrates an emphasis on a particular practice of looking, for seeing and watching enables one to recognise when these opportunities arise. I would also argue, then, for the valence of a sonic tactic. Through these tactics, soundscapes are democratised and the ocular is decentred as a way of structuring and experiencing a "sense of life in Singapore" (Tan 2006). While the narrative is structured around a seemingly disparate series of vignettes, Tan Pin Pin employs the technique of the sound bridge to foreground the heterogeneity of voices and sounds that comprise Singapore's "communal aural memory" (Tan 2006). The sound design is therefore a celebration and acknowledgement of difference that simultaneously embraces the power of connection.

88 *Sophia Siddique Harvey*

Each social actor featured in the documentary enacts his or her own iteration of sensuous citizenship. These social actors infuse Singapore's hyperbolic cityscape with the imprint of their idiosyncratic personalities. Through song, dance, play, music and speech, these social actors perform what it feels to be Singaporean – an embodied national identity that is steeped in nostalgia, and rooted in personal and collective memory. While the cast of social actors in *Singapore GaGa* includes cultural icons like the ventriloquist Victor Khoo and his childlike puppet, Charlee; Yew Hong Chow, a master of the harmonica; and radio news presenters who broadcast in Chinese dialects that are widely disappearing, I focus the remainder of my analysis on the following social actors: Melvyn Cedello, Gn Kok Lin (Ying), Margaret Leng Tan and Juanita Melson. In particular, these social actors remake the panoptical spaces of transportation (Mass Rapid Transport (MRT) subway) and housing (Housing and Development Board or HDB). The prose style of the chapter serves to evoke *Singapore GaGa*'s dialogical interplay of voices, sounds and language.

Opening credits and Melvyn Cedello: destabilising the narratocratic mode and the primacy of vision

Singapore GaGa opens to the crackle of exploding fireworks in celebration of Singapore's National Day. Residual smoke from the fireworks shrouds the frame in an almost sheer blanket of haze. Cheers from an undifferentiated mass of spectators emerge from the soundtrack. This collective cheer is anchored to the national imperatives of a common vision, social cohesion and solidarity; it is a celebration of unisonance. The sound of fireworks and cheering continue as the credit titles begin. As written text, these opening credits continue to displace the primacy of the National Day celebration as the dominant focus. A sound bridge continues to connect the spectator to the first social actor of the documentary to appear on-screen, Melvyn Cedello. He strums his guitar in a near empty Novena MRT station as he croons and laments:

> Wasted days and wasted nights,
> I had left for you behind
> For you don't belong to me
> Your heart belongs to someone else

Tan Pin Pin then connects the next verse to a subjective point of view (POV) shot of someone looking out of an aeroplane window.

> Why should I keep loving you?
> When I know that you're not true
> Then why should I call your name?
> When you're the blame for making me blue

I position this song as well as its performance and placement within the first minute of the documentary as a sonic tactic. Heard metaphorically, the song speaks to the pain, ambivalence and pathos of one's relationship with one's country. Each spectator is sutured into this melancholic gaze and must look through a window at an inscrutable landscape. While a map pinpoints the route and helps to geographically orient the spectator, it is the voice of the flight attendant that imbues the disparate series of images with an emotional anchor: "Welcome to Singapore, ladies and gentlemen. And to all Singaporeans and residents of Singapore, a warm welcome home." This sonic tactic serves to decentre vision as the dominant sense-making organ. It similarly destabilises the state's narratocratic mode by suggesting alternate sonic pathways towards Singapore's national imaginary.

Seizing the opportunity: Gn Kok Lin (Ying)

Ying is a street performer whose tactical performance site is the panoptic space of the MRT (subway station). Ying, a self-proclaimed 'national treasure' juggles while playing the harmonica and provides his own percussive accompaniment by tapping his clogs on the ground. Indeed, Ying literally marches to the beat of his own drum. Ying further insinuates himself intimately into this panoptic space through carefully selected material objects. He hangs a picture of himself on the wall (an act of domesticity) and places a bucket for donations by his feet (a signifier of his presence and purpose).

His kinetic yet slow shuffled movements suggest an itinerant mobility that redirects the seemingly efficient flow of commuters as they rush about their business. Tan Pin Pin's editing strategy evokes the syncopation with its staccato cuts and rapid beats. Ying tries his best to prolong his performance, but he is forced to leave on two occasions. On the second occasion, he is asked whether he has a licence to perform. Ying replies that he received one from the National Arts Council, but the woman, a bystander, seems confused and refuses to believe that Ying did indeed procure such a licence. While *Singapore GaGa* revels in such performative subjects of the city-nation, the film text seems ambivalent about the impact and role of the state as a force that shapes both Singapore and Singaporeans as pedagogical objects of the city-state.

Quotidian sounds: Margaret Leng Tan

The camera chronicles Margaret Leng Tan's performance of John Cage's 4'33" in one long take. In this signature piece, Margaret Leng Tan enters a void deck, sets up her toy piano, carefully assumes her position and commences with her rendition. Robbie Goh's article, "Things to a Void: Utopian Discourse, Communality and Constructed Interstices in Singapore Public Housing" (2003, 51–3), defines a void deck as:

> ...an architectural feature in public housing in Singapore which is unfortunately but somewhat appropriately named, since it is encountered as a deliberately-constructed absence (of history, the vernacular, specific function) which enables the presence of carefully-negotiated, overdetermined meanings

90 *Sophia Siddique Harvey*

> ... In addition, the structure of the void deck, with its openness unobstructed except for interspersed load-bearing walls, facilitates both ventilation and surveillance...

Here, Margaret Leng Tan literally insinuates herself into the alienated space of the void deck with her toy piano and stopwatch. According to Leng Tan, 4'33" (four minutes, thirty-three seconds) allows the listener to just concentrate and linger on sounds that would normally recede into the background and be rendered inaudible. In the long take, four minutes and thirty-three seconds pass with only ambient sounds infusing the soundtrack. Time beats to the cadence of traffic while space flows with the cacophony of sounds of everyday life. A man, for example, peers curiously at Leng Tan from the top left corner of the frame, recognising her alien presence but is mesmerised nonetheless. Leng Tan has succeeded, if for a brief moment, to disrupt this individual's sense of time and space by forcing him to furtively engage with sounds that are fleeting yet integral to his experience of the world around him.

This vignette is also powerful in that every audience member must hear the image in a double time. By this, I mean that each spectator is likewise aware of the ambient sounds of the theatre or exhibition venue itself, as coughs, clearing of throats, laughter, the creaking of seats and other sounds become foregrounded. Sounds that may have receded into the background or been coded as noises or disruptions, may shift in their meaning and become sonic elements contributing to a communal and connective space.

Voice of the MRT: Juanita Melson

The MRT is a ubiquitous presence in Singapore's urban landscape; more pervasive is perhaps the female voice that one hears on every MRT train and at each station. This seemingly dispassionate voice orients and helps commuters navigate the ever-evolving materiality of Singapore's physical landscape. The disembodied voice, however, also serves to promulgate codes of proper social conduct. This voice articulates a narratocratic mode in which certain behaviours or utterances are rendered intolerable, particularly if these acts of social disruption impede the engines of progress and efficiency. While Tan Pin Pin does not reveal an image that links a subject to the voice, she does incorporate interviews and supplies a name. The power of that impersonal voice is diffused through an act of personalisation. Melson speaks with a similar cadence and intonation but this voice reminisces about school girl memories of proper grammar usage. She chafes at the incorrect pronunciations of La*ven*der by Singaporeans speaking Singlish, in direct contrast to the correct pronunciation of *La*vender.

Tan Pin Pin echoes Michel Chion's seminal work on sound by deliberately challenging our conceptions of image–sound relations. In this sense, Tan Pin Pin does not presume that a voice must be accompanied by an image of its source. She similarly does not assume a sonic hierarchy in which sound is continually yoked in service of the image. Tan Pin Pin creatively explores the power, allure and contradiction of the acousmêtre. Chion (1999, 21–4) writes

> When the acousmatic presence is a voice, and especially when this voice has not yet been visualized - that is, when we cannot yet connect it to a face – we get a special being, a kind of talking and acting shadow to which we attach the name acousmêtre ... The powers are four: the ability to be everywhere, to see all, to know all, and to have complete power. In other words, ubiquity, panopticism, omniscience, and omnipotence...

Tan Pin Pin chooses not to reveal the face of Juanita Melson. While the image is withheld, the latent subjectivity beneath the voice, its intonations, grain, texture and accent are revealed. There is a person behind and beneath this implacable voice. I would argue that a degree of the disciplinary sway of this voice is lessened; no spectator will ever quite hear that voice along the same registers of power.

Singapore GaGa ends in much the same manner as it began. Shots of scenes from the official annual National Day Parade are punctuated with national signifiers such as the Singapore flag. This time, however, the undifferentiated mass becomes somewhat recognisable as individuals. The crowds continue to wave and cheer as the narratocratic spectacle continues to unfold: "Stand up for Singapore" blares through the loudspeakers, neon glow sticks shine in solidarity, and a man climbs the pinnacle of a giant peak, waving a Singapore flag after a successful summit. To counter this narratocratic spectacle, Tan Pin Pin uses a sound bridge to take us back to Melvyn's lament of wasted nights and lost loves. A metaphorical ambivalence serves to counter the certainty and ideological call to stand up for Singapore.

Sensuous citizenship: reception

Singapore GaGa's communal aural memory does not merely exist within an inert filmic object, one exhibited only within the air-conditioned confines of a darkened theatre. Tan Pin Pin sought to "...take *Singapore GaGa* out of cinemas" and to "the people" (Tan 2006). For example, Tan Pin Pin screened the documentary in school auditoriums, thereby reconfiguring the space of exhibition to accommodate alternate ways of viewing, listening and experiencing the film. From Tan Pin Pin's observations and narrative accounts, schoolchildren engaged in a participatory dialogue with the social actors and images on-screen; they cheered, they sang, they appeared to be "...peering curiously at the screen, watching themselves..." (Tan 2006). The power of *Singapore GaGa* lies precisely in its ability to touch audiences, to reach within them and ignite a conversation of what it means to feel not only a collective Singaporean identity but an individual one as well. Tan Pin Pin's exhibition and distribution strategies therefore imbricate *Singapore GaGa* and its diverse audiences in a phenomenologically intimate way. Jennifer M. Barker speaks to this when she writes that the relationship between film and viewer ought to be positioned as "...intimately related but not identical, caught up in a relationship of intersubjectivity and co-constitution, rather than as subject and object positioned on opposite sides of the screen" (2009, 12–13).

92 *Sophia Siddique Harvey*

Conclusion

Davide Panagia (2009, 15) articulates the possibilities of imagining perceptual alternatives when he writes:

> ...that though we might ordinarily engage with objects in a narratocratic mode, there is nothing in the activity of critical political theorizing that requires individuals to have to accept or submit to narratocracy as the standard by which actions, events, and subjectivities are at once articulated and rendered meaningful.

Singapore GaGa's sensuous vernacular speaks of Singapore's "semantic openness" (Short 2011, 8). Tan Pin Pin and her social actors "reclaim it [Singapore] for ourselves and define it [Singapore] for ourselves" (Tan 2006). This political intervention is particularly potent given the state's current preoccupation with the guiding principles of *Singapore 21*. The introduction to *Singapore 21* (8) states:

> Modern Singapore has achieved its present level of peace and progress, thanks to the ideals of a far-sighted and dedicated founding generation of leaders and citizens. Building on this firm foundation, Singapore 21, launched by Prime Minister Goh Chok Tong in 1997, seeks to articulate a vision that Singaporeans can reach out for together to build the society we want for the year 2000 and beyond...

This is narratocracy at its most palpable; it is a grand vision of forward propulsion. It is vital that cultural texts such as *Singapore GaGa* and the other films I analyse offer their own constructions of sensuous citizenship that destabilise this narratocratic imperative. *Singapore GaGa* calls for an alternative mode of speaking that asks the viewer to pay attention to the politics of listening to and with the nation.

References

Barker, Jennifer M. *The Tactile Eye: Touch and the Cinematic Experience.* Berkeley: University of California Press, 2009.

Bhabha, Homi K. "DissemiNation: Time, Narrative, and the Margins of the Modern Nation." In *Nation and Narration*, edited by Homi K. Bhabha, 291–322. New York: Routledge, 1990.

Chion, Michel. *The Voice in Cinema.* Translated by Claudia Gorbman. New York: Columbia University Press, 1999.

Chua, Beng Huat. *Communitarian Ideology and Democracy in Singapore.* New York: Routledge, 1995.

de Certeau, Michel. *The Practice of Everyday Life.* Translated by Steven F. Rendall. Berkeley: University of California Press, 1984.

Goh, Robbie B.H. "Things to a Void: Utopian Discourse, Communality and Constructed Interstices in Singapore Public Housing." In *Theorizing the Southeast Asian City as Text: Urban Landscapes, Cultural Documents, and Interpretative Experiences*, edited by Robbie B.H. Goh and Brenda S.A. Yeoh, 51–75. Hackensack: World Scientific Publishing, 2003.

Lee, Terence. *The Media, Cultural Control and Government in Singapore*. London: Routledge, 2010.

Marks, Laura U. *The Skin of the Film: Intercultural Cinema, Embodiment, and the Senses*. Durham: Duke University Press, 1999.

Panagia, Davide. *The Political Life of Sensation*. Durham: Duke University Press, 2009.

"Singapore 21 Report." www.singapore21.org.sg/s21_reports.html (accessed 11 May 2011).

Short, Sue. *Cyborg Cinema*. London: Palgrave Macmillan, 2011.

Sobchack, Vivian. *The Address of the Eye: A Phenomenology of Film Experience*. Princeton: Princeton University Press, 1992.

Tan, Kenneth Paul. *Cinema and Television in Singapore: Resistance in One Dimension*. Leiden: Brill, 2008.

Tan, Pin Pin. "Singapore GaGa Tours Singapore." *Criticine: Elevating Discourse on Southeast Asian Cinema*, 4 May 2006. http://www.criticine.com/feature_article.php?id=30 (accessed 15 June 2011).

Wee, C.J.W.-L. *The Asian Modern: Culture, Capitalist Development, Singapore*. Hong Kong: Hong Kong University Press, 2007.

7 Popular music and contemporary Singaporean cinema

Liew Kai Khiun and Brenda Chan

Introduction

Music in film has the primary functions of conveying emotions and providing lenses through which the audience may understand the inner thoughts of the characters or the overarching themes of the film. Film music also allows spectators to imagine, and identify with, the context of the narrative which may be remote from the audience's everyday life (Green 2010, 82–6). Film music is usually categorised into *diegetic* music (music that is part of the narrative world of the film and is "heard" by the characters) and *non-diegetic* music (music that is heard only by the audience) (Ramsey 2002, 314; Brown 1994, 67). This chapter examines the diegetic and non-diegetic popular music used in the soundtracks of a range of Singaporean films from the 1990s to 2011. Collectively, these soundtracks represent Singaporean filmmakers' attempts at seeking the voices and identities of Singaporeans, as they negotiate tensions between the English-speaking, Mandarin-speaking and dialect-speaking segments of the ethnic Chinese community in Singapore.

Discussions of the soundtracks of films in this chapter will be undertaken in two parts, namely the use of nostalgia in resurrected songs of the recent past as cinematic acts of reminiscence in diegetic styles, as well as the more original Chinese songs in the films of Jack Neo that deal with the struggles of the present in a non-diegetic manner. Although veering in opposite directions, the soundtracks of these films are crucial in the broader negotiations of Singapore's soundscapes in cinema against the displacements – real and perceived – arising from the rapid pace of urbanisation, immigration and modernisation in the city-state.

Popular music and nostalgia in Singaporean films

Nostalgia films seek to recapture the fashion styles and atmosphere of a bygone era (Jameson 1991). David Shumway (1999, 40) argues that "music is the most important ingredient in the production of the affect of nostalgia" in such films, as it has the power to recreate the alternative world of a fictionalised and idealised past for the viewer, even if he or she may not have lived through that era. In this section, we will analyse the ways through which popular music is used to produce

Popular music 95

nostalgia in two locally produced films, *Forever Fever* (1998) and *It's a Great Great World/Da Shi Jie* (2011).

Forever Fever (1998), directed by Glen Goei, approximates Jameson's notion of the postmodern nostalgia film as a work of pastiche blending elements from Bruce Lee's martial arts films with John Badham's *Saturday Night Fever* (1977, starring John Travolta). Set in 1978 Singapore, the central character of the film is Hock (played by Adrian Pang), a grocery clerk who idolises Bruce Lee and joins a disco competition in order to win cash to buy a motorcycle (Uhde and Uhde 2000). The film was bought by Miramax and later released in the United States as *That's The Way I Like It*, making it the first Singapore film to break into the international market beyond the film festival circuit (Berry and Farquhar 2006). Moreover, international audiences find resonance with *Forever Fever*'s soundtrack of disco hits such as "Kung Fu Fighting" and "Jive Talking", covered by local Singaporean artistes. These disco songs alternate between their functions as diegetic and non-diegetic music in the film, in addition to referencing memorable scenes in *Saturday Night Fever*. For example, prior to Hock's first visit to a discotheque, he undergoes a makeover – buying a glossy body-hugging shirt and perming his hair – after which he is seen strutting down the streets, with "Staying Alive" as the extra-diegetic music in the background. In this scene, the camera first focuses on Hock's brand new shoes and slowly moves up to his bell-bottomed pants and then his new neon-yellow shirt, and finally his smug expression of newfound self-confidence. The camerawork in this sequence closely mimics the opening credits of *Saturday Night Fever*, with Tony Manero (John Travolta) walking down a busy street to the tune of "Staying Alive" by the Bee Gees.

An example of music serving a diegetic function in *Forever Fever* is Hock's climactic solo performance on the dance floor during his first visit to the discotheque, where he reprises John Travolta's classic solo dance sequence in *Saturday Night Fever*, using the same song "You Should Be Dancing" and similar dance moves. While both Hock and Tony Manero exude masculine sexuality as well as athletic and acrobatic dexterity in their dance performances, Hock infuses an added air of narcissism and incorporates kung fu moves into his dance, not unlike his idol Bruce Lee.

As Chris Berry and Mary Farquhar (2006, 221) have pointed out, Hock's "double mimicry" of Bruce Lee and John Travolta, two well-known global stars, speaks to the hybrid East–West identity of the Singaporean subject; and by extension, the survival of the nation state of Singapore within the transnational capitalist order. Similarly, Khoo Gaik Cheng (2004) argues that Hock represents a post-colonial hybrid masculine identity within a society that has integrated its vernacular languages and traditional Asian values with the consumption of imported Western popular culture. The opening scene of *Forever Fever* drives home this hybridity through its display of:

> a world map which locates Singapore spatially and audibly within the global spread and "flow" (Appadurai 1996) of disco fever as the sound of radio deejays introducing disco in various languages is accompanied by dots of

96   *Liew Kai Khiun and Brenda Chan*

radio stations on the global map lighting up across continents. Temporally, the year 1977 appears juxtaposed on the map to signify the moment of disco's arrival or, rather, the arrival of American cultural and neo-economic imperialism in Singapore.

(Khoo 2004, 3–4)

Not only was Singapore one of the nodal points in the global circulation of Western popular music, it was also situated at the crossroads of the transnational flows of Chinese popular music – a scenario that still remains today. This is because the ethnic Chinese community in Singapore has been bifurcated into English-educated and Chinese-educated segments, as a result of the co-existence of English-medium schools and vernacular schools in Singapore during the colonial days. The vernacular schools for the Chinese, Malay and Indian students were important institutions in maintaining ethnic identities and boundaries (Chiew 1997). In the days before independence, the textbooks used in the Chinese-medium schools were oriented towards China, while those in the English schools were oriented towards Britain. So, despite being of the same ethnicity, the English-educated and the Chinese-educated were very different in terms of cultural outlook, political inclination and language use (Lau 1999; Kwok 1994). The English-educated Singaporeans listened to Western popular music, while the Chinese-educated consumed Mandarin popular music imported from Taiwan and Hong Kong, as well as popular songs in Chinese vernacular languages such as Cantonese, Hokkien and Teochew. In a more recent film *It's a Great Great World* (2011), Mandarin popular music was appropriated in the construction of nostalgia for an imagined past of Singapore in the 1950s and 1960s.

Directed by Kelvin Tong, *It's a Great Great World* (hereafter abbreviated as *Great World*) features the life stories of a street vendor (Ah Meng), a carnival shooting gallery operator (Mei Juan), a nightclub singer (Mei Gui) and a clown (Ah Boo), all of whom worked at the Great World Amusement Park. The real Great World Amusement Park in Singapore history was a popular entertainment venue that was first built in the 1930s, used as a prisoner of war (POW) camp during the Japanese Occupation (1942–1945), and was reopened in 1958 with a ferris wheel, children's rides, restaurants, four cinemas and a cabaret. After the amusement park was closed in 1964, the cinemas and restaurants continued to operate before finally closing down in 1978 (Tong 1997).

In the film, the stories of the main characters occurred between the 1940s and 1960s; for instance, Ah Meng's wedding banquet took place in the Wing Choon Yuen Restaurant in Great World on the night that the Japanese bombed Singapore, while Ah Boo's story was about his attempt to take a picture with Elizabeth Taylor when she visited Sky Theatre in 1958 (Han 2011). While the director Kelvin Tong has attempted to recreate the façade of Great World in the film set, popular music proved to be the more powerful element in the film for evoking the atmosphere of the 1950s and 1960s. The story of Ah Boo opened with the lively strains of Ge Lan's "I Love Cha-Cha/ Wo Ai Cha Cha", a sub-theme from *Mambo Girl/Manbo Nülang*, a 1957 Mandarin film produced in Hong Kong. Ah Boo (played by Henry

Thia) was seen dancing and singing to the song as he dressed for work. Another Mandarin song by Ge Lan, "Jajambo/Shuo bu chu de kuaihuo" (1960), is featured in another segment of the film, in the form of a cover version performed by ageing cabaret singer Mei Gui (played by Xiang Yun). Mei Gui has been pining for her long-lost lover, but eventually learns that he has married a Thai woman. With her dreams shattered, Mei Gui decides to put her past behind her and performs a new song, "Jajambo", for her audience. "Jajambo" is a fast-paced sensuous number taken from *The Wild, Wild Rose/Ye Meigui Zhi Lian* (1960), an award-winning film adaptation of Bizet's *Carmen* by Hong Kong director Wong Tin Lam (Teo 1997). The name of the Great World songstress Mei Gui, meaning "Rose" in English, also plays upon Ge Lan's role in *The Wild, Wild Rose* as a nightclub singer nicknamed Ye Meigui (Wild Rose) for her feisty, sexy and flirtatious character.

Ge Lan, also known as Grace Chang, was the "most representative musical star-cum-actress" during the heyday of Mandarin musicals in Hong Kong cinema in the 1950s and 1960s (Teo 1997, 34). The popular Mandarin songs that she sang in her films are still referenced today in Chinese-language cinema, including Singaporean films. Another Singaporean director, Royston Tan, used Ge Lan's "I Don't Care Who You Are/Wo Bu Guan Ni Shi Shui" as the extra-diegetic opening music to his short film, *Hock Hiap Leong* (2001), which captures the last days of business in a fifty-five-year-old coffee shop before it is slated for demolition by the republic's urban renewal authorities. In the second half of Tan's short film, the young man lamenting the impending demolition of the coffee shop leads a group of men and women clad in 1960s fashion in a campy and comical song and dance segment, lip-syncing to Ge Lan's "I Love Cha-Cha". Royston Tan's *Hock Hiap Leong* clearly draws its inspiration from Tsai Ming-liang's *The Hole/Dong* (1998) (Millet 2006, 111), as the latter features five fantasy musical sequences set to Ge Lan's "I Want Your Love/Wo Yao Ni De Ai" (adapted from Georgia Gibbs' "I Want You To Be My Baby"), "I Love Calypso/Wo Ai Ka Li Su" (from the Mandarin musical *Air Hostess/Kongzhong Xiaojie*, 1958), "Vixen/Yanzhi Hu", "Sneezing/Da Pen Ti" (adapted from The McGuire Sisters' "Achoo Cha Cha") and "I Don't Care Who You Are/Bu Guan Ni Shi Shui" (from *The Loving Couple/Xin Xin Xiang Yin*, starring Grace Chang in 1960).

Corrado Neri (2008, 400) opined that the use of Ge Lan's music in *The Hole* expresses nostalgia for "a past where emotions were still conceivable", contrasted against a dystopic commodified society in the present in which human relationships are cold, repressed and dysfunctional. However, Jean Ma (2011) argues that such a reading obscures the fact that Ge Lan's films and songs were produced and consumed in the highly commercialised context of the studio era in post-war Hong Kong cinema. In fact, we would argue that Ge Lan's music is a floating signifier of nostalgia in contemporary Sinophone cinema. While *The Hole* and *Hock Hiap Leong* employ fantasy song and dance sequences to Ge Lan's songs to highlight the sense of alienation and loss of community in urbanised societies, *Great World* takes on a different mood with a more realist mode of storytelling, composed primarily of flashbacks as the aged Ah Meng recalls the various characters working in the Great World Amusement Park, including his own life story.

98   *Liew Kai Khiun and Brenda Chan*

All the snippets in Kelvin Tong's film have happy endings that bring a smile to the old man recounting the stories. For example, when Mei Gui realises that her years of waiting for her fiancé have come to nought, she revitalises her flagging career with a new song, and discovers that her nightclub boss is actually in love with her. It is a reversal of the archetypal character of the tragic songstress in the romantic melodramas of Hong Kong cinema in the 1950s and 1960s (Teo 1997), or even Ge Lan's role in *The Wild, Wild Rose* as a sultry nightclub diva who is eventually killed by her own husband. Devoid of the melancholy characterising Tsai's and Tan's films, and unlike Royston Tan's critique of the destructive forces of progress in *Hock Hiap Leong*, Ge Lan's songs in *Great World* merely transports audiences to the old-world charm of Great World in the 1950s and 1960s. The film is but memories of a lost past without a tinge of bitterness or regret; after all, many older Singaporeans remember the amusement park as a place of fun and pleasure in their childhood, and it was simply destined to go when it was surpassed by other forms of entertainment (such as television).

Both *Forever Fever* and *Great World* represent instances of commodified nostalgia. According to Shumway (1999, 39–40), commodified nostalgia

> involves the revival by the culture industry of certain fashions and styles of a particular past era … Such commodified nostalgia evokes the affect of nostalgia even among those who do not have actual memory of the period being revived.

Popular music belonging to a certain era may be revived in films that repackage the past as a commodity to audiences. In so doing, argues Shumway (1999), such films often obscure the original subversive quality of the music in its actual history, as well as the cultural conflicts associated with the era from which the music is taken. For example, *American Graffiti* (1973) recreates the idealised aura of the 1950s through its rock and roll music, displacing a historical understanding of the past, and thereby providing "its post-Vietnam, post-1960s audience a glimpse of the America it would rather see, one that has no apparent connection to the war and protests that dominated the news media" (Shumway 1999, 42). When the film is consumed by those who have actual experience of that past as well as those who do not, the latter may often assume that the representation in the film is authentic due to their lack of first-hand knowledge of that bygone period in history (Shumway 1999).

Against the strains of Ge Lan's popular songs in *Great World* is the cacophony of different Chinese dialects spoken by various actors in their everyday dialogue. For example, two chefs in a Chinese restaurant converse in Hainanese as their boss reprimands them in Cantonese, while the lead waitress tries to appease customers in Teochew. While this is a brilliant attempt by the director in emphasising the diversity of dialects spoken by the Chinese community in pre-independence Singapore (which has now been flattened by the Singapore government's policy to promote Mandarin as the lingua franca of the Chinese), the ethnic diversity in the original amusement park is completely ignored. The Malay *ronggeng* dancers and *their* music, which was extremely popular in the historical Great World Amusement Park, is only briefly mentioned in the dialogue, but never featured in the film. In this sense, the film music in *Great World* falls short in capturing the true sonic richness of the historical Great World Amusement Park at the height of its popularity.

Similarly, *Forever Fever*'s remembering of the import of disco music into Singapore is a case of commodified nostalgia – the disco music that arrived in Singapore in the 1970s, as well as the selected disco tracks in *Forever Fever*, are purely mainstream commercial disco music stripped of the original underground qualities of the genre and its association with homosexuality (Khoo 2004). Khoo (2004) suggests that the only hint of disco's early association with queerness in *Forever Fever* is the male protagonist's transsexual brother. Otherwise, the film

> is colored by the same commodified global re-nostalgia that spurred the recent vintage fashion explosion and saw the production of *Boogie Nights*, *Summer of Sam*, *The Last Days of Disco* and other films set during the 1970s.
>
> (Khoo 2004, 9)

Both *Forever Fever* and *Great World* drew upon mainstream popular music from bygone decades to evoke feelings of nostalgia – disco music in English for the former, and Mandarin songs in the latter. In contrast, the soundtracks to some Singaporean films include original compositions written specifically for the films concerned. This is most notable in Jack Neo's films such as *Money No Enough* (1998) and *I Not Stupid* (2002). Jack Neo is the most successful commercial film director in Singapore with a series of box office hits, among which *Money No Enough* (1998) is the top grossing locally produced movie of all time (Tseng 2008).

In the 1990s, Jack Neo's films stood out because of his heavy use of Hokkien dialogue in his productions. Hokkien is a Southern Chinese dialect and was, up to the 1970s, widely spoken in the ethnic Chinese community in Singapore. However, with the introduction of the Speak Mandarin Campaign in 1979, Hokkien and other Chinese dialects had been banned on television and systematically marginalised in various spheres of life in Singapore. The use of Hokkien in Jack Neo's films "staged a 'return of the repressed'" (Chua 2003, 171). In the next section, we will examine the Hokkien songs in the soundtracks of Jack Neo's films and explore the ways in which they became voices for the working class in Singapore struggling to survive in its affluent and materialistic society emphasising capitalistic competition and progress.

Jack Neo's un-nostalgic sonic money-scapes

Theme songs of Jack Neo films are inserted predictably into the timelines at three distinct stages, namely the usual introduction and end credits, as well as the cinematic ebb in the narrative. Predominantly sung in a mix of Mandarin and colloquial Hokkien, the tracks characterising his productions are often composed

100   *Liew Kai Khiun and Brenda Chan*

along mainstream popular music styles with deliberate emphasis given to the clarity of vocals over that of instruments. Ranging from slow to at most medium beats with simple riffs, the songs are tuned to allow listeners to follow the lyrics and their corresponding subtitles in both English and Chinese more closely. For audiences exposed to Hong Kong cinema, it is also evident that the musicological styles of Neo's theme songs in his productions are inspired heavily by the vernacular aspects of Hong Kong Cantonese popular music, or Cantopop styles of Sam Hui with strong working class narratives.

Such a practice reflects the commercial considerations over the contrasting and diverse linguistic literacies of Singapore society arising from both historical migratory trends as well as the educational and media policies that privilege English and Mandarin over the provincial regional Chinese dialects. Hence, the soundtracks of the films have to be tailored to a simultaneously older generation of viewers who are more familiar with Chinese dialects, and the younger counterparts schooled in the official languages so completely that the mother tongues of their grandparents would seem alien. Among other considerations would be that of the concerns about the export market where Neo's productions do have an audience in Hong Kong, Taiwan and China, as reflected in the more formal use of the Chinese language in the subtitles to denote other more colloquial local phrases. In this respect, Neo tries to simultaneously ground his productions as local Singaporean, and within the orbit of transnational Chinese films based in Hong Kong and Taiwan.

Reflecting the narratives of his productions closely, the contents of Neo's theme songs in his productions follow the materialist–conservative trajectory of the struggles and angst in the pursuit of wealth in the republic against the maintenance of traditional notions of family and filial piety. Opening theme songs from films like *Money No Enough* (1998), *The Best Bet* (2006) and *Money No Enough 2* (2010) humorously but fatalistically highlight the realities of a moneyed society that reiterates the primacy of material wealth in determining success and recognition. In Neo's *Money No Enough*, the introductory theme song opens with scenes of ordinary cultures of materialism around Singapore. Within the backdrop of scenes of gambling, bidding of gold-plated religious statues during festivals, swiping of credit cards, filling up of lottery tickets and price tags on every single fruit item in the marketplace, Neo sings in Mandarin on the collective greed of society. With the end credits at the closure of the film, Neo again reinforces the centrality of money and materialism in his song that uses both Hokkien and Malay words to underline the frustrations of ordinary citizens struggling in Singapore. It is only in a comfortable resolution of the narrative where the protagonists managed to extricate themselves from a spiralling cycle of failed businesses, uncontrollable bad debts and broken families that the song can be played in a more light-hearted manner.

Demonstrating the centrality of the capitalism in Singapore, especially among the working classes whose outlets seems to be that of lottery tickets, the introduction of *The Best Bet* (2004) sees Neo, whose face is virtually superimposed on a hundred dollar note, rapping entirely in Hokkien on the promises and myths of investing in the weekly lottery, which is seen as the poor man's quick road to wealth. Neo's films have also been a platform for his critiques on government policies in generally a less subtle manner. However, in the second instalment of *Money No Enough 2*, Neo combines both his trademark rhymes on materialism in Singapore with thinly veiled displeasure at that which he perceives to be unreasonably high taxes on vehicle road usages in Singapore in the opening theme song parodying one of the official songs "We are Singapore" that is often sung on the republic's National Day parades.

Packaged as light-hearted pop tunes, these songs serve as less solemn versions of the national anthem that citizens can sing along joyously in unison without forgetting the nation's struggles and achievements or national unity and cohesion. In Neo's parody, juxtaposed against the computer-animated skyline of the towering and slick urban cityscape, it seems momentarily that the opening scene of *Money No Enough 2* resembles another reaffirmation of the triumphant narrative of the state moving confidently into the cyber future. Sung in Hokkien right from the beginning, audiences familiar with Neo's cinematic template would have been prepared to expect a perspective that is less agreeable to the original version. In addition, with this song, audiences familiar with the local context would also be reminded of the specific reference made by an annoyed former Singapore Prime Minister Goh Chok Tong to a satirical Singaporean website (talkingcock.com) that had playfully subverted the lyrics of *We are Singapore* to *We are Jing-kang-khor* (Singapore Government Press Release 2002). In Hokkien, this phrase implies a condition of "great difficulty" (真艰苦), used commonly to denote hardship or on annoying persons. From this juncture, the narrative takes a less reverent turn as electronic toll gantries (known as Electronic Road Pricing, commonly abbreviated as ERP) pop up rapidly to meet the audience, serving as reminders of an imposing nanny state eager to milk its citizens. At this moment, parodying the state's constant justification of its fiscal policies entailing financial handouts to mitigate the cost of living and reduce tax burdens, the lyrics are quick to remind audiences of the constant generosity of a paternalistic government that leaves them with few choices. Suggesting a sense of fatalistic resignation with the system, this remaining portion of the excerpt of the opening theme song paints a highly unequal relationship between the strong state and the helpless masses. In reference to the successive electoral victories of the ruling party since 1959 and the systematic emasculation of political dissent, this track begins Neo's film on the daily struggles and negotiations of ordinary people under the watchful eyes and visible hand of the state.

For more than a decade, Neo's exposure of the realities of materialism in Singapore underlies his highly commercialised film templates mixing slapstick comedy, moralising narratives and emphasis on individual diligence towards success. His screen protagonists are largely disenfranchised Chinese working class players caught in the ferris wheel of the Anglocentric capitalist modernity disguised under lexicons of meritocracy, pragmatism and development by the Singapore state. As vernacular cultural resources, his theme songs – many of which are original compositions – have also sonically exposed the harsh realities of contemporary Singapore's soulless money-scapes. Relegated by the official promotion of Mandarin to that of a crude and parochial dialect with little economic value, Neo's use of Hokkien in his song ironically mirrors the crudities of the inequalities and marginalities of Singapore society. While Neo may be criticised for reinforcing the stereotypes of the buffoonish working classes in his films, his soundtracks remain one of the most poignant reminders of the stubborn presence and the noise of the underbelly of the city-state aspiring to "world class" status.

Conclusion

Generally, the soundtracks of contemporary films in Singapore can be placed under the nostalgic productions favoured by more independent filmmakers and the contemporary dominated by the commercialised productions of Jack Neo. Even as the former unearths forgotten popular songs of the past, while the latter dredges into the everyday of the present vernacular vocabularies for inspiration, they commonly share the efforts to control the temporalities of Singapore's historical trajectories as well as the soundscapes of the city-state. In many ways, these soundtracks also represent both the outcome as well as the responses to the ideological scripting and socio-cultural engineering of Singapore society by the post-colonial Singapore state.

Both scholarly and popular explorations of contemporary Singapore films have not placed attention on the kinds of diegetic and non-diegetic music in these productions. This chapter has demonstrated their significance in providing the critical sonic-scapes for the articulation of these visual narratives. Together with the moving images, the theme songs and soundtracks of these films have contributed to the cinematic recreation of otherwise suppressed and forgotten memories that were left behind by the passing of time or sacrificed to the demands of development, order and stability. These songs have also opened up sonic spaces for the social underbelly of Singapore to make their voices heard through the comical and crude Hokkien voices of the unfavoured working class. In a nutshell, music in Singapore films – be it the dances in *Forever Fever* or *Money No Enough* – becomes a consciously strenuous act of not forgetting.

References

Appadurai, Arjun. *Modernity at Large: Cultural Dimensions of Globalization*. Minneapolis: University of Minnesota Press, 1996.
Berry, Chris, and Mary Farquhar. *China on Screen: Cinema and Nation*. New York: Columbia University Press, 2006.
Brown, Royal. S. *Overtones and Undertones: Reading Film Music*. Berkeley: University of California Press, 1994.
Chiew, Seen Kong. "The Socio-cultural Framework of Politics." In *Understanding Singapore Society*, edited by Ong Jin Hui, Tong Chee Kiong, and Tan Ern Ser, 86–106. Singapore: Times Academic Press, 1997.
Chua, Beng Huat. *Life is Not Complete Without Shopping: Consumption Culture in Singapore*. Singapore: Singapore University Press, 2003.

Green, Jessica. "Understanding the Score: Film Music Communicating to and Influencing the Audience." *Journal of Aesthetic Education* 44, no. 4 (2010): 81–94.

Han, Wei Chou. "Celluloid time machine: 'It's a Great Great World'." *Channel News Asia*, 3 January 2011. www.channelnewsasia.com/stories/moviesfeatures/view/1107477/1/.html (accessed 22 August 2011).

Jameson, Frederic. *Postmodernism, or the Cultural Logic of Late Capitalism*. Durham: Duke University Press, 1991.

Khoo, Gaik Cheng. "The Asian Male Spectacle in Glen Goei's Film *That's The Way I Like It* (a.k.a. *Forever Fever*)." Asia Research Institute Working Paper Series No. 26. Singapore: Asia Research Institute, 2004. www.ari.nus.edu.sg/docs/wps/wps04_026.pdf (accessed 23 August 2011).

Kwok, Kian Woon. "Social Transformation and the Problem of Social Coherence: Chinese Singaporeans at Century's End." Working Paper No. 124, Department of Sociology, National University of Singapore, 1994.

Lau, Wai Har. "Bridging the Gap Between the Two Worlds: The Chinese-educated and the English-educated." In *Our Place in Time: Exploring Heritage and Memory in Singapore*, edited by Kwok Kian Woon, Kwa Chong Guan, Lily Kong, and Brenda Yeoh, 199–207. Singapore: Singapore Heritage Society, 1999.

Ma, Jean. "Delayed Voices: Intertextuality, Music and Gender in *The Hole*." *Journal of Chinese Cinemas* 5, no. 2 (2011): 123–39.

Millet, Raphaël. *Singapore Cinema*. Singapore: Editions Didier Millet, 2006.

Neri, Corrado. "Tsai Ming-liang and the Lost Emotions of the Flesh." *Positions: East Asia Cultures Critique* 16, no. 2 (2008): 389–407.

Ramsey, Guthrie P. Jr. "Muzing New Hoods, Making New Identities: Film, Hip-Hop Culture, and Jazz Music." *Callaloo* 25, no.1 (2002): 309–20.

Shumway, David R. "Rock 'n' Roll Sound Tracks and the Production of Nostalgia." *Cinema Journal* 38, no. 2 (1999): 36–51.

Singapore Government Press Release. "Remaking Singapore – Changing Mindsets." National Day Rally Address by Prime Minister Goh Chok Tong at the University Cultural Centre, NUS on Sunday, 18 August 2002, at 8.00 PM. www.nas.gov.sg/archivesonline/speeches/view-html?filename=2002081805.htm (accessed 15 September 2015).

Teo, Stephen. *Hong Kong Cinema: The Extra Dimensions*. London: British Film Institute, 1997.

Tong, Kelvin. "Once, the WORLD was GREAT." *The Straits Times*, 17 October 1997. http://ourstory.asia1.com.sg/neatstuff/places/great.html (accessed 22 August 2011).

Tseng, Douglas. "The Superpower of Sequels." *The Straits Times*, Life Section, 19 January 2008, 2–3.

Uhde, Jan, and Yvonne Ng Uhde. *Latent Images: Film in Singapore*. Singapore: Oxford University Press, 2000.

Vasil, Raj. *Asianising Singapore: The PAP's Management of Ethnicity*. Singapore: Heinemann Asia, 1995.

8 Off with the shaking heads! Reel-ising the "Singapore Indian" in the local Tamil films, *My Magic* and *Gurushetram – 24 Hours of Anger*

Nidya Shanthini Manokara

Ethnic and language representations in Singapore film

Singapore is a small and thriving cosmopolitan city-state that often boasts of its multicultural and multi-ethnic demography. Neatly categorising its citizens and permanent residents into ethnic origins of Chinese, Malay, Indian and Others (CMIO), the state tends to homogenise the otherwise heterogeneous composition found within each ethnic group. Printed as "Race" on the National Registration Identity Card (NRIC), this ethnicity aims to label and reinforce one's identity. Moreover, in line with the state's bilingual policy, the Chinese, Malay and Indian (CMI) racial categorisation is then tagged to a specific language. Mandarin, Malay and Tamil represent the "official" ethnic languages of the Chinese, Malays and Indians respectively. Alongside English, these languages are celebrated as the official languages of Singapore.

Like the other ethnic communities, the Indian community is diverse and comprises different Indian regional groups, each with its distinct linguistic characteristics. Malayalam, Telugu, Hindi and Punjabi are some languages that some Indians speak. While such heterogeneity has been in place since the formative years of the nation state and has become more pronounced in recent times due to the influx of foreign Indian immigrants, the decision to officially represent the Indian community with the Tamil language attests to the large number of Tamil-speaking Indians present in Singapore's early years. As of September 2014, 7.4 per cent of Singapore citizens are classified as Indians; of these Indians, half are literate in Tamil (National Population and Talent Division 2014). Although Tamil-speaking Indians are a size-able minority group with constitutional rights in this Southeast Asian city-state, this ethnic and linguistic group is sadly underrepresented in Singapore film.

From the early years of P. Ramlee movies to more current contemporary reflections of Singapore in local films such as *12 Storeys* (1997), *881* (2007) and the *Ah Boys to Men* trilogy (2012–2015), little Indian minority representation is visible. Exceptions include films like *Saint Jack* (1979) where Indians are portrayed through the pivotal characters of the prostitute and innkeeper. Thereafter, there has been a lull in the presentation of the Indian community in Singaporean film. The tokenistic portrayal or complete absence of the Indian community is strongly marked, especially in films from the mid-1990s. Primarily shot in Chinese dialects, inclusions of the stereotypical Indian were made either for comic relief or as a notionary representation of the multicultural nature of Singapore (Tan 2004).

In other local films, Indian characters service the main protagonist, and hence play secondary roles. These characters are built around stereotypes to function as buffoons like the effeminate Kenny Pereira in *Army Daze* (1996), soccer coach turned drunkard security guard Sammy in *One Leg Kicking* (2001), and the irksome Inspector Suresh who speaks with a thick accent in *The Blue Mansion* (2009). In *Army Daze*, the dream sequence where Krishnamoorthy and Lathi dance around trees is reminiscent of stereotypical representations of the ethnic group. In other instances, the Indian characters remain marginalised, as Raj was in *The Blue Mansion* (2009). Thus, it is apparent that the Indian community – a race other than the one featured primarily in most of the local films – is unrepresented, underrepresented or presented as caricatures.

Including Tamil-language films into the rhetoric of Singapore cinema

In this chapter, I argue for the inclusion of two pioneering local Tamil films, Eric Khoo's *My Magic* (2008) and T. T. Dhavamanni's *Gurushetram – 24 Hours of Anger* (2010), as part of Singapore cinema. Both these movies are pivotal to the development of Singapore cinema for two closely related reasons. First, they are filmed almost entirely in Tamil, which is both an official language of Singapore and the indicative language of the Singaporean Indian community. Second, both films heavily feature the otherwise marginalised Indian, and more specifically Tamil-speaking local community. I propose that both these films offer a counterpoint to the existing and dominant Chinese dialect films. At the same time, both Khoo and Dhavamanni appear to undertake a conscientious effort to omit prevalent Indian stereotypes including the constant head shaking and dancing around coconut trees featured in movies from India and Singapore alike. Instead (an) other plausible image for Singapore Tamils is recreated on-screen. *My Magic* and *Gurushetram* wilfully position themselves as the vectors of economic adversity and social deviance by showcasing the underground activities of the community such as alcoholism and drug syndicate operations respectively.

To a significant degree, both directors have tapped into various cultural capital to perform their perspectives of the Indian community on film. This has then resulted in the reception of the films by the local community; with the latter better received than the former. This chapter will analyse the various cultural economies and some inherent tensions that allowed the formation of the directors' versions of a Singaporean Indian/Tamil identity. Last, I will investigate the ways in which these films individually and collectively function as Tamil films in Singapore cinema. In using the Tamil language and foregrounding social issues that are more prevalent to this community, I propose that both *Gurushetram* (2010) and *My Magic* (2008) can be seen as responses to the otherwise Chinese dialect dominance in Singapore cinema.

Tapping into patterns of reception

My Magic is directed by Eric Khoo, and is jointly written by him and Wong Kim Hoh. Produced by Zhao Wei Films in association with Infinite Frameworks, this movie was released in Singapore on 26 September 2008. New faces Bosco Francis and Jathishweran were cast as the main characters, and portrayed an estranged father–son relationship between Francis and Raju. Distributed in France by ARP and its international sales managed by Wild Bunch, *My Magic* earned S$29,911.50 at the box office. It is the first local film nominated for the Palme d'Or at the Cannes Film Festival in 2008, and was Singapore's official entry for the 2009 Oscars (Zhao Wei Films 2013). Francis's bizarre magic acts of eating glass and fire breathing feature heavily in the film; these magic tricks and his final electrocution explicate the visceral aspects of pain, and highlight his horrific return to magic "to redeem himself and win his son's love and respect" (ibid.). Although the Tamil language and Indians feature predominantly in the film, the Hokkien vernacular and Chinese gangsters are equally significant to the plot.

With the screenplay written by T. T. Dhavamanni and Chong Tze Chien, *Gurushetram* is jointly presented by Blue River Pictures in association with the Singapore Film Commission. Dhavamanni also produced the film. The involvement of European director of photography Lucas Jodogne and acclaimed Chennai-based editor Praveen K. L. highlight this film as a transnational collaboration. Distributed locally by Golden Village (GV) Pictures, *Gurushetram* was released in Singapore on 8 April 2010 and earned S$99,453 at the box office (Blue River Pictures 2010). T. T. Dhavamanni's *Gurushetram – 24 Hours of Anger* takes on another perspective of the Tamil-speaking community. Set against the stringent drug trafficking laws in contemporary Singapore anchored by the Central Narcotics Bureau (CNB) officer Anbarasan, the movie foregrounds a personal vendetta between a drug syndicate uncle–nephew duo Vinod and Prakash. Familiar artistes from Singapore's official Indian television channel *Vasantham*, Mathialagan Manikkam, Sivakumar Palakrishnan and Vishnu Andhakrishnan play the CNB officer, drug ringleader uncle and nephew respectively. Similar to the Chinese dialect films, the dominant Indian representations in *Gurushetram* appear to suggest an ethnic enclave too.

The way each film was marketed accounted largely for the levels of reception within the local Tamil community. Since *Gurushetram* was targeted at the local Tamil community, the state-sanctioned Tamil print media, radio and television channels of *Tamil Murasu*, *Oli* and *Vasantham* respectively lent their support to fervently advertise the local Tamil-language film directed and produced by a local Tamil-speaking director. There was a tinge of linguistic pride in social media websites like Facebook, where the movie was touted as "Singapore's first local Tamil feature film". Furthermore, the official release of the movie in Singapore coincided with the national Tamil Language Festival in 2010 organised by the Tamil Language Council, an annual festival aimed at promoting the Tamil language in Singapore (Tamils Representative Council 2010). The gala event on 6 April 2010 at GV Vivocity was presided by then President of Singapore, His Excellency

Off with the shaking heads! 107

S. R. Nathan. Other prominent attendees included Minister of State S. Iswaran, Nominated Member of Parliament Viswa Sadasivan and *Tamil Murasu* chairman S. Chandra Das (ibid.).

Given that Singapore's Tamil-speaking citizens make up about 7 per cent of the total population, *Gurushetram*'s premiere at the GV Vivocity cinema further highlights the enviable socio-political position of Tamils in Singapore. In contrast, despite the rave reviews of the use of Tamil language in the film, its use in *My Magic* remains underappreciated. Yet, this Tamil-language feature film toured the international film circuit. It was presented at the Montreal World Film Festival, Rio de Janeiro International Film Festival, Pusan International Film Festival (now known as the Busan International Film Festival), Ghent International Film Festival, Tokyo International Film Festival, Taipei International Film Festival, Stockholm International Film Festival and International Film Festival Rotterdam (Zhao Wei Films 2013). Although the narrative is easy to follow and Bosco Francis had received a fifteen-minute standing ovation at Grand Théâtre Lumière during the 61st Cannes Film Festival (Yong 2008), this film was not as well-received as *Gurushetram* by the local Tamil-speaking population. What accounted for Singapore's Tamil-speakers reception of *My Magic*?

The long duration of each of Khoo's shots and low-key lighting for most frames, indicative of arthouse cinema influences, drew much attention to the characters and their relationships. Although *My Magic* was not exclusively targeted at the Tamil-speaking minority community, Khoo's cinematic style may have been difficult to follow for the uninitiated. Most locals are familiar with mainstream Tamil films from India where villages and even anti-heroes are often glorified through the cinematography like in *Paruthiveeran* (2007). They are also probably more familiar with film techniques that cross-cut lush greenery and extreme close-ups of the heroine's blinking eyes with the fluttering wings of a butterfly and low-angle shots to depict powerful and confident heroes. Moreover, in gangster–thriller films like *Billa* (2007), the guns and car chase sequences echo Hollywood movie sensibilities. As these film-editing techniques form the dominant reception patterns of the local Tamil-speaking community, the decay depicted through the film stock of *My Magic* becomes a sharp departure. Thus, Khoo's treatment of a Singapore underbelly may offer little pleasure for the Tamil filmgoing audience members.

By contrast, the reception of *Gurushetram* was almost on par with many mainstream star-studded Tamil films from India. Like many others in the local Tamil community, I was extremely excited to watch *Gurushetram* primarily due to the familiar faces that were part of the cast and crew. Similar to Jack Neo's incorporation of television celebrities in his initial movie directorial period, T. T. Dhavamanni relied on young Tamil television culture and its fan following for the film. Moreover, many of the camera angles, mid-range shots, seamless editing and fast cutting found in the trailer, and especially in the dance and fight sequences, are reminiscent of mainstream Tamil films enjoyed by the local population.

This reception is, in part, indicative of the ways in which the state-mandated television channel has shaped a particular kind of Tamil audience through the careful broadcast of mainstream movies from India and local programmes. Since the early years of limited Tamil programmes broadcast over *Channel 8* (the current Mandarin-language channel) in the 1970s and 1980s, artistes involved in variety shows like *Malai Madhuram* and social dramas such as *Nadaga Arangam* have enjoyed some fan following. However, the increased airtime for Tamil and other Indian languages over TV channels including *Channel 12* (1984–1995), *Vasantham Central* (2000–2008) and currently *Vasantham* (2008–), has increased the visibility of the artistes and the Tamil language in locally produced dramas (MediaCorp 2010). In today's tech-savvy context, online catch-up TV mediums like *Toggle.sg* and *xinmsn* provide users with the ease of watching *Vasantham* shows at their preferred time. Roadshows held at heartland malls and even in Malaysia further reinforce the popularity of shows like *Vettai* in the region, and provide more opportunities for interactions between audiences and media artistes (Channel News Asia 2015). Moreover, social media outlets, including Facebook and Twitter, aim to strengthen ties between both parties.

T. T. Dhavamanni's cast selection is sensitive to Singapore Tamil television culture's fan following, as seen in the *Gurushetram* publicity poster and trailer. Much like Hollywood and Tamil film conventions from India, the poster is hero-oriented and foregrounds a male-dominated brotherhood film. A familiar face on *Vasantham*, Vishnu Andhakrishnan (the actor playing the protagonist) has hosted many variety shows and had also directed well-received travel guide cum info-education programmes such as *Uncle! Taxi Engeh Poguthu?* (Uncle, Where is the Taxi going?) (2011–2012). Judging from the reception whenever Vishnu hosts programmes like *Dhool* (2007), he appears to be a heartthrob for many young girls (Astro Ulagam 2014). With his distinct voice and fan following, the *Gurushetram* trailer pervaded *Vasantham*, and to a larger extent, social media websites like Facebook and YouTube.

Actors Sivakumar Palakrishnan and Mathialagan Manikkam, while actively involved in productions for *Vasantham*, have also penetrated into the English-speaking local arts scene. Sivakumar is probably best remembered by the English-speaking community in Singapore as the old-fashioned discipline master Mr Raju in the Channel 5 production *First Class* (2008). Mathialagan had clinched the Best Actor award during the Asian Television Awards 2006 ("Mathi's ATA Awards '06 – Best Actor" 2008). As the first Tamil actor in Asia to have received such a prestigious accolade, he made the headlines in both the official English and Tamil newspapers, *The Straits Times* and *Tamil Murasu*, and had a congratulatory minute-long feature aired on *Vasantham* ("Mathi's Asian Television Awards 2006 Best Actor Promo" 2008). The music director Rafee, who makes a cameo in the film, also indicates the ways in which the local Tamil music industry has matured over the years. Since "Manthiram vetchayeh" from *Karupaayee* (1994), Rafee has sung for such India Tamil films as "Jumbalaka" from *En Swasa Kaatre* (1999) with A. R. Rahman, and has composed the music for *Jaggubhai* (2010). Therefore, in incorporating currently prominent local performers into *Gurushetram*, T. T. Dhavamanni harnesses "local stars" who are increasingly becoming part of the Singapore Tamil community's cultural capital.

Off with the shaking heads! 109

At the same time, T. T. Dhavamanni is also a prominent director within the Tamil-speaking community in Singapore. He introduced the docudrama style of narration to Tamil television viewers with the telemovie *Match'Stick – The Musical* (2003), which was later awarded the Certificate of Distinction at the New York Festivals in 2004, Certificate of Recognition at ABU/CASBA UNICEF Child Rights Award in 2004, and was also mentioned at the *Pradhana Vizha* Awards ceremony in 2004. He also veered off comedy serials and variety shows broadcasted on *Vasantham*. By mainly using actors from the younger generation, T. T. Dhavamanni has a pool of artistes who frequently appear in his productions, including Sivakumar and Vishnu. His teleplay series *Guru Paarvai* (2004), *Guru Paarvai 2* (2008) and *Guru Paarvai 3* (2009) dealt exclusively with school life, while further reiterating his directorial style to the local population. Slow panning and long takes allow each actor added screen presence, and visible editing techniques like fades and slow swipes initiate audiences in the experience of watching a T. T. Dhavamanni production. Thus, local Tamil television culture provides *Gurushetram* with the necessary scaffolding.

In discussing the polyphonic nature of local films, the Media Development of Authority (MDA) of Singapore states: "MDA recognises that films can be an important medium to promote our Singaporean identity and can help reach out to and engage our people" (Ministry of Communication and Information 2011). I propose that different kinds of "Singaporean identity" are constructed in *Gurushetram* and *My Magic*. While both films utilise the Tamil language (in which I am fluent), T. T. Dhavamanni and Eric Khoo tapped into different cultural capital to validate their unique perspectives on Singapore. As many local Tamil-speakers are well-accustomed to *Vasantham* dramas and Tamil films from India, *Gurushetram* and *My Magic* each construct a different imaginary view of Singapore and force a new kind of spectatorship.

Representing Singapore Indians as Tamils in *Gurushetram*

In *Gurushetram*, T. T. Dhavamanni incorporates multiple signifiers to root the film in the Singapore context. As he had mentioned in an interview with an India-based newspaper *The Hindu*, Dhavamanni had turned down offers to work in the film industry in India primarily because he wanted to direct a Singapore film, with a Singapore storyline and made in Singapore (Kumar 2010). This desire to make a Singapore film with a locally relevant plot has allowed him to be more sensitive to the construction of the Singapore Indian identity in *Gurushetram*. The most culturally specific frame would be the opening sequence of Changi Prison where Shanthi was rightly sent to the gallows on a Friday morning. Moreover, the inclusion of the CNB team and its crackdown on illegal activities reflects an important aspect of the Singapore legislative system. Other signifiers include the lingua franca, small one-room Housing and Development Board (HDB) flat, constant referencing to the neighbourhood Marsiling (an area where many Indians reside), Comfort Taxis, the Singapore car licence plate of the old blue Volkswagen van, and the Singapore flag-inspired tattoo on Prakash. Hence, Dhavamanni has

Figure 8.1 Mohan, sons and social worker in L-shaped flat.

carefully grounded elements of reality as a register of legitimacy and sincerity to his imagined Singapore.

Furthermore, personalities from the Indian community were also presented in the film, further entrenching it within the Singapore Tamil context. The dance competition scene and its Singapore context are legitimised through the inclusion of prominent television dancers Ramesh, Sree Devy and Manimaran, known for their filmic dance, contemporary Bharata Natyam and folk dance respectively. Moreover, the character Marsiling Baby is also reminiscent of the 2009 incident where twenty-three-year-old Pathip Selvan Sugumaran (known as "Marsiling Baby") confessed to killing his eighteen-year-old girlfriend for infidelity (Singapore Law 2010). The constant reference to the name, the actor's hairstyle and the climactic moment where he actually stabs his unfaithful girlfriend seem to collide with the real crime. In this manner, T. T. Dhavamanni used images and signifiers that are part of the local Tamil community's existing cultural economy to validate his depiction of Singapore and its Tamils on film.

> "It's also stated in it [NRIC] that my race is Indian. Are we Indians? We're Tamils; Singapore Tamils. It's all stated wrongly."

This statement given by Prakash, during the interrogation with CNB officer Anbarasan, is a central theme in the movie. In the cinema, this line received a couple of claps and faint whistles, highlighting the agreement of those watching it. While drug trafficking propels the plot, the issue of identity and belonging surfaces at various points. For a Singaporean "Indian" who speaks Tamil as well, one's identity is hardly a simple construction. Instead, it is a delicate

Off with the shaking heads! 111

Figure 8.2 Prakash's interrogation scene.

balance that needs nations like Singapore, India, and to some degree, Malaysia. *Gurushetram* offers a reassemblage by first adapting the cultural economy of Singapore Tamils, and then using Tamil Nadu cinematic conventions to perform its Indian community.

Since its inception in Singapore, the Tamil-medium television station has churned out social dramas suggestive of the conditions of the Tamil-speaking community. Functioning as state-driven tools, Tamil television programmes in Singapore included the awareness and protection against alcoholic husbands, wife battering and child abuse, and often showcased the living conditions of lower-income families. In more recent dramas and reality shows, the emphasis has shifted towards education and upgrading oneself. *Gurushetram* appears to be an extension of these social dramas insofar as it highlights an underbelly community amidst the prosperous nation state. Furthermore, the local community appreciated the casting of actors who were already accepted and recognised in specific role types. This, consequently, made the movie more accessible to local Tamil-speaking audiences.

Gurushetram also provoked much excitement and frenzy because it was released in both Malaysia and India. These nations are important for the identity formation of the local Tamil-speaking Indian population primarily due to the migrant society from which contemporary Singapore has emerged. The predominantly Tamil-speaking migrant population from South India who had arrived in Singapore and Malaysia's formative years now form the bulk of the Indian citizenry in these two countries. Moreover, the merger and split between Malaysia and Singapore in the post-war era are important for the collective memory of the Tamil-speaking population as well. The release of Dhavamanni's *Gurushetram* in India also adds to the repertoire of non-India made Tamil movies alongside those

112 Nidya Shanthini Manokara

that survived the civil wars in Sri Lanka. At the same time, the socio-political ties between Singapore and its neighbouring country are brought to the fore due to the theme of travelling to and from Malaysia in *Gurushetram*.

As it needed to travel across the national boundaries of India, Malaysia and Singapore, *Gurushetram* should be viewed as a transnational film. In discussing transnational films from South Asia, Jigna Desai posits that some inherent themes may be viewed as "cinematic Mcnuggets" that are often "Western friendly" (Desai 2004, 4–5). To her, those cinematic Mcnuggets allow movies to travel across political and linguistic borders. While the drug trafficking landscape of Singapore is crucial to *Gurushetram*, other themes allow it to travel as a transnational production. The violence, brotherhood of gang members, and intimate brotherly relationship between Prakash and Subra, are easy to follow topics that are "tasty, easily swallowed, apolitical global cultural morsels" (ibid.). Anti-heroes, docudrama style, dance and comedy thus become gateways for the global audience to familiarise themselves with this perception of Singapore that T. T. Dhavamanni has created on-screen.

The fallen heroes in *Gurushetram* including the divorced CNB officer Anbarasan, the bachelor drug syndicate leader Vinod, and Prakash who cares for his mentally challenged brother Subra, resonate with trends found in Tamil cinema from Tamil Nadu in India. In movies like Vishnuvardhan's *Pattiyal* (2006) and M. Sasikumar's *Subramaniapuram* (2008), there is greater emphasis on the anti-hero and brotherhood of the male protagonists, and the diminished importance of the female lead. This also enables the diasporic Tamil audience to identify with a trend in Tamil movies from the 1980s. Sathiavathi Chinniah (2008, 35) writes:

> The "angry young man" genre attained importance in Tamil cinema in the 1980s. This type of film, made popular in Hindi cinema through Amitabh Bachchan, was represented in Tamil cinema largely through the superstar Rajinikanth. In many of these films, the hero, initially an honest person, turns into an angry young man when faced with the attempted or actual rape or murder of his sister, girlfriend or mother.

This mainstream Indian cinema crime noir gained popularity in Singapore in the 1980s and shaped local Tamil viewership. In *Gurushetram*, Prakash may be likened to the angry young man. However, unlike Tamil films showcasing the protagonist avenging hegemonic forces gone wrong, Prakash in *Gurushetram* needs the CNB's help in order to avenge his mother's death. In doing so, the nation state regains its position of power.

There are a growing number of Tamil films from India also advocating the docudrama style of narration. This is especially true of the movie *Kadhal* (2004), which popularised Italian neo-realism through its blunt and in-your-face style of filmmaking (Krishnan 2008, 139). The director Mysskin's low-angle frames and shadow-cast shots in films like *Anjathe* (2008) offer innovative ways of propelling the plot. In a similar manner, the camera angles trying to convict all members of Vinod's gang for being a police confidential informant, from Karthik to Sundeli, seem to echo such an approach in *Gurushetram*. Nonetheless, this style seems to sit well with T. T. Dhavamanni's direction and reinforces the familiar viewership patterns for the local population.

In discussing Bollywood trends and the dominance of dance sequences, Ian Garwood writes: "Song sequence is a crucial part of the branding of Bollywood in Western film territories. [It is] the single most identifiable element that marks its territory from its Hollywood counterparts" (Garwood 2006, 348). While he references only Hindi Bollywood movies, one can argue that South Indian films have songs and dance sequences differentiating it from non-Indian films as well. However, in *Gurushetram*, the inclusion of the dance does not arrest the moment as in conventional Indian films. Instead, it follows the trend of current Tamil cinema and progresses the plot. The tongue-in-cheek rendition of the local song *Thozha!* (Friend) at the "Xplosion Nite" dance competition allows the audience to enjoy short snippets of song and dance sequences from India and Singapore. Through the editing, the competition reintroduces the earnest social worker Revathi, and the viewers are introduced to the rivalry between Prakash and Karthik. Moreover, we witness a glimpse of drug peddling and observe the CNB officers apprehending a different group.

In spite of its serious undertones, *Gurushetram* has many comical elements that are suited for both local non-Tamil-speakers as well as a transnational audience. These scenes are interspersed between more emotionally charged instances. One such comic element occurs when non-Tamils read the English subtitles in Vinod's interrogation scene. When asked about his wrongdoings, he confesses to entering Johor Bahru (in Malaysia) on half a tank of petrol instead of the legally stipulated three-quarters tank and knowingly purchasing contraband cigarettes. Moreover, Baby's character provides for timely comic relief. For instance, Baby

Figure 8.3 Marsiling Warriors dancing during X-plosion Nite dance competition.

Figure 8.4 Prakash and Subra looking at "snow".

stutters unrelated words at Vinod's entrance when Prakash is giving Subra a shower. In another instance, the scene of tender brotherly affection where Prakash and Subra enjoy snowfall is punctured when Baby and others frantically try to blow Styrofoam beads to create the effect. Baby's dialogue, "I told you not to let him watch Disney cartoons!" in the local Tamil lingua franca becomes comical in this instant. Thus, the timely comedy not only resembles filmmaking styles from India, but also allows the audience to enjoy the film.

Besides these transnational themes, homage is also paid to Tamil cinema's reliance on real-time violence in *Gurushetram*. The killing of Karthik is especially distressing and may cause one to cringe in the seat. The camera that follows him as he enters Vinod's compound and house stops the moment he enters the room and sits on the only chair. Furthermore, there is no background score when Karthik is stabbed by Prakash. This allows for a display of the crime, a model common to Tamil films from India. Nonetheless, the medium close-up of Karthik's slouched position on the chair after he is stabbed, Vinod walking into the frame and gently holding his head, and the final black out suggesting Vinod snapped Karthik's neck, makes the event rawer, more dramatic and almost graphic.

However, the way in which violence is celebrated in *Gurushetram* differs from its treatment in Tamil films from India. In *Gurushetram*, there is often no public display of violence. Even in Karthik's murder, the onlookers like Loga and Kanna are part of the gang, and the action is confined within Vinod's compound. Moreover, the scene where Baby stabs his girlfriend is done in the dark and without an audience. The final face off between Prakash and Vinod at their Ulu Tiram family home follows suit. The long take follows Tamil film conventions and aims to heighten the audience's excitement. There is some grandeur in the fight, even though there is no display to the public. Vinod and Prakash fling each other into glass tables and windows, and finally plunge from the rooftop in front of the house into the pond.

Off with the shaking heads! 115

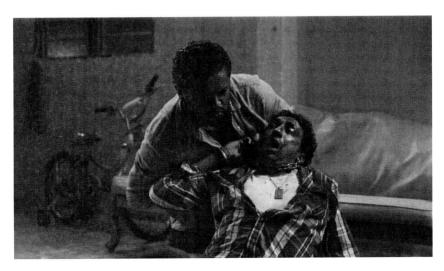

Figure 8.5 Vinod restraining Prakash with a bicycle chain.

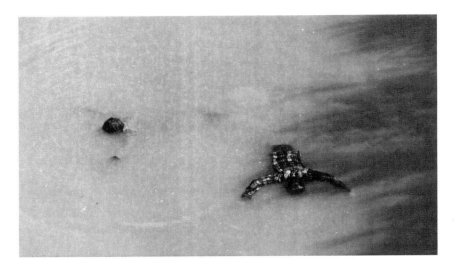

Figure 8.6 Dead bodies floating on pond.

After the mayhem and bloodied bodies, we are left with the stylised image of two bodies floating in the pond – a popular image of death circulated on film.

The spectacular violence is poignant primarily due to the space in which it occurs. The Malaysian home, as depicted in the flashbacks, had been a perfect place for Prakash's nuclear family until the arrival of Vinod from Singapore. Encouraged by Vinod to traffic drugs, the family leaves the rural home for urban Singapore. Prakash's peace is then shattered when the law punishes his mother. By returning to this nostalgic space, the film seems to be highlighting the subtle

116 *Nidya Shanthini Manokara*

importance of Malaysia in the formulation of the Singapore Tamils' identity as well as the migratory patterns of the Tamil community in Singapore post-1965.

Therefore, in *Gurushetram*, there is a deliberate amalgamation of signifiers grounding the film in the Singapore context and current Tamil Nadu cinematic conventions to perform a Singapore Tamil identity. By harnessing the language, space and timeframe within a contemporary Singapore, the living culture of the community is performed as the sensitive space pulling together India, Singapore, and to a lesser degree, Malaysia. Since the circulation of Tamil movies is so high in Singapore, use of those conventions grants the audience greater familiarity into the narrative. Moreover, these cinematic conventions can travel across geographical boundaries and serve the transnational Singapore Tamil community.

Representing an Indian identity in *My Magic*

While *Gurushetram* strives to create an identity rooted in a linguistic marker, *My Magic* offers an identity bound by ethnicity. Almost in line with state-dictated demarcations of race and language, Tamil language in *My Magic* is indicative of the Indian ethnic community in Singapore. Director Eric Khoo voices one reason for such an appropriation: "Since both Bosco and Jathis are Indian, I wanted them to speak in their mother tongue because it is more authentic" (Zhao Wei Films 2013). Acknowledging that the language was alien to him, Khoo still braved through, relying on the translation skills of the bilingual actors. Here, ethnicity and language are conflated as a tool for the "authentic". To a large degree, this use of Tamil in *My Magic* allows Khoo to validate his depiction of the ethnic Indian minority community.

In a cosmopolitan nation like Singapore, it is difficult to compartmentalise each cultural group without accounting for the Asian values and Western ideologies that coalesce to create a distinct Singaporean culture. The boundaries between each ethnic group are constantly blurred due to the close ties in which they work. Given this context then, perhaps the notion of authenticity forwarded by Khoo needs some unpacking. Referencing Third World Cinema as a restraining framework for audiences with cinematic mobility where political and geo-social boundaries are blurred, Ezra and Rowden explain the limits for cultural authenticity:

> A certain anxiety of authenticity underlies the notion of culturally "correct" filmmaking, which assumes a heightened representational access by ethnic and cultural insiders to a stable and culturally distinct reality. But because transnational cinema is most "at home" in in-between spaces of culture, in other words, between the local and global, it decisively problematizes the investment in cultural purity or separatism.
>
> (Ezra and Rowden 2006, 4)

I suggest that a similar situation also holds true for the reception of Khoo's *My Magic*. To a large extent, the familiarity of *Vasantham* artistes and Dhavamanni's cinematic style offer an insider's perspective of the local community. However,

Figure 8.7 Opening scene with Francis and bartender.

it does not suggest that an outsider, like Khoo, has a non-authentic imagination of the Singapore Indian community. In Khoo's case, he is simply looking at the community from the outside-in. This, I argue, is a valid and unique position that has been shaped by the Singapore nation state, its policies and Khoo's interaction with the people from the local Indian community.

My Magic piggybacks on the *Vasantham* social dramas dealing with alcoholism and a dysfunctional family. The opening shot of Francis at a pub during the day immediately foregrounds the popular social understanding of Indian males and their alcoholic tendencies. Through this social indicator, this image allows both local Indians and non-Indians access into the film. As Francis demands more drinks, he slowly becomes more aggressive and even hits the bartender, which is again a stereotypical representation of drunken behaviour. However, this representation is broken when Francis is seen eating the glass bottle. In the domestic sphere, the topless Francis moves towards Raju, repeatedly telling him to sleep even as the latter says that he has to study for a test. Here, the drunkard representation is accompanied by care for his son's wellbeing instead of violence. Similarly, when he talks to the Indian prostitute after cleaning the pub, his low-paying job, the code-switching to Tamil and the cross-cutting to the prostitute as she listens highlight the vulnerable side of Francis. It is this atypical element departing from *Vasantham*'s depictions of drunkard behaviour that makes the film accessible to audiences.

Similar to *Gurushetram*, the absent mother in Raju's life reiterates the theme of the dysfunctional family common in *Vasantham*'s social dramas. With the low-key lighting and long takes, Raju's observations of a mother–son duo in the mall, and specifically his conversations to his deceased grandmother as to whether his mother will return since he has aced his exams while sitting on an old and decaying picnic bench, allows empathy to be created for this forgotten child. The

Figure 8.8 Francis and Raju in the L-shaped flat.

close-up of the image of the Hindu god framed as a family unit that cuts to Raju consuming a packet of *mee goreng* (fried noodles) and Yeo's Ice Lemon Tea further foregrounds the boy's lonely status. Moreover, the close-ups of Raju constantly cleaning up Francis's vomit, the decay highlighting the film stock and the drunkard forcing the child to sleep when he was working further emphasise the estranged father–son relationship.

Moreover, the extreme close-ups of Francis piercing a needle through his skin and mid-range shots of salivating during the electrocution scene force one to see the grotesque presentation of the Indian male body. Most local Tamil-speaking viewers are unaccustomed to the depiction of visceral pain in the extreme close-ups on Francis eating fire or lying on glass pieces. Francis towing a large group on people with two hooks attached to his shoulders is almost reminiscent of acts seen during the Hindu *Thaipusam* procession. Moreover, the Indian *tabla* percussion framing this instance forces the urban audience to reflect on the similarities and the "magic" offered in *My Magic*. Hence, even though the movie is grounded in Singapore through familiar spaces such as Little India, the high degree of the grotesque potentially distances the local Tamil community from embracing the film.

In his discussion on Third World literature in modern times, Fredric Jameson asserts that "the story of the private individual destiny is always an allegory of the embattled situation of the public third-world culture and society" (Jameson 1986, 69). Even when audiences are mindful of the maturity that Singapore cinema has seen and varying directors' perspectives on the nation, something in Raju's longing resonates with an ongoing Singaporean anxiety – the lack of a past. For this reason, I suggest that *My Magic* and Raju's personal story are allegories for the nation. Singapore is closely related to the *tabula rasa* condition premised on

Off with the shaking heads! 119

Figure 8.9 Close-up of needle piercing through the skin.

Figure 8.10 Electricity being passed through Francis.

state-sanctioned social collectivity that is built upon erasures of the past and inclusion of new (more modern) cultural signifiers. Raju's absent mother in the film and the constant references to her in the film trailer seems to suggest an inherent Singaporean anxiety of knowing one's roots.

To a large degree, the glitz and glamour prevalent in Tamil films are consistently absent in *My Magic*. It is this non-conformity of the familiar that makes

Figure 8.11 Raju with the framed photograph of his young parents.

the audience doubly aware of the intimate subject matter. *My Magic* offers the audience a means of cultural identification through the most personal father–son relationship that transcends ethnic and linguistic boundaries. The grand acts of inflicting pain on himself, while grotesque, allows the audience to slowly sympathise with his plight of only having this skill to earn himself a living and his son a future. The scene where Raju turns over in bed to see the fresh wounds on his father's back from the night's act highlights the visceral feeling of pain. Although the ambient music and lighting does not permit everything to be seen in detail, this is the moment where Raju and the audience begin to change their perspectives on the drunkard. The low lighting in the scene where Francis wakes Raju, and Raju's quivering voice as he asks about the wounds and blood, amplify the fear of father and son as well as their need to get away.

Beyond signifiers like the sari-clad mother in the final scene and the use of the Tamil language, the idea of "Indianness" gives way to the construction of a Singaporean identity that is recognisable to the foreign eye. The very construction of the personalised father–son relationship around which the plot progresses, allows the movie to be read as a unilateral representation of family dissonance. The inclusion of Chinese gangsters does become racially problematic, but it further illustrates distinctions between the private family relationship and the public one. Thus, when Francis and Raju are left in the dilapidated building towards the end, *My Magic* becomes a story about their relationship rather than their ethnic identity. Therefore, Singaporean and foreign audiences can look beyond the language attached to this movie and access it as Khoo's depiction of a father–son relationship.

In my view, *My Magic* more so than *Gurushetram*, implicates the audience to become postmodern flâneurs to understand the urban phenomena and modernity set up by Khoo. This could have been the main reason for *My Magic*'s success

Figure 8.12 Francis and Raju sleeping in the dilapidated building.

in the international film circuit. This urban phenomenon occurs at a global level, which allows a greater portion of the international audience – mostly from developed countries facing such a problem – access into the simple father–son narrative. Writing about Eric Khoo's iconic *12 Storeys*, Olivia Khoo explains that the film

> represent[s] the darker side of Singapore's economic modernization; the dispossession and discontent, exploitation and alienation felt by those marginalized by the modernising process (for example, the working class, or the youth). The filmic images ... enact the failed processes of an Asianized modernity at a vernacular or everyday level and in doing so represent the artistic modernity of contemporary Singaporean films.
>
> (Khoo 2005, 13)

Such an economic climate of *12 Storeys* is also visible in *My Magic*, and offers an alternative version of the nation state presented by the Singapore Tourism Board (STB) and statesman Lee Kuan Yew. As modern urban spectators, the audience is forced to encounter the failed patriarch Francis alongside their familiar reality. In doing so, viewers also formulate their own perspectives of the imaginary nation that they are watching.

New trajectories for Singapore film

Despite their differing content, portrayal and treatment of the Singaporean Indian Tamil identity, both *My Magic* and *Gurushetram* still function as Tamil films in Singapore. Collectively, they enter a local film market that was dominated by

Malay-language movies during the golden age in the 1950s–1960s and currently by movies in Chinese languages. The use of the Tamil language in *My Magic* and *Gurushetram* allows Singapore cinema to move into a young and new trajectory. The inclusion of such marginalised languages and linguistic groups inevitably challenges the dominance of recent Chinese dialect movies that are representative of the films from Singapore and have travelled the international film circuit.

The styles of *Gurushetram* and *My Magic* follow the conventions of local television and other Singapore films respectively, thus contributing towards the continuation and lineage of Singapore cinema. While neither movie sets out explicitly to question what it means to be a "Singaporean Indian", they manifest the socio-political and cultural particularities of the local Indian community by harnessing an official language of Singapore. In doing so, these movies also present something culturally specific to the nation state that constitutes part of its national cinema.

Much like other local films including *Saint Jack* (1979) and *Money No Enough* (1998), both *My Magic* and *Gurushetram* are records of Singapore's developmental phases and changing infrastructure. The orange coin payphones in *My Magic* and the well in *Gurushetram* offer nostalgic echoes of a Singapore that once was. The specific recurrence of the old rail in both films suggests an important relationship between the local Indian population and Malaysia. The vaulted Tanjong Pagar Railway Station in *Gurushetram* through which the brothers leave the country and the silver train in the background as Raju talks to his grandmother in *My Magic*, serve as reminders to Tamil-speaking Indians who may have once lived in Malaya. Since that same railway, once an important mode of commute for people between Singapore and Malaysia, had shut its operations in 2011, its image on film captures an important cultural memory of the local community (Jayakumar 2011).

Figure 8.13 Prakash and Subra boarding a train at Tanjong Pagar Railway Station.

Off with the shaking heads! 123

Gurushetram also influenced the type of television dramas made, most notably the *Vettai: Pledged to Hunt* (2011) series by EagleVision Productions focussing on the police force tracking down a drug syndicate. Although there was an informant from within the police, the force retains its integrity when the law punishes him too. Thus, there is a feedback loop where the movie – that borrows in part from some of the conventions of the television series – now serves as inspiration for other television serials. Therefore, *Gurushetram* played a pivotal role for Tamil film and television culture when it was first released.

The popularity of *Gurushetram* within the local Tamil community suggests a prevailing genre preference. It is one that is in line with the more established Kollywood cinematic conventions. This preference of the local Tamil population has victimised the themes and issues in *My Magic*. The 2011 local Tamil movie *Pickles* by Tantra Films appears to be a comedy modelled after Tamil movies from India as well. However, unlike *Gurushetram*, *Pickles* includes songs composed by both locals and artists from India. Songs such as "Nalla sarakku" and "Engeyo izhukkuthayya", though not made exclusively for the movie, often function as refrains over the Singapore Tamil radio station *Oli*, at Indian functions, and even at clubs. Thus, the maturation of the Tamil music industry occurs alongside its alignment with mainstream reception of Tamil movies from India.

Since Tamil movies in Singapore as a collective is in its infancy stages, it is difficult to access its position in relation to the larger oeuvre of Singapore cinema now. Individually, *My Magic* and *Gurushetram* are the directors' reflections on Singapore and a single perspective of the nation. As they try to operate in the transnational circuits, directors of both films require some sense of rootedness to the space and culture in order to depart from them. This "space" and "culture" often become sites of contestation and confrontation, as they are only representatives of the directors' image of the national.

Singaporean audiences are at once global and local citizens. For this reason, one should view *My Magic* and *Gurushetram* as catalysts that allow the audience to negotiate the familiar – established through state-sanctioned media and STB promotions as well as their daily experiences – with that which is represented on-screen, and formulate their own perspectives of the imaginary nation they see in the films. Some form of reflexive mapping between the text and audience for movies like *My Magic* and *Gurushetram* is important, for it demonstrates the films' use as plausible cultural capital for later projects, while positing Tamil films' lineage within the Singapore cinema industry.

References

Astro Ulagam. "Yutha Medai Hosts-Vishnu." Malaysia: Astro Broadcasting Television Network Satellite Pay TV Service, 2014. www.astroulagam.com.my/yuthamedai/theshow/Vishnu (accessed 12 February 2015).

Blue River Pictures. "Gurushetram Production Notes." Singapore: Blue River Pictures, 2010. http://gurushetram.com/gurushetramproductionnotes.pdf (accessed 5 March 2011).

124   Nidya Shanthini Manokara

Channel News Asia. "Vasantham's First Roadshow in Malaysia Draws over 5,000." *Channel News Asia*, 23 February 2015. www.channelnewsasia.com/news/entertainment/vasantham-s-first/1674648.html (accessed 23 February 2015).

Chinniah, Sathiavathi. "The Tamil Film Heroine: From a Passive Subject to a Pleasurable Object." In *Tamil Cinema: The Cultural Politics of India's other Film Industry*, edited by Selvaraj Velayutham, 29–43. London: Routledge, 2008.

Desai, Jigna. *Beyond Bollywood: The Cultural Politics of South Asian Diasporic Film*. London and New York: Routledge, 2004.

Ezra, Elizabeth, and Terry Rowden. "General Introduction: What is Transnational Cinema?" In *Transnational Cinema: The Film Reader*, edited by Elizabeth Ezra and Terry Rowden, 1–12. London and New York: Routledge, 2006.

Garwood, Ian. "Shifting Pitch: The Bollywood Song Sequence in the Anglo-American Market." In *Asian Cinemas: A Reader and Guide*, edited by Dimitris Eleftheriotis and Gary Needham, 346–57. Honolulu: University of Hawai'i Press, 2006.

Gurushetram – 24 Hours of Anger. Directed by T. T. Dhavamanni. Malaysia: Suara Networks AV, 2010.

Jameson, Fredric. "Third-World Literature in the Era of Multinational Capitalism." *Social Text* 15 (1986): 65–88. www2.warwick.ac.uk/fac/arts/english/currentstudents/undergraduate/modules/fulllist/special/newlits/jameson3rdworldlit.pdf (accessed 5 March 2011).

Jayakumar, S. "POA Deal a Win–Win – Eventually." *The Straits Times*, 2 July 2011. www.straitstimes.com/news/singapore/transport/story/poa-deal-win-win-%E2%80%93-eventually-20110702 (accessed 15 February 2014).

Khoo, Olivia. "Slang Images: On the 'Foreignness' of Contemporary Singaporean Films." Asia Research Institute Working Paper Series No. 40. Singapore: Asia Research Institute, May 2005. www.ari.nus.edu.sg/wps/wps05_040.pdf (accessed 26 February 2015).

Krishnan, Rajan. "Imaginary Geographies: The Makings of 'South' in Contemporary Tamil Cinema." In *Tamil Cinema: The Cultural Politics of India's Other Film Industry*, edited by Selvaraj Velayutham, 139–53. London: Routledge, 2008.

Kumar, S. R. Ashok. "Slice of Singapore." *The Hindu*, 19 December 2010. www.thehindu.com/todays-paper/tp-features/tp-cinemaplus/slice-of-singapore/article961862.ece (accessed 22 December 2010).

"Mathi's Asian Television Awards 2006 Best Actor Promo." YouTube video, 0:59, from the congratulatory video televised by MediaCorp Vasantham Central, n.d. Posted by Mathialagan M. on 28 July 2008. www.youtube.com/watch?v=jVULF0Jg2vw (accessed 5 March 2011).

"Mathi's ATA Awards '06 – Best Actor." YouTube video, 1:31, from Asian Television Award 2006 televised by MediaCorp Channel 5, n.d. Posted by Mathialagan M. on 28 July 2008. www.youtube.com/watch?v=0la65g3R4kk (accessed 5 March 2011).

MediaCorp. "MediaCorp Interactive History." Singapore: MediaCorp, 2010. Last updated 2011. www7.mediacorp.sg/interactivehistory/?p=3 (accessed 15 February 2015).

Ministry of Communication and Information (MCI). "The Committee of Supply 2011 on Ensuring Quality PSB Programmes and Local Films, and Fostering the Discerning Use of Media – Response by Mr Sam Tan." Singapore: Ministry of Communication and Information, 2011. www.mci.gov.sg/mobile/news/media/the-committee-of-supply-2011-on-ensuring-quality-psb-programmes-and-local-films-and-fostering-the-discerning-use-of-media--response-by-mr-sam-tan (accessed 10 August 2011).

My Magic. Directed by Eric Khoo. Singapore: Zhao Wei Films and Scorpio East Entertainment, 2008.

National Population and Talent Division (NPTD). "2014 Population in Brief." Singapore: National Population and Talent Division, 2014. www.nptd.gov.sg/portals/0/homepage/highlights/population-in-brief-2014.pdf (accessed 26 February 2015).

Singapore Law. "Public Prosecutor v Pathip Selvan s/o Sugumaran [2010] SGHC 335." Singapore: Singapore Law, 2010. www.singaporelaw.sg/sglaw/laws-of-singapore/

case-law/free-law/high-court-judgments/14361-public-prosecutor-v-pathip-selvan-s-o-sugumaran-2010-sghc-335 (accessed 13 June 2011).

Tamils Representative Council. "The Charity Gala Premiere of *Gurushetram – 24 Hours of Anger.*" Singapore: Tamils Representative Council, 16 April 2010. www.trc.org.sg/resources/2010/6Apr10.htm (accessed 20 February 2015).

Tan, Kenneth Paul. "Ethnic Representation on Singapore Film and Television." In *Beyond Rituals and Riots: Ethnic Pluralism and Social Cohesion in Singapore*, edited by Lai Ah Eng, 289–315. Singapore: Eastern Universities Press, 2004. https://lkyspp.nus.edu.sg/wp-content/uploads/2013/03/Chapter_11_289-315.pdf (accessed 16 September 2015).

Yong, Shu Chiang. "15-Minute Standing Ovation." *AsiaOne News*, 25 May 2008. http://news.asiaone.com/News/The+Straits+Times/Story/A1Story20080525-66887.html (accessed 12 February 2015).

Zhao Wei Films. "My Magic (2008)." Singapore: Zhao Wei Films, 2013. http://zhaowei.com/my-magic-2008/ (accessed 20 February 2015).

Part III
Cine-cityscapes

9 Singapore v. Foucault

Biopolitics and geopolitics in contemporary queer films

Jun Zubillaga-Pow

In February 2011, the Singapore state censors ordered that the American film *The Kids Are All Right* be limited to a single print and be restricted to audiences twenty-one years old and above. Some members of the public expressed disappointment with the bureaucratic decision regarding the story of a lesbian family drama set in suburban California. They contended that the maintenance and sharing of a household, as well as the personal interactions on an everyday basis, can be as daunting for gay parents as they are for straight parents. Not only is family life physically intrusive, but it is also mentally challenging (Chen 2012; Au 2011). Among other aspects of life, most homosexuals, like heterosexuals, also wish to find a partner and settle down. For gays and lesbians, the additional hurdle to establish or locate an appropriate "gay-friendly" space makes the initial process more vexing. Regrettably, mainstream Queer scholarship has often overlooked the intimate aspect of gay and lesbian personhood, and more often than not has unknowingly misrepresented gays and lesbians by casting homosexuality in rather stereotypical frames.

While the word "Queer" is used to refer to a certain Foucauldian strand of theoretical underpinnings connoted with political resistance and emancipation from the normative and heteronormative, I use the terms "homosexual", "queer" and "gay" in this chapter to differentiate the respective definitions of the biological, theoretical and socio-cultural constructions. In tandem, my argument herein coheres with the critique of a normative gender/culture synchrony, where sexuality and its corporeal performativity are not correlative, empirical or otherwise (Muñoz 1999; Butler 1990). In this sense, my chapter aims to counter two of such essentialist perspectives using the case study of Singapore Queer Cinema.

One prevalent mistake in contemporary society is the identity or identification of homosexuals as interacting or doing things only with bodies of the same gender. Within a social interactionist paradigm, the body and its behaviour are actually not distinctive categories that generate differentiable discourses of sexuality and society. Physical actions are always already constructed via socio-cultural regulations. In addition, it is also a common oversight to situate what Guy Hocquenghem (1993) calls "homosexual desires" as residing mainly within "other" spaces, spaces that are alternative or lying outside the hegemonic purview. Rather, the heteronormative spaces are themselves in fact not as resistible

130   *Jun Zubillaga-Pow*

to critical re-territorialisation as they are perceived to be. Based on the Foucauldian method of negation, it is clear that these sites of heteronormativity, whether real or imaginary, can afford to be reclaimed by non-normative subjects in the form of biopolitical resistance, and that this repose made visible through recent ethnographical and filmic resources acts as a geopolitical strategy towards the creation of a Queer screen cartography. However, the Singaporean case studies immediately thwart such de Certeauian tactics and instead persistently support the bio-spatial demarcations between sexual beings (Ahmed 2006, 91). In accord with these filmic narratives, sexuality in Singapore remains a social determinant of dissident places and placements: the decadent West, indecent public sex, and obscenities and profanities on-screen, etc. Liberal sexual attitudes and practices are being suppressed in the geopolitical arenas within and without local contemporary queer films.

I

Geopolitics in this chapter is understood as the dynamic interactions between subjects and objects, including those abstract or ungraspable, as limited by a geographical setting on which politics and aesthetics intersect. One good example of a less abstract relation is Fredric Jameson's notion of the "geopolitical unconscious" within world cinema (1992). For Jameson, filmic media have come to be projects for proper geopolitical scrutiny in the past decade. Despite the increase academic interests in geo-cinematic analyses, scholars often privileged the popular perspective over those of the formal and practical (Power and Crampton 2005). Queers, however, have never been covered in geopolitical cinema studies. This chapter, located within the discipline of cultural studies, emphasises the significance of sexual differences in geo-cinematic analyses. I supplement Michael Shapiro's theory of a "violent cartography" (2008) in Western war cinema with the equally harrowing experiences of forbidden and unrequited desires. To the extent that Shapiro's idea of violent imaginaries is predicated on identity difference – in our case, the enmity between heteronormative and homonormative attitudes, as well as Singaporean and Western cultures – Singapore cinema conveys a rather unconscious geopolitical violence seemingly unable or uninterested in transcending that which Jacques Rancière calls "the mimetic regime of art" (cf. Tan 2008). Whether imitating or imagining the gay or lesbian communities in Singapore, the narratives and affects of the short films discussed herein do not subscribe to the theoretical agenda of decolonial geopolitics (Maldonado-Torres 2004) or alternative geopolitics (Koopman 2011). Instead, the critical interrogation of queer bodies on mundane cinematic spaces does not reveal any re-territorialisation of desexualised space, but rather upholds an unconscious complicity with the hetero/homonormalising nature of a neoliberal geography (Puar 2002).

That said, more pertinent within the decolonising world today is that engaging in counter-arguments against Eurocentric dialectics, sexual or otherwise, is already an *a priori* discursive defeat. Even if the gradual displacement of British colonial attitudes and American neoliberal globalisation by the enforcement of Asian values and Confucian thought patterns has had any impact on the Singaporean civility, the validity of a post-colonial Queer discourse would have lost its place in the very test of apprehending heteronormativity with or against a Singaporean identity (cf. Hawley 2001). On the one hand, the contingency of this discussion can only be predicated upon relatively contemporaneous contexts because the supporting evidence, which hereby determine increasing queer visibilities on film, is restricted within the first decade of the twenty-first century. This means that the longitudinal progress of gay and lesbian livelihood in Singapore cannot be fully accounted for. On the other hand, the filmmakers' encapsulation of each semi-fictitious episode subtends the possibilities of gays and lesbians imagining the aestheticisation of private and public spaces, and re-inscribing "homo-ness", to use Leo Bersani's coinage, as a pragmatic method of geopolitical re-territorialisation.

The reading of these cultural artefacts must nonetheless be situated within the socio-political perspectives of the *hic et nunc*, the here and the now. A constitutional prominence of the 2007 Parliamentary discussions and 2013 court rulings concerning the repeal or retention of Section 377A of the Singapore Penal Code, which criminalises all acts of gross indecency between men, must form the backdrop of this and any other post-Victorian Queer thesis. The immediate reason is that the explicated viewpoints expressed within this socio-legal milieu correspond acutely to the refined nexus of attitudes held by the political representatives of this country debating for and against homosexuality and heteronormativity. If most of the perspectives had reflected a conservative projectile, then this is what gays and lesbians in Singapore have learnt to circumvent and acculturate against an incumbent biopower that is obsessed with neoliberal geopolitics (cf. Amirthalingam 2009).

In another sense, this chapter also charts a historical reappraisal of the way Singaporean gays and lesbians have, over time, learnt to negotiate the subjectifications instigated by biopoliticians and geopoliticians alike by orientating towards an anti-Foucauldian decorum against the Victorian policing of sexuality. In fact, some studies have suggested that Singapore is an exact representation of an authoritarian Victorian society with the retention of a Westminster legislative Parliament and the revision of the British constitution, among other factors (Ho 2012). If these theoretical underpinnings prove themselves to be empirically cogent, I conclude by seeking a redress to understand why the application of these Foucauldian critique onto the context of queer Singaporean culture tends to amplify the datedness and denigrating efficacies of Queer Theory vis-à-vis the idiosyncrasies of queer life in everyday Singapore, cinematic or otherwise.

One of the grounded realities remains that, even if homosexual themes and characters have appeared *straightforward* to film viewers, the inherent dimension of Queer biopolitics and geopolitics among other discourses are mostly opaque to the uncritical spectacle. Singapore Queer Cinema as a niche category henceforth continues to be sidelined by other aspects of film and cinema studies. Precisely because of the absence of a Singapore Queer Cinema collective, the impetus for a critical appraisal within contemporary scholarship should not be disregarded. Making the selection as inclusive as possible, I will examine Eric Khoo's

132 *Jun Zubillaga-Pow*

Be With Me (2005), Kan Lume's and Loo Zihan's *Solos* (2007), Boo Junfeng's *Tanjong Rhu* (2008), Loo Zihan's *Threshold* (2009), Royston Tan's *Anniversary* (2009), Sun Koh's *One* (2010), Lincoln Chia's *Sisters* (2011), Regina Tan's *Transit* (2011), Jerome Won's music video 逃离思念 (2012), and *Purple Light* (2014) by Cecilia Ang, Javior Chew and Charlene Yiu.

II

In his 1967 lecture to architects at the *Cercle d'études Architecturales* (Circle of Architectural Studies), Foucault borrowed the term heterotopia from the medical terminology to classify spaces of otherness. It was to become an episteme that deviated critically from the standard methods of spatial management. According to Foucault:

> This space of localization opened up with Galileo ... [is] a space that was infinite, and infinitely open ... A thing's place was no longer anything but a point in its motion, just as a thing's rest was nothing more than its motion indefinitely slowed down.
>
> (2000, 176)

Alternatively, these real spaces, as opposed to the imaginary places of utopia, are also open spaces to be "located" and "localised" by objects that have been "violently displaced". This is understood by Foucault's choice of the French word *localisation*, as derived from *localiser*, which signifies the different meanings of "to locate" and "to localise". With the aid of six principles identified by Foucault in his address, I will compare and contrast the *imaginary* cinematic frameworks of the abovementioned films with my own ethnographic observations of everyday life to buttress the thesis that queer spaces in Singapore have deviated from the critical ideals of a Foucauldian heterotopia and are becoming akin to an assimilated homotopia.

First, a heterotopia is considered to be a space of deviation and crisis because their inhabitants do not partake in the organic function of a creedal union between a man and a woman (Foucault 2000, 180). The amorous relationship of gays and lesbians, who deviate from the *doxical* sexual practices of the Judeo–Christian or Confucian family structures, is relevant here. According to Foucault, "religion can play the double role of nature and of rule, since it has assumed the depth of nature in ancestral habit, in education, in everyday exercise, and since it is at the same time a constant principle of coercion" (1989b, 231). Comparatively, gays and lesbians behave similarly to people who are mentally challenged residing in an asylum that is segregated from the "rational" majority. Both groups exist under the shadow of a deontology that adheres to heteronormative dogmas as if they lack the ability to know and to reason. Foucault deems such a heterotopia as "a juridical space where one is accused, judged, and condemned, and from which one is never released except by the version of this trial in psychological depth – that is, by remorse" (1989b, 256). One literary example is the narratives of the novelist Philip Pullman, whose stories have been described as a queer heterotopia of shame (Munt 2008, 199).

In Singapore, some gays and lesbians have refused to be "imprisoned in [such] a moral world" (Foucault 1989b, 256) despite being restrained by the sickle of a juridical "adumbration", that is the local penal code. Instead, they are starting to construct their personal Queer ethics. For instance, some local clubs such as Zouk and the now-defunct Butter Factory organised "polysexual" events that aptly enact a symbolic resistance against the moral configuration as imposed upon by the heteronormative state. This phenomenon is reflected in a brief scene in Boo Junfeng's *Sandcastle* (2011) where a young heterosexual couple was filmed clubbing in one of the bars in Singapore's gay enclave. In contrast to the queer gentrification of heteronormative spaces, this scene represents the first moment where Singapore, as a geopolitical *location*, disavows Foucault's framing of non-hegemonic spaces as deviant. Instead, the gay bars achieve social saliency by affording interactions between heterosexuals and homosexuals.

Another case study that deviates from Foucault's heterotopic classification is Lincoln Chia's *Sisters*. The short film uses the Chinese custom of fetching the bride from her maiden home as the setting of the plot. The climax of the film occurs at the moment when the bridegroom is tricked into proposing to the bride's brother as part of the playful ceremony (Figure 9.1). The scene portraying the confession of love to each other happens right in the middle of the apartment amidst the gathering of family members, young and old. The position of the two gay men surrounded by family members dislodges the possibility of establishing a heterotopia of deviation and crisis. It is at the very moment when the protagonist utters the words "I do" in front of the entire family that homosexuality comes to

Figure 9.1 Film still from *Sisters* (2011), directed by Lincoln Chia.

134   Jun Zubillaga-Pow

reclaim the traditional notion of the creedal act. With more and more gay couples in Singapore getting recognised by their families over the past decade, this form of non-judgemental acknowledgement can be considered as a demarcation of transgressive boundaries via an extension of homosexual relationships into familial spaces.

However, a different observation is made from Sun Koh's *One*, where a single long take shows an East Timorese family loading goods onto their boat and returning home to celebrate Christmas. The people who are invisible to the audiences are the filmmaker herself and her partner, a UN peacekeeper. While East Timor has regained sovereignty and security since 2006, the legal crisis that separates the lesbian couple remains unbeknownst to both the viewers and the family featured in the film. From a human rights perspective, any possibility of a cinematic heterotopia is already foreclosed since the non-diegetic representation of queerness escapes all audiovisual recognition in the five-minute short film. Hidden behind the scenes of subaltern geopolitics is the (hetero)normalised façade of two foreign women who cannot digress from their professional mission, lest they are rejected by the staunchly Catholicised local population. This is instantly a show of defiance against Western film philosophy by Singapore's Queer filmmakers, who thwart Jacques Rancière's observation that the visible brings about a contradiction to the narrative signification (Rancière 2006, 22). Instead, filmmakers either make queer bodies and affects apparent and logical to the plot or become invisible within the mainstream cinematic cartography that sustains the geopolitical antinomy.

III

Before the 1980s, places in Singapore where gay men socialise were restricted to a few bars and clubs, although they were often interrupted by frequent police surveillance (Heng 2001). With the advent of gay bathhouses and an active cyber-culture in the late 1990s, the transition, as allegorised by the sociologist Manuel Castells, "from the bars to the streets, from nightlife to daytime, from 'sexual deviance' to an alternative lifestyle" contributed to the crucial development of the community and marked the birth of the "gay village" (Castells 1983, 141). In the last dozen-odd years, these spaces, patronised mostly by gays and lesbians in Singapore, have undergone tremendous changes from both social and geographical perspectives. Congruent with the spatial history of homosexuals and queer people particularly in the more progressive West (Ingram *et al.* 1997), the local movement of homosexuals in Singapore diverges from Foucault's historicised analogy of the cemetery as a heterotopia (2000, 180). This alternative space, with its association with death, becomes sacrilegious and defiled; it moves gradually into the geographical periphery away from the city centre.

Akin to the social critique of Castells, such affective and contagious extensions of the "queer diaspora" is befitting of the Foucauldian heterotopia (Puar 2007, 170). However, such an enlargement of queer embodiment in reality does not advance any geopolitical territorialisation. On the contrary, the clamour for such a categorical subversion of the "queer heterotopia", understood as "spaces where the infinite performances of queerness can exist and flourish free from regulation and marginalization" (Jones 2009, 5) fails to eliminate the amount of police surveillance and public discrimination in Singapore.

On the one hand, the resistance to any "localisation" of such "queer heterotopia" is inculcated firmly within the Singaporean consciousness. Nowadays, many gays and lesbians refuse to be seen lingering on the few streets where the bars and clubs are located. If the Queer scholar Warren Hoffman argues that "walking into a gay bar is a momentous act in the life history of a homosexual, because in many cases it is the first time he publicly identifies himself as a homosexual" (quoted in Fouz-Hernandez 2008, 154), then the Singaporean homosexual would perpetuate a self-censorship of the gay locale, both in everyday life and on film. Notwithstanding the "polysexual" moment in *Sandcastle*, the very absence of films with gay characters in a gay locale, be it real or propped, is acutely indicative of the disavowal of Queer spatial configuration as an anti-Foucauldian geopolitics.

Rather, gay apparel shops in Singapore are tucked away in obscure corners, while the saunas cropped up at dull and odd "para-sites" trying to blend in with the conservative streetscape (Tattelman 1997). Bearing similar attitudes to how Terry Sanderson describes the British scene of "cottaging" as "dirty, undignified, nerve-wracking and dangerous" (1991, 64), the infiltration of gay or queer businesses into the Singaporean suburbia, or "heartlands" in the colloquial catchphrase, failed in the long run to attract any gay men and women to these places due to economic inflation and inaccessibility. Eventually, these heterotopias of displacement were forced to quickly liquidate. Such a goal of erecting a queer heterotopia in Singapore takes on the metonymic self-annihilation of what Hocquenghem has claimed as the "accursed race" (1993, 88).

In contradistinction, a subplot from the film *Be With Me* (2005) by Eric Khoo depicts with higher accuracy the social movement of lesbians in everyday life. The intimacy of two teenage girls engaging in public displays of affection forms a third of the film, which consequentially received a M18 ("above 18") rating by the Board of Film Censors in Singapore. These scenes of same-sex interactions are critically significant not because of what the girls are doing in front of the camera, but because of what they are *not* doing on-screen. Through the non-diegetic gaze, one sees the lovers being totally oblivious to the people around them as if the heteronormative periphery has "liquefied". Whether they are taking a picture, cuddling in the theatre, or feeding each other in the ice cream parlour, the lesbians *locate* their acts of homosexuality right within public gaze. Even though the kissing scene is set on the rooftop of a high-rise building away from public access, this cinematic framing, given the dense geography of Singapore's residential topography, is symbolic of the Foucauldian panopticon where the homonormative act remains subjected to the surveying glance.

In this sense, the characters are establishing an agenda, whether conscious or unconscious, to re-territorialise public spaces as their own in disparate moments of Queer time. This public display of their same-sex love for each other shares precedences with, say, the final scene in the British film adaptation of Jonathan Harvey's *Beautiful Thing* (1996) by Hettie MacDonald, in which the protagonists

136   *Jun Zubillaga-Pow*

enact a public "outing" in full endorsement by the residents of the neighbourhood. Representing the "enlightened" homosexuals, who have been relieved of a parochial culture, the youngsters refused to be socially and spatially alienated. They deny being disenchanted by the theocratic or other forms of ethics that demand such behaviour to be conducted in private spheres. Via these performances of homosexuality in a public environment, the characters reclaim the erstwhile heteronormative spaces as if it were a geopolitical task that redefines the gay migratory census.

IV

Foucault identifies the third principle of the heterotopia as one where a single real space is able to juxtapose several otherwise incompatible sites (2000, 181). As a parody of the theatre and cinema, this is a place of performativity where one need not exit to do that which one wants. Exemplarily, Singapore, as a planned economy, does not reserve such multivalent spaces for homosexuals. The gay locales continue to be dispersed, causing these places to be out of sight and out of sync. As a consequence, gays and lesbians remain just as suppressed as the heterosexuals, living alongside the intersections of compulsory heteronormativity and contingent homosexuality (Ahmed 2006). In addition, the sites where gay men cruise gradually become "localised" at many secluded spots, such as parks, reservoirs and the beaches on the Eastern coast.

In his film *Tanjong Rhu* (2008), Boo Junfeng recollects the story of one of twelve men caught in a police operation at Fort Road beach in 1993. The portrayal of young gay men looking for sex was filmed on location in the darkness of bushes, shrubs and a small forested area, away from the concrete façades of urban Singapore. This is obviously not a multifaceted heterotopia where dissimilar activities occur at the same time; the people who track these paths have only one purpose and that is to fornicate. In other words, the yearning for company, sexual or otherwise, is realised by both filmic speech and gestures. These cinematic tropes often take on a "localised" reference: "do you come *here* often?" or the twisting of the head as a vectorial gesture to lead and follow: "come". The act of being voyeuristic is coupled with a desperate search for companionship; and, given the country's meagre size and authoritarian politics, this personal navigation within the available spatial limits continues to be etched illiberally within the Singaporean social psyche for both the public majority in general and the homosexuals in particular.

In Boo's short film, there is a split-second shot of the clothed groin area to set the tone of the entrapment scene, but this, I believe, is more indicative of the way in which the queer use of space has veered away from the theatrical aspect of Foucault's heterotopia. Rather, several pressing issues are eked out in the film as it unfolds with the speech-acts derivative of social realism. Such a rhetorical device has been acknowledged as an artistic style prevalent among contemporary Singaporean filmmakers (Yao 2007, 149). The filmviewers are invited into the past and present lives of the protagonists, each of whom only shares a brief encounter with one another on the beach. Yet, unlike the juxtaposition of picnicking, hiking

Singapore v. Foucault 137

and cruising that exemplify the multivalent utilities of, say, the European outbacks of Hampstead Heath in London or Alberoni Beach in Venice, the film portrays the Singaporean terrains as a dystopic and displaced site, where queer repression becomes inevitable and real.

The administered deterrence towards public cruising in the undeveloped spaces is a resistance against the "homonormalising" act, one that is deemed antagonistic to the current heteronormative and monopolistic ideology (Edwards 1994, 100). Hocquenghem may have likened the utilitarian function of the "pick-up scene" to a "system in action, the system in which polyvocal desire is plugged in on a non-exclusive basis" (1993, 131); but, in Singapore, this system of polyvalent expression is annihilated and suppressed time and time again due to the unregulated legal practice and misinformed red tape, among other factors. This phenomenon is most acute in the urban landscape shown in the music video, 逃离思念 (*táo lí sī niàn*), that accompanies Jerome Won's song of the same name. Two young boys infatuated with each other are seen loitering at the basketball court, the bus stop and the car park, all of which are transient places where bodies appear ephemeral and movement perpetual. Bearing expressions of innocent love, the boys finally get to meet each other as the teleological narrative preaches dogmatically the virtue of patience and the righteousness of romantic fidelity. There is a stark censure of sexual plurality, or a heterotopia of promiscuity, especially not within the local affective economy.

V

As with the previous heterotopic principle, a well-planned space is able to stand the test of time, acting as both a heterotopia and a heterochrony. Like the artefacts and books in the museum and library respectively, allowing its inhabitants to capture history at its most quintessential moment is the primary objective of a heterotopia (Foucault 2000, 182). In any one gay location, an older person should be able to reminisce over his past upon seeing a younger person, who would correspondingly emulate the moral or other good of the older other. This fluidity of temporal differences enables life in the gay locale to uphold a positive image by following Foucault's advocacy of a way of life that "can be shared among individuals of different age, status, and social activity. It can yield intense relations … a culture and an ethics" (1998, 138). Moreover, the lives of gays and lesbians can be encased within a queer territory, resembling the Polynesian inhabitants on their own islands, enjoying the heterotopia of festival and eternity or, as Foucault indicates, living simultaneously within the instant and the infinite.

If the above scenario has a regular place in Queer progression, then Singapore is directed as an anti-example, where older gays and lesbians seem to have disappeared almost entirely from the local scenes. One does not have to make wild guesses as to where they have gone; the lack of role models for the younger generations of gays and lesbians today is because their older counterparts have either formed reclusive partnerships, whether straight or queer, or are seen loitering around in public toilets and changing rooms as the "perverted old man".

138   *Jun Zubillaga-Pow*

The ancient Greek model of the *erastês* and *erômenos*, or the conducive, pedagogic man–boy relation, is culturally extinct in a non-affective Singaporean regime (cf. Dover 1989).

Such male–male interactions among three generations of hetero- and homosexual people is intrinsic to the plot of Loo Zihan's short film *Threshold* (2009), which won in the category of Best Script at the Singapore Short Film Awards 2010. The plot surrounds an arranged gay threesome in a dingy motel room between a young drug dealer who is about twenty years old and two officers from the CNB posing as interested parties. While the more senior sergeant is more understanding of the inspector's sexual urges and even initiated to bring him to the red light district, the mid-career inspector around thirty years of age turns out to be struggling with his own sexuality and cannot forgive the promiscuous behaviour of the gay medical student.

In twenty minutes, the film sets out to present the numerous past experiences and current dilemmas of the three characters. Again, the positioning of the characters in places of transient temporality – that of a motel room and, like in Boo's film, a forested mirage – immediately thwarts the very idea of a heterotopia of festivity and didactic exchange. Instead, these sites reveal the severe communication fault-lines among people of different generations, gay or otherwise. The rapid urbanisation of Singapore has resulted in such disparate changes to homosexual behaviour and ways of life to the large extent that there is neither shared time nor space for older and younger persons to relate to and with each other, or even among themselves. As revealed in Loo's script, almost everyone is concerned with their own state of affairs, promotions and other personal interests. Representative of Tan See-Kam's cinematic analogy of Singapore as a "society of strangers" (2009), Loo's filmic narrative resembles a neoliberal dissolution of the Foucauldian project to erect a heterochrony.

VI

Appropriating Foucault's proposition, the heterotopia is also a space of exclusion: exclusive to the minority, excluding the majority, and excluded from the majority (2000, 183). Akin to a barrack or brothel, that which one does within a queer heterotopia is unknown to those without. Gays and lesbians may engage in "tactical" homosexual acts similar to the way soldiers learn bayonet fighting skills in military camps: both maintain confidentiality from the public. Such a heterotopia is also "consecrated" to activities of purifications, such as the obedience to the scriptures, the discipline of a model soldier, the stringent adherence to gay mannerism and fashion, and the ascetic *dressage* to be the highest-earning rent boy.

Uncannily, this may be the only principle that is applicable to the Singaporean queer culture. The visibility of gay social activities in Singapore is relatively opaque that even biopolitical bureaucrats are misled by myopic assumptions and dishonest "astroturfing". This delocalisation buttresses Bersani's (1998) conception of "homo-ness" as one begetting a heterotopia denying aliens from any naïve

Singapore v. Foucault   139

penetration into what could be called a Lacanian *barred* system. According to Foucault, "one can enter only with a certain permission and after a certain number of gestures", specifically, "purification activities" (2000, 183). A parallel analogy is the military propaganda to assure citizens that soldiering is good for the progress of the country, whereby the inclusion and exclusion of information is managed bureaucratically. While the government promotes the defence of one's nation and international peacekeeping efforts, they disavow to educate the public on the ethics of war, violence and its exorbitant defence expenditure (Ministry of Defence 2006, 2009). This theory can be exemplified by the people and places in Royston Tan's short film *Anniversary*, which was written by the playwright Alfian Sa'at and released in 2009.

In several scenes, conversations about infidelity and HIV testing are heard among platonic friends of both sexes in fast food restaurants and coffeehouses. The dialogues are within audible proximity to the patrons nearby. Yet, these sexually coded euphemisms are tactically "barred" from any unacquainted person from knowing the contents of the exchange. The main reason rests in the fact that gays and lesbians have carved out a "heterotopia of purification" amidst the everyday dining and socialising locales as exclusive domains for the subsistence of gay and homosexual discourses. The use of words and gestures by the characters in the film escape their common vernacular connotations and encode a community into a heterotopia of exclusivity.

That said, these acts of camouflage are being obliterated, as homosexuals and transgenders begin to "come out" and explain themselves and their ways of life in hope of being included as a vital constituent of Singapore. On one hand, there are the promotional trailers shot by Boo Junfeng for the Pink Dot initiative from 2009 to 2013, which are analogous representations of the ways in which gays and lesbians have come to aspire towards social and national integration by veering away from the heterotopia of exception. On the other hand, the short documentary, *Transit* (2011), by Regina Tan showcases the achievements and aspirations of a Malay–Muslim, male-to-female, pre-op trans person, who expresses herself via dance and fashion. Her story is however portrayed uncritically through the filmic heterotopia of exclusion without the active participation of people who are neither Malay–Muslim nor transgender. The protagonist is essentially typecast as cinematically exceptional.

Inevitably, the queer heterotopia is also a phenomenon that has only evolved over the past half century. Foucault classifies it as the youngest of all colonies, a heterotopia of compensation occupied by a new group of people governed by different labels (2000, 184). In our case, these can only be none other than the gays, lesbians, trans, etc., who do not alter the sexual orientation or the lifestyles of the habitants from the area in which they come to territorialise. Their brand of biopolitics stops short of imposing gay laws or introducing any gay language upon the natives. They merely gentrify the space to allow themselves to live according to their needs, sexual or otherwise. Similar to the British or French colonies, these queer heterotopia are created "out of compensation" for the lack of gay spaces available in the heteronormative world.

140   *Jun Zubillaga-Pow*

As mentioned, Singapore does not partake in such geopolitics. The "delocalisation" process is characterised by the gradual closure of numerous bars and discothèques in the previous decade alongside the "return-of-the-closet" for many gay people and businesses. Like the fate of *The Kids Are All Right* mentioned at the start of this chapter, there continues to be a cultural deficit and censorship of gay performances and media visibilities in Singapore. The excellent feature film *Solos* (2007) by Kan Lume and Loo Zihan, which won the *Premio Nuovi Sguardi* Award at the Torino Film Festival, remains banned in the country.

There are numerous factors from this latter narrative that disavow the formation of such a queer colony even on local cinema screens: the explicit portrayal of three naked men having sex, the lack of fidelity and filial piety, the amorous relationship between the student and his teacher, and the decision of the protagonist to become an artist instead of the pragmatic routes of studying law, engineering or business. The state censors have established an administration of draconian control, which aligns acutely with Foucault's logic of censorship, that is "affirming that such a thing is not permitted, preventing it from being said, [and] denying that it exists" (1998, 84). Singapore is adamant that the Foucauldian heterotopia of colonisation does not propagate in the country. This doctrine is internalised in such a docile manner that it has become intrinsic to the subgenre. An epitome is the 2014 short film, *Purple Light*, in which two male soldiers quickly retreat "into the closet" after being punished for kissing during a field exercise as if the incident has not happened at all.

Finally, if Foucault has proclaimed the ship as the heterotopia *par excellence*, the queer film would be associated, albeit ironically, as the heterotopic *dystopia*. Unlike the Foucauldian boat, which gives itself "over to the boundless expanse of the ocean, and that goes from port to port, from watch to watch, from brothel to brothel, all the way to the colonies in search of the most precious treasures that lie waiting in their gardens" (2000, 185), all the films discussed in this chapter are set either in the immobility of dark and secluded outdoor places or the walled-in spaces of private residences or motel rooms. The absence of gay people, narratives or events taking place in sites of public accessibility such as the clubs, parades or shopping centres is representative of the ultimate liquidation of the Foucauldian heterotopia by Singapore Queer Cinema.

In aggregate, the film analyses presented here expose the underlying conventions of pragmatism upheld by a conservative Singaporean homosexual community as antagonistic to the generic Queer theorising in contemporary academic writings. Within and without the filmic ideological apparatus, such a refusal to engage in the Western derivatives of biopolitics and geopolitics is an indication of the vested interests of Singaporean gays and lesbians in gaining autonomy from the hegemonic imperialism, which shackles the notion of homosexuality to an uncritical dogma, aggravating the already precarious nature of being queer. In considering Foucault's concept of the heterotopia as a geopolitical ideological apparatus, a localised comparison between everyday life and its corresponding cinematic representations vis-à-vis the various filmic moments has propounded the irreconcilable dialectics between the politicised homosexual body and the geographical boundaries. In a nutshell, this research can be deemed both as a realignment of Orientalist meditations on queer subjects within a Foucauldian paradigm as well as a critical reformulation of the ways in which the creative narratives produced by queer Singaporean subjects have aggrandised a homonormative politics of sexual recognition and repression.

References

Ahmed, Sara. *Queer Phenomenology: Orientations, Objects, Others*. Durham and London: Duke University Press, 2006.

Amirthalingam, Kumaralingam. "Criminal Law and Private Spaces: Regulating Homosexual Acts in Singapore." In *Regulating Deviance: The Redirection of Criminalisation and the Futures of Criminal Law*, edited by Bernadette McSherry, Alan Norrie and Simon Bronitt, 185–212. Portland: Hart, 2009.

Au, Alex. "What's More Terrifying Than Sex? Family." *Yawning Bread*, 18 February 2011. http://yawningbread.wordpress.com/2011/02/18/whats-more-terrifying-than-sex-family/ (accessed 10 July 2014).

Bersani, Leo. *Homos*. Cambridge: Harvard University Press, 1996.

Butler, Judith. *Gender Trouble: Feminism and the Subversion of Identity*. New York: Routledge, 1990.

Castells, Manuel. *The City and the Grassroots: A Cross-Cultural Theory of Urban Social Movements*. Berkeley: University of California Press, 1983.

Chen, Loretta. "The Kids are *Not* All Right: The Curious Case of Sapphic Censorship in City-State Singapore." In *Queer Singapore: Illiberal Citizenship and Mediated Cultures*, edited by Audrey Yue and Jun Zubillaga-Pow, 175–86. Hong Kong: Hong Kong University Press, 2012.

Dover, K. J. *Greek Homosexuality*. Cambridge: Harvard University Press, 1989.

Edwards, Tim. *Erotics and Politics: Gay Male Sexuality, Masculinity and Feminism*. London: Routledge, 1994.

Foucault, Michel. *The History of Sexuality, Vol. 1: The Will to Knowledge*. Translated by Robert Hurley. London: Penguin Books, 1989a.

Foucault, Michel. "The Birth of the Asylum." In *Madness and Civilisation: A History of Insanity in the Age of Reason*, translated by Richard Howard. London: Routledge, 1989b.

Foucault, Michel. "Friendship as a Way of Life." In *Essential Works of Foucault 1954–1984 Volume 1: Ethics: Subjectivity and Truth*, edited by Paul Rainbow, 135–40. New York: The New Press, 1998.

Foucault, Michel. "Different Spaces." In *Essential Works of Foucault 1954–1984 Volume 2: Aesthetics, Method, and Epistemology*, edited by James D. Faubion, 175–86. London: Penguin Books, 2000.

Fouz-Hernández, Santiago. "School is Out: The British 'Coming Out' Films of the 1990s." In *Queer Cinema in Europe*, edited by Robin Griffiths, 145–64. Bristol: Intellect Books, 2008.

Hawley, John C., ed. *Postcolonial, Queer: Theoretical Intersections*. New York: State University of New York Press, 2001.

Heng, Russell Hiang Khng. "Tiptoe out of the Closet: The Before and After of the Increasingly Visible Gay Community in Singapore." *Journal of Homosexuality* 40, no. 3–4 (2001): 81–97.

Ho, Aaron. "How to Bring Singaporeans Up Straight." In *Queer Singapore: Illiberal Citizenship and Mediated Culture*, edited by Audrey Yue and Jun Zubillaga-Pow, 2–23. Hong Kong: Hong Kong University Press, 2012.

Hocquenghem, Guy. *Homosexual Desire*. Durham and London: Duke University Press, 1993.

142 *Jun Zubillaga-Pow*

Ingram, Gordon Brent, Anne-Marie Bouthillette, and Yolanda Retter, eds. *Queers in Space: Communities, Public Places, Sites of Resistance.* Seattle: Bay Press, 1997.

Jameson, Fredric. *The Geopolitical Aesthetic: Cinema and Space in the World System.* Bloomington: Indiana University Press, 1992.

Jones, Angela. "Queer Heterotopias: Homonormativity and the Future of Queerness." *Interalia* 4 (2009): 1–20. www.interalia.org.pl/index_pdf.php?lang=en&klucz=& produkt=1260885944-076 and www.interalia.org.pl/en/artykuly/2009_4/13_queer_ heterotopias_homonormativity_and_the_future_of_queerness.htm (accessed 10 July 2014).

Koopman, Sara. "Alter-geopolitics: Other Securities are Happening." *Geoforum* 42, no. 3 (2011): 274–84.

Lefebvre, Henri. *The Production of Space.* Translated by Donald Nicholson-Smith. Oxford: Wiley-Blackwell, 2004.

Maldonado-Torres, Nelson. "The Topology of Being and the Geopolitics of Knowledge: Modernity, Empire, Coloniality." *City* 8, no. 1 (2004): 29–56.

Ministry of Defence, Singapore. Speech, 26 July 2006. www.mindef.gov.sg/imindef/news_ and_events/nr/2006/jul/26jul06_nr/26jul06_speech.html (accessed 30 October 2014).

Ministry of Defence, Singapore. Speech, 20 November 2009. www.mindef.gov.sg/imindef/ news_and_events/nr/2009/nov/20nov09_nr/20nov09_speech.html (accessed 30 October 2014).

Muñoz, José Esteban. *Disidentifications: Queers of Color and the Performance of Politics.* Minneapolis: Minnesota University Press, 1999.

Munt, Sally R. *Queer Attachments: The Cultural Politics of Shame.* Aldershot: Ashgate, 2008.

Power, Marcus, and Andrew Crampton. "Reel Geopoltics: Cinemato-graphing Political Space." *Geopolitics* 10, no. 2 (2005): 193–203.

Rancière, Jacques. *Film Fables.* Translated by Emiliano Battista. Oxford: Berg, 2006.

Puar, Jasbir. "A Transnational Feminist Critique of Queer Tourism." *Antipode* 34, no. 5 (2002): 935–46.

Puar, Jasbir K. *Terrorist Assemblages: Homonationalism in Queer Times.* Durham and London: Duke University Press, 2007.

Sanderson, Terry. *Stranger in the Family: How to Cope if Your Child is Gay.* London: The Other Way Press, 1991.

Shapiro, Michael J. *Cinematic Geopolitics.* London and New York: Routledge, 2008.

Tan, Kenneth Paul. *Cinema and Television in Singapore: Resistance in One Dimension.* Leiden: Brill, 2008.

Tan, See-Kam. "Singapore as a Society of Strangers: Eric Khoo's *Mee Pok Man, 12 Storeys,* and *Be With Me.*" In *Chinese Connections: Critical Perspectives on Film, Identity, and Diaspora,* edited by Tan See-Kam, Peter X. Feng and Gina Marchetti, 205–19. Philadelphia: Temple University Press, 2009.

Tattelman, Ira. "The Meaning at the Wall: Tracing the Gay Bathhouse." In *Queers in Space: Communities, Public Places, Sites of Resistance,* edited by Gordon Brent Ingram, Anne-Marie Bouthillette and Yolanda Retter, 391–406. Seattle: Bay Press, 1997.

Yao, Souchou. *Singapore: The State and the Culture of Excess.* London and New York: Routledge, 2007.

Filmography

Ang, Cecilia, Javior Chew, and Charlene Yiu. *Purple Light.* Singapore, 2014.

Boo, Junfeng. *Tanjong Rhu.* Singapore, 2008.

Boo, Junfeng. *Sandcastle.* Singapore, 2011.

Boo, Junfeng. Pink Dot Promotional Videos. Singapore, 2009–2013.

Chia, Lincoln. *Sisters.* Singapore, 2011.

Cholodenko, Lisa. *The Kids Are All Right.* United States of America, 2010.

Kan, Lume and Loo Zihan. *Solos*. Singapore, 2007.
Khoo, Eric. *Be With Me*. Singapore.
Koh, Sun. *One*. Singapore/East Timor, 2010.
Loo, Zihan. *Threshold*. Singapore, 2009.
MacDonald, Hettie. *Beautiful Thing*. United Kingdom, 1996.
Tan, Regina. *Transit*. Singapore, 2011.
Tan, Royston. *Anniversary*. Singapore, 2009.
Won, Jerome. 逃离思念. Singapore, 2012.

10 Mapping Singapore's cinemas

Charley Leary

Daddy, what is a movie?
[…]
Daddy, Daddy! Then, where is this theatre?

IPOS trailer campaign against video piracy

Introduction

Those watching a film in a Singapore cinema in recent years would be familiar with the public service campaign trailer from Singapore's Intellectual Property Office against video piracy. This trailer, which is shown among the coming attractions, is set in a dystopic future where movie theatres no longer exist. In it, a child asks his father to explain the nature and purpose of a movie ticket – the object everyone in the audience would be holding – as the movie ticket had become a collector's item in the father's scrapbook as a remembrance of a bygone age. The solemn father, with an obvious sense of loss and mourning in his tone, then informs his son that movie tickets were used at places called movie theatres, places with "a big screen" and "a good sound system", where one would go to watch things called movies. While this short film affirms a unique sense of materiality and tactility in filmgoing, I do not suspect movie theatres will physically disappear from Singapore any time in the near future, precisely because characters like the father still exist in real life.

The frequent crowds at many cinemas in Singapore provide sufficient proof of this, and are a testament to the intense cinephilia of Singaporeans (Lai 2010). According to a recent survey by the United Nations Educational, Scientific and Cultural Organization (UNESCO) Institute of Statistics, Singapore had the fourth highest cinema attendance per capita worldwide (2009), with South Korea and Hong Kong ranking second and third respectively. Singapore was also in the global top ten in this survey. In 2009, Iceland ranked first, America second and Australia third. However, a number of cinemas no longer exist in Singapore. This is inevitable due to changing film exhibition technologies across the world and the changing environment of the city. The primary objective of this chapter is to outline the diverse history of film exhibition and spectatorship in Singapore, for this diversity is unique and unlike that of many other film cultures across the world.

Mapping Singapore's cinemas 145

I hope to document this cultural heritage by producing a map of cinemas, extant and non-extant, in Singapore.

Major research programmes in the discipline of film studies in recent years have interrogated the relationship of cinema and modernity, situating the cinema among other forms of cultural production in the construction of modern life. Film exhibition and film spectatorship are central to this question of modernity for cinema. Consequently, this chapter aims to contribute to that ongoing research through the case of Singapore film exhibition; and in so doing, place Singapore among other cosmopolitan centres (e.g. Shanghai, Tokyo, New York, Paris, Buenos Aires, London) critical to the invention of modern life (Important studies of cinema's relationship with modernity include Charney and Vanessa, 1995, Hansen, 1991, Zhang Zhen, 2005). While there has been research on such theoretical points of departure done on Singapore, more remains to be done. Through use of some of the methodologies described below, more perspectives on Singapore modernity, as well as its cultural connections with East and Southeast Asia can be gleaned.

The locations of film culture

The distinctive quality of different spaces for film exhibition in the history of Singapore film culture can be qualified, for instance, by the variety of films in various languages, as well as by the various exhibition formats and architecture. Today, most cinemas in Singapore show Hollywood films in English or Hong Kong films dubbed in Mandarin. Of course, this is far from an absolute rule, as there are numerous other film venues and places to see films besides popular Hollywood imports. One ready example would be the recently refurbished Rex Cinema, showing Tamil language films (Figure 10.1). The Picturehouse by Cathay Organisation screens international arthouse films. In the past, one would also find a greater number of theatres showing films in Malay, as well as in different Chinese dialects. Indeed, some theatres would show a film in Cantonese and others would show the same film in Mandarin. For example, in 1980, one could watch the Taiwan martial arts film, *The Legend of Sister Lin-tou* (1979), in Mandarin at the Yangtze Cinema on Eu Tong Seng Road, or see the Hokkien version at New City Cinema in Geylang Serai.

Throughout the twentieth century, Singapore employed a variety of physical structures for film exhibition such as the grand picture palace, for which Singapore has had a number of magnificent examples. The Cathay Cinema was housed in the Cathay Building, the seat of power for the Cathay Organisation. It also became a landmark, as the tallest building in the city until the 1960s. Even after ceasing operations of its Malay-language film studio in Singapore, and establishing the Motion Picture and General Investment Company in Hong Kong (becoming a major producer in the golden age of Hong Kong Mandarin films), Cathay retained images of the Dhoby Ghaut building for the logo in its Hong Kong films. The original building with the cinema on the ground floor alongside huge billboards of movie posters was demolished and rebuilt as a shopping mall and residences. In

Figure 10.1 Rex Cinemas, 2010.
Source: C. Leary

the new premises, the cinema was moved to the higher floors as multiplexes. The only trace of the original structure is in the replica concrete art deco façade faintly fronting the gleaming glass building. The Capitol Theatre, opposite City Hall, was one of the grandest picture palaces until its closure in 1998. The Capitol is now set to reopen after extensive renovation, and will be integrated within a larger commercial complex, in time to celebrate the 50th Anniversary of Singapore's independence. As part of the celebration, five old films – Malay action drama *Chuchu Datuk Merah* (1963), post-war Singapore's first Chinese film *Lion City* (1960), Hokkien/Amoy opera *Taming of the Princess* (1958), early P. Ramlee drama *Patah Hati* (1952), and Tamil romantic comedy *Ninaithale Inikkum* (1979) – were screened for free on 20–23 August 2015 at the newly reopened Capitol Theatre (Sinema 2015; See 2015).

Singapore film culture featured more informal spaces for film viewing as well. For example, mobile film units would travel to *kampongs* to project films in communities with less access to picture palaces. An ideal map of Singapore cinemas would trace the routes and destinations of these travelling film operators. In addition, neighbourhood community centres, during the colonial period, postcolonial era and the present-day, have served as locations for the screening of educational films. During the colonial period, army and air bases featured their own cinemas, operated by distribution networks such as Astra and Army Kinema Corporation. Other more contemporary alternative sites include venues for screening independent, avant-garde, and experimental films and videos, such as The Substation or The Arts House at the Old Parliament Building.

The identification of the first place of film exhibition in Singapore remains a matter of historical debate. Uhde and Ng Uhde claim the first public screening was held in a tent erected in an empty lot near Fort Canning by Hill Street in 1902; with no electricity available, limelight was used for projection (2010, 188). That this first site of film exhibition was held outdoors is telling, for the open-air cinema is another unique site in Singapore film history. Although not nearly as prevalent in other major world cities, open-air cinema has had both permanent and temporary structures in Singapore. Given the warm and humid climate of Singapore, open-air cinemas provided a comfortable exhibition space before the greater predominance in Singapore of that which the late Lee Kuan Yew, Singapore's Prime Minister of three decades, considered one of the great inventions of the twentieth century to improve quality of life and productivity, particularly in tropical climates: air-conditioning (George 2000). Another short-lived version of an open-air cinema in Singapore was the drive-in theatre, the only one in Singapore's history being the Jurong Drive-in Cinema operated by Cathay, which opened in 1971 and closed in 1985. However, there are occasional revivals of the drive-in cinema in car parks. For instance, occasional drive-in revivals have been held at Paya Lebar car park, Kallang car park and the NTUC club at Pasir Ris (Ahmad 2004).

The sensory experience and material culture of Singapore film culture has changed over the years as well. In open-air showings at major halls, tickets for wooden benches at the front of the hall would be bought at cheaper prices than those for more comfortable seats in the rear. Instead of popcorn, *kachang putih* (roasted nuts wrapped in used paper sheets into mini cone shaped containers) and *satay* (meat skewers) were popular snacks to eat during and after film shows. Adjacent to one of the earliest cinemas, the Marlborough Cinema, for example, was the popular "Satay Club" on Hoi How Road, off Beach Road, which was once a major film theatre district. This legacy still remains on Beach Road, as a few cinemas remain along this strip. While ticketing and seat selection today is computerised, the common previous practice involved the ticket seller using a wax pencil to mark the seat number on individual tickets before giving them to the patron at the ticket counter.

Many of the picture palaces and standalone neighbourhood cinemas are gone, but Singapore has re-established itself at the forefront of film exhibition with the arrival of the Golden Village Corporation in 1992, becoming the first country in Asia to adopt the multiplex configuration for cinema architecture that now dominates the space of filmgoing across the world. Since its beginning, Singapore film culture has been a hub of local and global cinema. In order to detail the unique status of Singapore as an international film capital, this project aims to trace the shifting patterns in cinema construction by mapping the locations of past and present cinemas, and analysing them against urban development in Singapore.

Cinema mapping

The first step in researching the history of film exhibition in Singapore is determining the locations of cinemas and other places of film exhibition within the colony/nation state – both operational in the present-day and no longer in operation. This research is done through a variety of methods: consulting building plans, archival photographs, street maps, recollections and oral history, as well as simply strolling through the streets of Singapore. The list below includes cinemas whose physical structures still remain even though they have ceased operation. A not uncommon practice in Singapore and across the world is for avid filmgoers to take advantage of the interior auditorium structure of a theatre by transforming it into a parish where they may engage in a local secular worship of film idols (Figure 10.2). Useful secondary sources found below in the list of references include published monographs on the history of Singaporean cinema and two unpublished theses from the National University of Singapore (NUS) and Nanyang Technological University (NTU) from the 1980s. A very valuable undergraduate thesis from the NUS geography department, written in 1984 by Anne Kang Joo Lian, situates a few cinemas among surrounding retail, entertainment and food establishments; another undergraduate thesis from the NTU Department of Mass Communications by Koh Ah Noi, gathers a wealth of data on the development of the film industry in Singapore.

The sheer number of cinemas that have existed in Singapore is testament to its status as a very cinephilic state. The condition of cinephilia refers not only to loving movies, but also an obsession about movies and their presentation. Cinephiles who consider themselves purists, seeking that which they deem to be an authentic cinematic experience, may prefer not to watch films on home video. To these purists, the film must be encountered in its proper habitat, in the cinema,

Figure 10.2 Faith Community Baptist Church, formerly Liberty Cinema, 2010.
Source: C. Leary

Mapping Singapore's cinemas   149

where the object is not only to read a text, but also to engage in a sensory experience. Compiled below is a list of approximately 180 cinemas that have operated in Singapore since 1904:

Alhambra Theatre, Beach Road
Alsagoff Open-air Cinema, Jalan Alsagoff
Astra Changi, Changi Base
Astra Tengah, Tengah Airbase
Atlantic Theatre, Great World
Balestier Community Open-air Cinema, Balestier Road, Singapore Improvement Trust (SIT) Flats
Bedok Cinema, New Upper Changi Road
Bright Cinema, Upper Paya Lebar Road
Broadway Cinema, Ang Mo Kio
Broadway Cinema, Joo Chiat Road
Buller Terrace, Buller Terrace, Open Space
Canberra Theatre, Naval Base
Canton Cinema, Great World
Capitol Theatre, Stamford Road
Cathay Cinema, Bukit Timah Road
Cathay Cinema, Dhoby Ghaut
Causeway Point, Woodlands
Central Mall, Clarke Quay
Central Theatre, Jalan Eunos
Changi Cinema, Changi Road
Changi Theatre, New Upper Changi Road
Chinatown Complex, Chinatown Point
Choa Chu Kang Cineplex, Choa Chu Kang
Ciros Theatre, Telok Blangah Road
Clementi Theatre, Clementi
Dalit Cinema, Bukit Merah
Da Dong Ya Amusement Park (Greater East Asia Amusement Park), Upper Bukit Timah Road
Diamond Theatre, North Bridge Road
Eastpoint, Simei Street
Empire Cinema (Chungking Theatre), Tanjong Pagar Road
Empire Theatre, Serangoon Road
Empress Cinema, Clementi
Eng Wah Open-air Cinema, Holland Village
Gala Cinema, Beach Road
Gala Cinema, Upper Bukit Timah Rd
Galaxy Cinema, Geylang
Garrick Theatre, Geylang Road
Globe Cinema, Great World
Golden City, Queenstown

150 *Charley Leary*

Golden Sultan Theatre/Plaza, Jalan Sultan
Government Servants' Club Open-air Cinema, Haig Road
Grand Theatre, New World
Great View Cinema, Punggol Road
Guo Hua, Upper Serangoon Road
Hollywood Theatre, Tanjong Katong Road
Hoover Cinema, Balestier Road
Imperial Theatre, Upper Thomson Road
Jade Theatre, Shaw Towers
Jalan Kayu Theatre, Jalan Kayu
Joo Seah Cinema, Lim Chu Kang Road
Jubilee Cinema, Ang Mo Kio
Jubilee Theatre, North Bridge Road
Jurong Drive-In, Yuan Ching Road
Kallang Cinema, 1 Stadium Walk
Kembangan Open-air Show, Jalan Kembangan
Kent Cinema, Dover Road
Keppel Cinema, West Coast Road
Kim Chuan Theatre, Kim Chuan Road
Kim Seah Open-air Cinema, Thomson Road
King's Cinema, Toa Payoh
King's Theatre, Kim Tian Road
Kok Wah Theatre, Yio Chu Kang Road
Kong Chian Open-air Cinema, Toa Payoh Lorong 4
Kong Eng Cinema, Changi Road
Kreta Ayer People's Theatre, Kreta Ayer
Kwang Liang Open-air Cinema, Chye Kay Village
Lay Wah Open-air Cinema, Kampong Tengah
Lee Kong Cinema, Bukit Timah
Leisure-Drome Theatre, Kallang Park
Liberty Cinema, Marine Parade Central
Lido Cinema, Orchard Road
Liwagu Theatre, Changi
Majestic Cinema, Eu Tong Seng
Mandarin Theatre, Kallang Bahru
Marlborough Theatre, Beach Road
Matsuo Cinema (Harima), North Bridge Road
Mercury Theatre, Upper Serangoon Road
Metropole Cinema, Tanjong Pagar Road
Nee Soon Theatre, Seletar Road
New City Cinema, Geylang Serai
New Crown Cinema and New Town Cinema, Ang Mo Kio Town Centre
New Happy Cinema, Gay World
New Starlight Cinema, Pasir Panjang Road
New Victory Theatre, Gay World

Ocean Theatre, Upper East Coast Road, Siglap
Odeon Cinema, North Bridge Road
Odeon Cinema, Batu Road
Odeon-Katong, East Coast Road
Oriental Theatre, North Bridge Road
Pacific Cinema, New World
Palace, East Coast Road
Paramount, Serangoon Garden Estates
Paris Cinema, Victoria St
Pasir Panjang Open-air Cinema, West Coast Road
Pavilion Theatre, Orchard Road
Pei Li Cinema (Seletar Cinema), Nee Soon Village
Picturehouse, Dhoby Ghaut
Premier Cinema, Orchard Towers
President, 350 Balestier Road
Prince Theatre, Shaw Towers
Princess Theatre and Raja Theatre, Bedok North
Pulau Brani Open-air Cinema, Pulau Brani
Pulau Ubin Open-air Cinema, Pulau Ubin Jetty
Queen's Cinema, Guillemard Road
Queensway Theatre, Commonwealth Avenue
Railway Recreation Club Open-air
Regal Cinema of the Army Kinema Corporation (AKC), Gillman Barracks
Regal Cinema, Bukit Merah
Republic Theatre, Marine Parade Central
Rex Cinema, Mackenzie Road
Riverside Point, Clarke Quay
Roxy Cinema, East Coast Road
Royal Theatre, North Bridge Road
Ruby Cinema, Balestier Road
Singapore Harbour Board (SHB) Boys' Club Open-air Cinema, Keppel Road
Savoy Theatre, Boon Lay
Sea View Hotel Open-air Cinema, Tanjong Katong
Seng Wah Cinema, Near Tampines Road, 9th mile
Serangoon Cinema, Serangoon
Serangoon Garden Sports Club, Serangoon Garden
Shaw Plaza, Balestier Road
Siglap Open-air Cinema, East Coast Road
Silver City Theatre, Gay World
Sin Wah Theatre, Bukit Panjang Road
Singapore Open-air Cinema, Changi Road
Singapura Theatre, Geylang Serai
Sky Cinema, Great World
Somapah Open-Air Cinema, Somapah Village
South Country Open-air Cinema, Braddell Road

152 *Charley Leary*

Star Open-air Cinema, Upper East Coast Road
State Theatre, New World
Straits, Woodlands
Sultan Cinema, Sembawang Road
Sun Cinema, New World
Sun Plaza, Sembawang Drive
Sun Seng Cinema, Smith Street
Taj Cinema, Changi Road
Talib Open-air Cinema and Stage Show, Pulau Damar
Taman Jurong Open-air Cinema, Taman Jurong
Tampines Open-air Cinema, Tampines Road
Theatre Royal, North Bridge Road
Tiong Wah Theatre, Bukit Timah Road
Tivoli Cinema/Theatre, North Bridge Road
Town Hall (later Victoria Theatre), Empress Place
Venus Theatre, Queenstown
Vision (Hougang), Upper Serangoon Road
White Sands, Pasir Ris
Woodlands, Woodlands Centre Road
Yangtze Cinema, Eu Tong Seng
Yi Lung, Dover Road
Yio Chu Kang Road Community Centre, Yio Chu Kang Road
Zenith Theatre, Tampines

Drawing upon the list above, I have composed a rudimentary map using Google Maps and a form of Geographic Information System (GIS) software (Figure 10.3). GIS technology is used for urban planning, and in more academic endeavours, often used by geographers, archaeologists and anthropologists tracing intangible/ tangible cultural heritage. This map shows that the downtown and Central Business District areas have not changed significantly in the number of cinemas, even though there are now fewer cinemas in the Kreta Ayer/Chinatown area. Also noteworthy is the fact that the map shows a reduced number of buildings functioning singularly as cinemas in contemporary Singapore and an increased number of multiplexes within mega-malls. This may indicate further trends for the future, as audiences for smaller neighbourhood cinemas are accommodated by larger multiplexes located around major transportation hubs (all the multiplexes are, for example, around an MRT subway station), and cinema architecture becomes subordinate to the larger layouts of shopping centres.

One important measurement that this map does not show is change over time periods, which would give a more accurate description of the progressive changes in film exhibition in Singapore. The map in this chapter simply shows that which exists today and that which once was. It is also based on the current map of Singapore, which has also changed over time. Layers of historical maps of Singapore could be added to this map to make it more sophisticated. As it stands, some of the locations indicated are estimations of the current structures'

Mapping Singapore's cinemas 153

Figure 10.3 Map of Singapore's cinemas. Dark grey indicates extant cinemas, light grey indicates non-extant sites.
Source: Google Maps

whereabouts on the current map, and some are general estimations based on neighbourhoods.

Further directions

This mapping project raises a number of other questions that are worth pursuing. One might look for connections among the predominant language of the films (e.g. Malay, Chinese dialects, Tamil and English) shown at particular cinemas in relation to inhabited neighbourhoods, and consider these cinemas' relationships with the surrounding ethnic communities of those neighbourhoods as well as the changing demographics of such neighbourhoods; for example, *kampongs* giving way to public housing apartment blocks.

How did film exhibition come to Singapore and subsequently develop? What relationship does such development have with the history of modern Singapore? How has government policy shaped Singapore's film culture, and what place does film heritage share with urban development? Where are cinemas in proximity to public housing estates and other forms of entertainment (such as gaming centres and karaoke establishments)? In conjunction with above considerations, one could calculate the number of Singaporeans that are likely to patronise each cinema, taking into account, for example, population increase. What would be the maximum distance a Singaporean needs to travel in order to reach a cinema? We

154 *Charley Leary*

might think about the change of cinema architecture over time in connection with length and types of films, and whether they were part of ancillary attractions (for example, cinemas in entertainment complexes such as Great World Amusement Park operated by Shaw Brothers) (Wong and Tan 2004)? What has become of these buildings and structures; can and should they be preserved? What is the reuse value of some of these remaining structures?

All this data offers a measurement of the film heritage of Singapore, and may provide urban planners and heritage groups with an idea of the places to preserve in Singapore. One such example – not a cinema itself – but a film-related site that I think invites consideration for preservation and restoration, is the former Malay Film Productions and Shaw Brothers Studio on Jalan Ampas, the source of much of Singapore's film history and some of the most important films made in Singapore. The site also highlights Singapore films' connections with Southeast Asia and East Asia (in particular, Hong Kong and Mainland China). As the buildings still remain and there is a Singapore Heritage Board marker indicating the historical significance of the place, it seems an ideal place for repurposed use as a cinema or film museum. While other cosmopolitan areas in Asia, such as Hong Kong, Shanghai and Tokyo, garner more recognition as capitals of film culture, this project will underscore the richness of Singapore's film history and history of filmgoing, and showcase Singapore as another cultural capital of Asia.

References

Ahmad, Nureza. "Infopedia: Jurong Drive-in Cinema." Singapore: National Library Board, 2004. http://eresources.nlb.gov.sg/infopedia/articles/SIP_478_2005-01-22.html (accessed 6 October 2011).

Charney, Leo, and Vanessa R. Schwartz, eds. *Cinema and the Invention of Modern Life*. Berkeley: University of California Press, 1995.

George, Cherian. *Singapore: The Air-Conditioned Nation: Essays on the Politics of Comfort and Control, 1990–2000*. Singapore: Landmark Books, 2000.

Hansen, Miriam. *Babel and Babylon: Spectatorship in American Silent Film*. Cambridge: Harvard University Press, 1991.

Kang, Anne Joo Lian. "Cinemas in Singapore." B.Soc.Sci. thesis, National University of Singapore, 1984.

Koh, Ah Noi. "Development of the Movie Industry in Singapore." B.Sc. thesis, Nanyang Technological University, 1980.

Lai, Chee Kien. "Patron's Portions." Unpublished conference paper presented at "Singapore Cinemas: The Locations of Film Exhibition." Singapore: Asia Research Institute, 22 May 2010.

Roy, Anjali Gera. "Performing *Des* [Home] in a Jaded Space." Unpublished conference paper presented at "Singapore Cinemas: The Locations of Film Exhibition." Singapore: Asia Research Institute, 22 May 2010.

See, Joyce. "The Capitol Theatre is Doing Free Screenings of Old Singaporean Films: Catch a Glimpse of Singapore in the '50s and '60s with These Five Films." *SG Magazine: The Insider's Guide to Singapore*, 27 May 2015. http://sg.asia-city.com/events/news/free-screening-old-local-films-capitol-theatre#sthash.sxPHZ1Rx.dpuf (accessed 27 May 2015).

"The Capitol Theatre is doing screenings of old Singaporean films." *Sinema: Independent Film News Portal*, 29 May 2015. www.sinema.sg/2015/05/29/the-capitol-theatre-is-doing-free-screenings-of-old-singaporean-films/ (accessed 25 June 2015).

Uhde, Jan, and Yvonne Ng Uhde. 2010. *Latent Images: Film in Singapore.* Reprint, Revised Edition. Singapore: Ridge Books, 2010.

UNESCO Institute of Statistics. "Cinema: Attendance Frequency Per Capita." http://stats.uis.unesco.org (accessed 6 October 2011).

Wong, Yunn Chii, and Kar Lin Tan. "Emergence of a Cosmopolitan Space for Culture and Consumption: The New World Amusement Park-Singapore (1923–70) in the Inter-War Years." *Inter-Asia Cultural Studies* 5, no. 2 (2004): 279–304.

Zhang Zhen. *An Amorous History of the Silver Screen: Shanghai Cinema 1896–1937.* Chicago: University of Chicago Press, 2005.

11 Going to the movies in *Pardes*

Anjali Gera Roy

Introduction

Carl Plantinga argues that psychological film studies have so circumscribed the terms "pleasures", "desires" and "fantasy" that it has become imperative to expand the understanding of the pleasures of viewing films and the functions of fantasy and desire within narrative. Plantinga also interrogates the notion of pleasure as defined in screen studies and maintains that "the spectator's pleasure in viewing mainstream films is more complex and contradictory than screen theory allowed" (Plantinga 2009, 19). Using a "cognitive–perceptual approach" to the movie-going experience (Plantinga 2009, 39), he identifies five sources of audience pleasure in mainstream films, namely: (i) cognitive play, (ii) visceral experience, (iii) sympathy and parasocial engagement, (iv) satisfying emotional trajectories rooted in narrative scenarios, and (v) various reflexive and social activities associated with film viewing such as criticism and appreciation (Plantinga 1995). He also regards the intratextual experience of viewing films to be as important as the intertextual and extratextual. In an earlier essay, Plantinga and Tan engaged in an exchange about the global nature of film affect and concluded that "the study of affect is best initially approached at the local level, as the attempt to isolate and describe individual affects or affect trajectories, and the structures that elicit them" (Plantinga and Tan 2007, 16). They proposed that "at the global level, we can best approach a film as an intentional orchestration of multiple affects, rather than as a text that generates a single, overarching affective or emotional state" (Plantinga and Tan 2007, 16). Overarching theories of film affect fail to elucidate the multiple affects of Hindi films for South Asian viewers, particularly diasporic viewers, for whom the pleasures of the cinematic text are invariably imbricated in the extratextual pleasures of the sensuous geographies they evoke. Viewing cinema as an event, this chapter traces the history of film exhibition in Singapore to unpack the meanings of going to the movies for Singapore's diverse ethnicities. It begins by providing a brief overview of the history of cinematic exhibition in Singapore and the social centrality Indian films have traditionally performed among Singapore's diverse ethnic groups, before focussing on a cineplex exclusively dedicated to the screening of Hindi films. The description of this experience is based on personal observation, open-ended interviews with cinemagoers

Going to the movies in Pardes 157

in July 2009, 2010 and October 2011 as well as on information obtained from internet chats and blogs.

Complicating the filmgoing experience and film affects

While the phenomenology of film experience and affects of films have attracted considerable attention in cinema studies, most film scholars have largely focussed on text-based theories of affect. In contrast to early studies on Indian cinema (Mishra 2002; Prasad 1998; Chakravarty 1993) that largely devoted themselves to the textual analysis of canonical texts with the objective of elucidating their social, cultural and political meanings, new research has shifted the focus of South Asian film studies to film distribution, exhibition, spectatorship, audience and affect. Instead of inquiring into the meaning of particular films and the pleasures of viewing films, these studies have embedded them in a wide range of practices that constitute the cinematic experience. Instead of viewing films as texts or narratives, they perceive them as a performance, event or assemblage (Devadas and Velayutham 2012; Hughes 2010; Rai 2009; Dudrah 2006). Beginning with Marie Gillespie's ethnographic work on television and Steve Derné's on North Indian men watching films, Shakuntala Banaji, Jigna Desai, Rajinder Dudrah, Raminder Kaur and others have unravelled home and diasporic practices in which Bollywood films acquire a social centrality (Banaji 2006; Desai 2006; Dudrah 2006; Kaur and Sinha 2005; Derné 2000; Srinivas 2000a and 2000b; Gillespie 1995). Drawing on Laura U. Marks's notion of haptic visuality and rasa theory (Marks 2000), Dudrah examined the sensuous geographies in which the narrative diegesis produces meaning. While Jigna Desai (2006) uncovered a performative economy of music and dance to second-generation Indian Americans, Brian Larkin brought amazing evidence from Kano in Nigeria to examine the influence of Bollywood song on Bandiri music (Larkin 2003). Among the studies that have appeared more recently, those of Amit Rai (2009), Bhrigupati Singh (2003), and Vijay Devadas and Selvaraj Velayutham (2012), deserve particular mention as they engage with the practice of cinema-going in India and the diaspora by locating them in a complex media assemblage through which the cinematic text acquires social centrality.

Devadas and Velayutham shift the view of film and cinema "as something to be analysed for meanings and representations to one that approaches it as cartography or as an event; something experienced as a dynamic exchange, as activities, in motion" (Devadas and Velayutham 2012). Arguing that the notion of *assemblage* offers, specifically in terms of exploring Tamil cinema, a conceptual tool for thinking about cinema's complex entanglement with different modes of sociality; its relationship to the production and consumption of other commodity forms the ways in which it "blocks, or makes possible other worlds" (Fuller 2005) they call on us to "attend to the ways in which people position or embody themselves (or are marked) as bearers of identity within particular social and institutional networks" (Singh 2003), and propose the notion of "cinema in motion" (Devadas and Velayutham 2012). Turning to the sensory experience of the exhibition space,

158   *Anjali Gera Roy*

Devadas and Velayutham discuss three narratives briefly and weave them into each other to exemplify the intricate and complex ways Tamil cinema connects with human bodies, lives, experiences and different social worlds. Devadas and Velayutham's narratives are valuable for encapsulating the history of the exhibition of Indian films in Malaya/Singapore from the tent cinemas in plantations to the theatres by comparing and contrasting the experiences of three generations of spectators. Although it focusses on the history of Singapore cinemas in general, Erik Holmberg's research on "Cinema in Singapore from 1896 to 1910" can throw light on the interactions between members of different ethnic communities in Singapore (Holmberg 2010). Similarly, Timothy Barnard and Ho Hui Lin's work on "'World' Cinemas in Singapore before World War II" that looks at the films shown at these cinemas (Barnard and Ho 2010), can tell us how films fitted within the larger entertainment venue and how they reflected subtle differences in the audience who frequented them.

Going to the movies in a tent cinema, going to the movies in a theatre

Singapore's retention of an Indian space might be equally viewed as a reflection of its celebrated multiculturalism or of the long history of film exhibition beginning in the silent era when Indian renters carried their tent cinemas to plantations in British Malaya and followed the screening of European films with Indian ones with the coming of sound (Guy 2010). Although documentation of these screenings is limited to anecdotal allusions and oral narratives, Ravi Vasudevan (2010), Priya Jaikumar (2006) and others have demonstrated that the screening of Indian films in the colonies was encouraged by the introduction of the Cinematograph Films Quota Act of 1928 through the stipulation that a certain percentage of films produced in the British Empire would be shown. The movement of films to this region confirms Hughes's observation on "the mobility of early cinema in India" and its "spatial movement throughout South Asia" and beyond (Hughes 2010). This spatial movement of early cinema from India to other British colonies abroad, where the tent theatres Samikannu Vincent had introduced in Chennai travelled to the plantations in Malaya, Fiji and Mauritius (Guy 2010), is borne out in Devadas and Velayutham's reproduction of the testimony of Mala – part of the second-generation Indian diaspora in then Malaya:

> …When we were in the estates, they [the estate owners and bureaucrats] used to show a film once a month, sometimes once every two months. They would bring along a white screen-cloth and projector and we [the estate community] would set up our mats on the ground, and get our munchies ready for the show. This was a big night for the estate; and everyone came with his or her families, mats, gunnysacks, blankets and food. When the sun set, the show would begin, and usually, I would fall asleep soon after the samples were shown, and after I had my share of the kachangs [peanuts] and before the actual film begun because I was usually tired from having to work in the

Going to the movies in Pardes   159

oil palm plantation the whole day. But the film was not important; it was the experience of the day that mattered.

(Devadas and Velayutham 2012)

Tent cinema tickets existed in three classes, according to several accounts of Indian film history (New Tamil Cinemas 2011; Tamil Cinema Online; Siva 2008), namely the floor, bench and chair. Despite the hierarchy of the tent theatre continuing in perpetuating caste relations until recently, the floor ticket purchaser "enjoyed certain advantages that other patrons did not. He could sit as he pleased, or he could turn over and take a short nap when the narrative was particularly dull and roll back again when the action was again to his liking — luxuries in which the upper class could never indulge". As Mala recalls, she could not only sit as she pleased but also go to sleep even before the movie began; thus bearing out Gillespie's (1995) notion that watching Hindi films at home was a "family centric leisure activity" where "notions of togetherness take precedence" over watching the film. But Mala's testimony of watching films in tent cinema in the 1960s also throws new light on the overlap between old and new modes of film exhibition in Singapore, as picture palaces had been established elsewhere in both Malaysia and Singapore way back in the 1930s. While Devadas and Velayutham effectively establish the social centrality of cinema for the diaspora, their essay does not delve into the relationships between films and other forms of entertainment, and the subtle differences between exhibition venues and the class, ethnicity and gender of the audiences. Nor does it address the segregationist policies governing exhibition in Malaysia and Singapore, which offer an instance of disjuncture in the understanding of cinema as a great equalizer in India.

Singapore and Malaysia had three different kinds of theatres during this period, namely first run, second run and third run. The post-war years had a few first run (Royal on North Bridge Road) and second run theatres (Ciros and Canberra) exclusively dedicated to the screening of Indian films, which appear to have included both Tamil and Hindi hits. It was at the Taj, one of these theatres dedicated specially to the screening of Indian movies, that Mala watched her first film in a theatre in 1967:

> I never went to a theatre until I came to Singapore in 1967. Once a month, my husband's siblings and I would go to the Taj Theatre in Geylang. The Taj used to show Tamil, Hindi and English shows. We will only go on days that Krishnan, my brother, was working. He was the ticket seller and would smuggle us in for free. I watched lots of films there, MGR and Sivaji films.
>
> (Devadas and Velayutham 2012)

However, Mala's narrative is not exclusively Tamil because in Mala's cinematic imaginary, unlike that of Devadas, the experience of viewing a Tamil film is inextricably intertwined with that of Hindi movies. In fact, the first Hindi film she viewed in a theatre in Singapore is *Sangam* (1964) in the Garrick Theatre in Geylang.

160 *Anjali Gera Roy*

The first Hindi film I saw was *Sangam* [Confluence], at the Garrick Theatre, also in Geylang. Sangam had Raj Kapoor and Vyjayantimala and I loved the song Dost Dost Na Raha [My Friend Was No More My Friend]. [Mala breaks into the song]. I didn't understand Hindi, and the subtitles were in English or Malay and I didn't know either but it didn't matter. I followed the film through the actions: in fact I watched *Sangam* thrice. Like the estate days, it didn't matter what film was on, it was the fun of going to the theatre, getting away from housework which I had to do!

(Devadas and Velayutham 2012)

Mala's statement about the experience of the day mattering more than the film is reproduced in the experience of other South Asians on other continents. Separated from Mala by time as well as space, June Doe recalls going to repeat viewings of the same film cited by Mala, *Sangam*, at a drive-in theatre in Dar-e-salamin Tanzaniaon Sundays as a "fun" thing like an Indian National Day where everyone went to the movies with curry and raincoats (Doe, Interview with author, 12 April 2009). However, more surprising is the evidence of the popularity of the same Hindi film among Chinese audience such as, Edward, a sixty-seven-year-old Chinese taxi driver, who confessed to have acquired a love for Hindi films while working for British defence:

Where did I watch it? I always watched movies – when I was a young man – I went to many theatres. I don't remember. It will take time to recollect. I worked for the British defence. I had a few Indian friends too.

(Interview with author 19 July 2010)

Attributing his love for Hindi films to their dance and music, he broke into the same song from the film as Mala,

I liked Hindi films because of the dances – because in Hindi films, there were lot of dances – but also music, I liked the tempo of music. It was like yodelling. Dost dost na raha/pyar pyar na raha/wo mere dost tum hi ho … [breaks into song]. Hum tum se mohabbat karega … [chuckles] … The latest ones, I never watch. I like the old ones. Because I am old man you see. I am sixty-seven … What is the secret of my youth? Sing a song from *Sangam*.

(Interview with author 19 July 2010)

Unlike Mala, however, he could also follow details of dialogues as they were subtitled in English,

I could follow the conversation! They were subtitled in English. It [*Sangam*] is about a love triangle of two boys and a girl. The boys are very good friends. They are best friends. They are ready to sacrifice for one another.

(Interview with author 19 July 2010)

By 1970, Jubilee had become the popular haunt of Chinese mothers wishing to watch Indian films. A Malay woman in her fifties, Sahara, recalled her mother taking her to watch movies in a number of theatres in Geylang, including Singapura, Garrick and others during the 1970s (Interview with author, 8 October 2011). She loved those films because they had strong storylines, unlike the present lot that she describes as exhibitionist displays of beautiful bodies and costumes (ibid.). She had become such a great fan of Shashi Kapoor and Amitabh Bachchan during the 1970s that she still follows all the gossip about them.

Going to the movies in a cineplex

At present, Singapore is unique in that several cineplexes, including Jade in Shaw Towers, Rex on McKenzie Road and others in Yishun, are exclusively dedicated to the screening of Indian films. This is unlike other parts of Southeast Asia where cinematic exhibition of Indian films abruptly ended in the 1970s. Unlike the theatres established in the post-war era, Jade Cineplex in Shaw Towers – which included the largest theatre, Prince – does not seem to have been an Indian theatre when it opened in 1977, as filmgoers visiting the Shaw Towers theatres until the 1980s recall watching Hollywood hits like *Jaws*. Somewhere during its several transformations, Jade emerged as an exclusive Hindi film space, while Tamil films shifted to other theatres such as Rex. As Devadas (2011) points out in his essay on the social centrality of Rex to South Asian migrant workers, theatrical space in Singapore is segregated by class, gender and language. However, the bifurcation of the Tamil and Hindi cinematic spaces re-inscribes Jade as a Bollywood, rather than Hindi film space, reflecting the transition from the old to new migration patterns from India to Singapore. On the one hand, Singapore is unique in Southeast Asia in its dedication of an exclusive theatre for the screening of Hindi films because it emphasises the city-state's fabled multiculturalism. On the other, the allocation of an antiquated hall, rather than a state-of-the-art multiplex for the exclusive screening of Hindi films, accentuates the marginalisation of Indian popular culture in the global city. Rather than indentured fantasies of the *des* in Devadas and Velayutham's narratives, Jade reverberates with the post-1960s nostalgia observed by Dudrah in Queen's in New York (Dudrah 2006). Yet it produces a new Bollywood effect in which old Hindi film audience share space with new Bollywood fans frequenting Loews Theatre (Dudrah 2006). The Jade audience, on an average weekend, is divided by gender, age, class and ethnicity. Most importantly, it is the time of migration that separates old Hindi film lovers from new Bollywood fans. The audiences range from all male groups of students or young urban professionals, dating and married couples, middle-aged and senior couples as well as families of South Asian origin. Malays, both young and old, single, with partners or accompanied by families along with the lone elderly Chinese lady or gentleman on a night out introduce a disjuncture in the imagining of the *des*. The young woman at the ticket counter revealed that a number of senior Chinese come to watch all the films, particularly arthouse films, which also bring in European audience (Maria, interview with author, 8 October 2011).

162　*Anjali Gera Roy*

The ambience of the hall – seating, air-conditioning, technical failures, smells and so on – falls short of multiplex standards that the Jade audience have begun to take for granted, even in developing cities. A blogger, a marketing professional named Ekta, was deeply shocked by the disjuncture between the space of the global city and the Indian theatre:

> While I was still in this phase of being impressed of the city, we decided to go and watch a Bollywood film. So this was my first Bollywood cinema going experience in Singapore. It wasn't even like the movie going experience or cinema halls today in Mumbai. It was what cinema halls were 10 years back in Mumbai – the Chandan, Gaiety, Galaxy era. [sic]

Others complained about its lack of amenities – amenities that are included in the new multiplex package. Another blogger, one Archana said in an entry, titled, "Air Conditioner in Jade":

> Last Night I went to Jade to watch a movie with all the excitement of catching up with a new bollywood movie. I must say I had the worst experience sitting in the last row as the air conditioner was completely switched off. I literally felt difficult to breathe in the theater. As much I was enjoying the movie it became very difficult for me to sustain there. I was sweating as there was no air and it was my worst experience ever. I don't think I would ever go back to watch a movie in Jade again. I rather by [sic] a DVD for 15 dollars, Cozy up at home in front of my LCD with a couple of friends instead of wasting 10 bucks on the ticket, 10 bucks on my popcorn and 10 bucks on my cab after a night show. I hope they do something about this being the only bollywood theater in Singapore. [sic]
>
> (Posted on Sunday 8 November 2009 15:23:17)

Jade's lack of expected amenities was also highlighted by several interviewees in the Tabla! Section of an *AsiaOne News* article dated 6 March 2009:

> "I remember during one movie, when one of the reels finished, we had to wait about 15 to 20 minutes in the dark because the reel operator was not there," Prem Bhagat said.
>
> "The chairs are old, the cushions smell. Some of the seats are without handles. And recently the air-conditioning was not working," pointed out Zaliha Rashid.
>
> "The carpets are filthy and in some parts ripped. And if you sit at the back of the theatre, you can sometime smell the toilets, especially after intermission," said Karishmaa Pai.

The presence of a developing world exhibition space in a developed world city that continues to function as the nerve centre of Hindi film viewing despite the

Going to the movies in Pardes   163

litany of complaints from regulars necessitates an inquiry into the reasons why old Singaporean Indians; new professional Indian migrants; Nepali, Burmese, Bangladeshi and Filipino guestworkers; South Asian and non-South Asian tourists and old Hindi film audience like Malays, Chinese and others continue to frequent the cineplex. As Abhay, one of the respondents to Archana's post, said on Friday, 22 January 2010, 17:37:06: "Jade is like Indian politics" as it cannot be changed and cannot be resisted.

Laura U. Marks's notion of haptic visuality, which she borrows from Alois Riegl, presents a particularly useful tool for analysing "the multisensory quality of perception, the involvement of all the senses even in the audio visual act of cinematic viewing" (Marks 2000). Marks's suggestion that Gilles Deleuze's theory of time-image cinema permits a multi-sensory quality of cinema, which has a basis in Bergson's theory of memory being embodied in the senses, helps to elucidate the significations of intercultural films to show that vision can be tactile. In view of the alternative viewing options that Hindi film viewers have such as going to the other theatres in Yishun, watching films on television or buying DVDs of films, the drivers for "Jade-hopping" on weekends appear to lie in the haptic codes that recall exhibition practices in the *des* where the visual pleasures of the cinema intersect with other lines of complementarity such as those of touch, smell, sound and even taste, to produce a sensuous geography of home as well as that of early exhibition venues of Indian films in Singapore where they performed very different forms of social centrality. A visit to Jade on a weekend, or weekday, confirms the non-visual pleasures of going to the movies in India, which are reproduced in the Indian diasporas through the embedding of textual meanings in a set of socially embedded practices. Reading haptic visuality of the cinematic texts within the material practices that produce home can help to explain the reasons why South Asians continue to return to Jade, despite complaining about "stinking" toilets, uncomfortable seats and faulty air-conditioning.

The idea of a "cinematic 'machine' that produces concepts, percepts, affects, forms of life and modes of being-in-world" (Singh 2003) makes it imperative that cinema be located as part of a larger assemblage of things, objects, subjects, discourses. A blogger called Parikrama confessed to going to the movies as a perfect antidote to driving away Monday blues (Parikrama 5 July 2011):

> Watched Delhi Belly. I saw it on a typical Monday evening (7:35pm show). There is nothing more uplifting than chucking work at 6pm DOT on a Monday & heading out for a movie. It's perfect antidote to drive away those dreary Monday blues. What's more, it's easy on the wallet as well. The weekday shows are priced couple of dollars cheaper than the weekend shows & also the crowd is much much less. [sic]

For the Jade audience, the act of watching films is part of a larger assemblage of activities including eating an Indian meal, going to a Bollywood dance club to sing and dance to the songs in the film, or stopping to pick up some Bollywood fashions in the "Rang Fab" boutique strategically located right outside Jade. For

164 *Anjali Gera Roy*

example, Parikrama's visit to Jade to watch *Delhi Belly* was preceded by a dinner at Mumbai Café, whose "kitschy ambience", he quipped, set him and his wife in the perfect mood for Bollywood kitsch (Parikrama 5 July 2011):

> It's evening now, I meet my wife & we head for a relaxing early dinner at Mumbai Cafe Xpress. This Indian restaurant is located smack in middle of the Central Business District area. On a weekday, at 6:30pm it is practically empty. No! make that, it is completely empty. Throughbred desi's never eat dinner until it's well past 9pm. As a proof to this peculiar trait, there is not a single soul in sight. We are their first and only customers for the evening. We get to pick and choose our seats. But good well-mannered middle-class folks that we are, we decide to sit at a cramped table for 2 instead of hogging the 4/6 seater tables. Dinner menu is: Bhel Puri, Schezwan Fried Rice & Iced Lemon tea. We eat to strains of "Dil boley Shickdoom ShickDoom" played on the 3/4 wall mounted TVs. The theme of decor is "Bollywood". The walls are adorned with framed posters of blockbuster movies like "Kaalia", "Swades", "Murder" et al, with a huge blowup of Aishwarya Rai gazing menacingly down at the diners. The walls are painted garish purple. The chairs are garish purple and the menu card (yes, you guessed it right) is garish purple. The kitschy ambiance is perfect to get us in the mood for Bollywood kitsch, that's soon to follow.
>
> Dinner done with, we head to the theater. Much to our surprise, we discover that it's packed to the rafters. Seems like the Monday blues phenomenon has well & truly developed into a full blown pandemic! [sic]

In the following section, I share my own experiences of watching Hindi films in two theatres in Singapore to differentiate the differences in going to the movies in a cineplex like Jade and a multiplex on Orchard Road.

Watching Hindi films in two cineplexes

Sunny, the owner of Sunny Videos in Bangkok, had warned me: "the expectations of audience in India are very different from those here. People here don't view films with the critical eye that they do in India" (Sunny, personal communication, 12 July 2009). Priding myself on being a discriminating viewer who would agree to spare the mandatory two and a half hours for viewing a Hindi film only if the film had received favourable reviews in reputed newspapers and magazines, I found myself agreeing strongly with Sunny when going to watch two films in Singapore that were written off as resounding flops in India. The first film I chose to watch in Singapore was not a typical *masala* film in Jade, but a Warner Brothers India and China production in the Orchard Cineplex in the centre of the city. Elated by the release of a Bollywood film in a multiplex in the main shopping centre that typically screens Hollywood rather than Hindi films, I was disappointed to see that it was only half filled in the first week of its release. But I enjoyed the capers of an uncouth hawker assistant in old Delhi who finds himself in China,

Going to the movies in Pardes   165

presented in a slick Hollywood format, probably for the unfamiliar familiarity of the Bollywood plot and the Bollywood heartthrob Akshay Kumar's flair for comedy. As a result, I viewed the China–India angle less critically than I would have done had I watched it in India. The Orchard Cineplex boasted of a sophisticated cosmopolitan audience that included Indians, Chinese and Westerners. But the polite silence of the Chinese and Westerners and the suppressed laughter of the Indians made watching *Chandni Chowk to China* (2009) in this multiplex a less than Bollywood experience.

Going to the Jade to watch the Aamir Khan hit *Ghajini* (2008) that had beaten all records in India and abroad a few weeks later with an Indian couple underlined the difference in the spaces of Bollywood exhibition and their production of affects in the Bollywood audience in conjunction with the modes of sociality structuring the exhibition space. Unlike multiplex theatres that present a "nonspace" stretching from New York to Singapore and New Delhi, Jade, although a cineplex, reproduces a South Asian place through the repetition of rituals of belonging that are reminiscent of spectatorial spaces and practices of the India of the 1970s and 1980s rather than of the new millennium "malltiplex" (Rai 2009) in which global codes of conduct are conspicuously visible.

Outside Jade is a postmodern, super-organised space that produces a sense of the uncanny as it did in the blogger Ekta (12 June 2011):

> When I moved to Singapore from Mumbai, the city upgraded every part of my lifestyle. There was lesser travel time, no traffic, cleaner roads, no pollution, flashier malls; better shopping, good food, even the domestic helpers were more efficient. So all in all I was impressed and delighted with this elevation of my way of living.

The Orchard Cineplex, located on Orchard Road, is part of the heterotopia of the planned city of Singapore and is continuous with this super-organised space. Unlike the Orchard Cineplex where the act of viewing is structured by an impersonal speed and efficiency from pressing the elevator button to purchasing the ticket and being ushered in a state-of-the-art hall with globalised rituals of communication, Jade presents an unregulated space that disrupts the structured pattern of the city as well of the shopping mall. For Ekta, this was a source of disappointment (12 June 2011):

> Like the rest of the things in the city I expected the theater would be flashy, hi-tech, with lot of food stalls, smelling good etc. However the minute I entered Jade Cinemas, i entered to another world which didn't quite fit with rest of the city. [sic]

But for most viewers, the familiar world of smells, tastes and sounds produces a sense of familiarity through which one may belong. The aural, olfactory and tactile space of Jade, in addition to the visual, produces an illusion of home that enables the body to re-enact the memory of home through a different way of being in place.

166   *Anjali Gera Roy*

This way of being in place spills over from the pedestrian crossing leading into Shaw Towers to the corridors, the food courts and the escalators that usher one into the theatres. Moviegoers, looking for Jade, are literally guided into the theatre through sounds of the homeland right from the zebra crossing on Beach Road as groups of young urban professionals, chatting in either in Hindi or Tamil, cross the street to step into Shaw Towers through the side entrance. The moment they step into Shaw Towers, they are transported to the bustling lanes of old Delhi and Kolkata via the Chaat corner, "On a Roll: From Chandni Chowk to Chowringhee", offering a familiar world of gastronomic delights. In contrast to the usually silent Singapore escalators, the escalator leading to the ticket window and the screens violates Singaporean etiquette through loud conversations and laughter, shouted greetings and instructions as moviegoers make their way up and stare into the display window of a boutique called Rang Fab showcasing the latest Bollywood fashions. The narrow approach to the ticket counter compels them into such proximity that it replicates homeland behaviour of young men passing loud remarks, young women giggling, families speaking at the top of their voices and children running amok.

Unlike Ekta, to whom Jade appeared as an anachronistic space that might diminish the pleasures of Hindi movie experience for the Y generation, the present generation appears to enjoy it being a throwback to movie-going behaviour in the 1990s (Ekta 12 June 2011):

> So while Bollywood and Mumbai itself has moved ahead in life but Jade Cinemas is still stuck in a period left far behind. May be it's meant to be reminiscent of Hindi movie watching experience back then. But then the next generation doesn't even know that. They just compare the experience of watching Kung fu Panda in Golden Villages of the city with watching a Hindi movie at this place and of course soon they may despise the Hindi movie experience. Well the hope is extravaganza of the Bollywood movie will still and always make up for the out datedness of the well! [sic]

As youths, young and middle-aged couples or families walk up the narrow passage to the ticket counter conversing loudly in ethnic Indian languages, shouting greetings to friends or hushing a crying baby, the modern multiplex acquires a carnivalesque air that carries over to the ticket queue where moviegoers continue to chat with each other as well as with the Malay and Chinese staff at the counter who volunteer information on the films in addition to selling tickets (Parikrama 5 July 2011):

> The lady at the booking counter politely asked – "Any children??". I blushed a shade of pink & replied "Not yet!" My coyness didn't impress her any bit. She looked annoyed and raised her voice to tell me in no uncertain terms – "(Bose D.K.!!) the movie is rated R18. Kids not allowed". I realized my folly and quickly reassured her that the tickets are meant for 2 responsible and rapidly aging adults.

The text continues to play a significant role in the decision to go to the movies, which explained the difference between the audience for youth-oriented films like

Going to the movies in Pardes   167

Kabir Khan's *New York* (2009) and Sabbir Khan's *Kambakkht Ishq* (2009), and an arthouse production like Nandita Das's *Firaaq* (2008). The production of *des* by the two films *New York* and *Kambakkht Ishq* was ironic since both, set in the US, centred on the lives of diasporic Indians in social contexts, an American university and Hollywood, far removed from India. However, the large turnout for the films foregrounded the difference in the extra-diegetic gratifications of watching films at home and abroad. One of the two, *Kambakkht Ishq*, excited interest in India for the new size zero look of the female lead and the stunts performed by the male than for the Indianness it signified to diasporic South Asians.

Moving from the ticket queue to the snacks queue within the cramped space appears like an automatic reflux of bodies bearing the trace of spaces in which popcorn and soda were inextricably woven with *samosas* and *bhelpuri* in the cinema-going experience. Settling into the few seats or standing with a drink in one hand and samosa in the other, while arguing about the physique or histrionics of one movie star versus the other, making plans for dinner after the movie or joking around with friends activates memories of viewing practices in the *des* where going to the movies presented forms of conviviality denied in other exhibition contexts.

Memories of subcontinental viewing practices etched on the bodies of even those who have been removed from the *des* accompany the audience, as they move to occupy their seats inside the theatre. Until the movie begins, conversation continues both face-to-face and on mobile phones; people shuffle about in their chairs or move in the aisles; gape at latecomers or check out each others' outfits. However, it is during the viewing of the movie that Marks's notion of audiovisual media like film not only representing but also activating non-audiovisual sense material strikes one as applicable to the viewing of Hindi films. Sighs and grunts, inclining forwards to pay close attention or sideways to whisper a comment are forms of embodied knowledge that reproduce, albeit weakly, the viewing contexts of the past or in B-grade theatres in India in the present where whistling, clapping, hooting or making loud comments is deemed appropriate cinematic etiquette that binds the Hindi film audience into a community. A young couple from Lucknow, Manas and Geetishree, admitted that they returned to Jade instead of watching films in the comfort of their home because of the cinema-going experience at Jade reproduced the movie-watching experience in India (Manas and Geetishree, Interview with author, 8 October 2011):

> Well, it's always better to watch in the theatre with public booing and all that. Yes, it happens on the first day, particularly during the first show! People whistle and hoot. Doesn't happen on weekdays, but on weekends when the hall is totally jam-packed. Friday shows and Saturday shows are full.

Marks's point about sense memory as an important source of cultural knowledge for all, especially for minorities, and about rituals, gestures and other embodied forms of memory because it is crucial as a repository of knowledge for those whose experience is not represented, is important to the understanding of how viewing films along with others whose sensorium is organised in a similar fashion

168   *Anjali Gera Roy*

intensifies the pleasures of viewing (Marks 2000). Parikrama sums up this communal act of film viewing in his description of watching Abhinay Deo's *Delhi Belly* (2011) in Jade:

> Cut to reality. Jade theatre.
>
> Right on cue, upon seeing the butt filling up the screen, a lady sitting in row behind us says to her hubby "Kitnaa natural dikhaa rahey hein na sabkuch?" [How realistic is the entire representation! Isn't it?]
>
> Well truth be told, things can't get any more natural than a man's butt cleavage creeping out of boxers while being fast asleep! Till then I had not warmed up to the movie. I was dreading for yet another Hindi comedy movie where the audience and I laugh out of sync. But that one succinct observation from the lady set the mood, it tuned me to the laugh track that everyone was laughing to. From that moment on the rest of the movie was a blast.
>
> So dear wise lady in the back row – Thank You. Thank you for making Delhi Belly doubly enjoyable. Cut. [sic]
>
> (Parikrama 5 July 2011)

Second, her idea of the extra-diegetic sensory experience informing our viewing of films suggests the wide-ranging ways spectatorship is embodied. For the few hours inside Jade, the sensuous geographies of the nation, activated by the visual images on the screen and rituals enacted outside, are reproduced in the bodies of the spectators to reproduce the sense of home. This goes on to prove that cinema, though it engages two senses, activates a memory that involves all the senses.

Even the sweat and the stink that patrons of Jade complain about embody cultural memories of watching films in other spaces, and activate memories of other rituals of watching films through which home is reproduced. A visit to the toilets, in fact, could be viewed as completing the Jade experience. The hygiene levels in toilets, by no means intolerable by Indian standards, would strike one as lower than those in an average Singaporean shopping mall. However, it is not the old-fashioned fittings in the toilets alone that contributes to this impression, but toilet etiquette, if one may call it that, that produces a comforting familiarity as women talk to their friends across dividers, exchange makeup tips at the washbasins or shout instructions to children. Even though they are attired in unfamiliar Western casuals, they carry over the habits and behaviour in public spaces of crowded Indian cities where one might casually strike a conversation with anyone.

Conclusion

Literature on embodied spectatorship has largely focussed on non-visual ways of seeing films and of an experience that is as tactile, aural and olfactory as it is visual, and engages with the sensory images evoked by the cinematic text rather than on the contexts of viewing films. South Asian viewers' return to Jade appears like a nostalgic return home in the highly sanitised, organised, ordered city of

Going to the movies in Pardes   169

Singapore. For these regular Jade moviegoers, there is a nostalgia for the disorder that is the Indian city or town as it harkens back to the pleasures of viewing movies in standalone theatres in pre-globalised India. The desire for the conviviality produced by the communal act of viewing films, even in the "malltiplex" – returns the audience not to the memory of contemporary exhibition spaces identical to those in other global cities, but to those forms of embodied experience that have been threatened with the emergence of the ordered world of "malltiplexes".

The co-existence of these theatres in Indian metropolitan cities alongside cineplexes caters to the nostalgia for the embodied experience of going to the movies that began with buying the ticket. The anticipation of watching a movie in the pre-internet, pre-mobile phone era when cinemagoers would have to join serpentine queues to buy tickets only to have the ticket window shut before their turn with the "House Full" sign, the scramble for an alternative for which tickets were still available, or the disappointed return home added to the pleasures of the filmgoing experience. Alternatively, there was the thrill of being handed the last few tickets and being ushered in the cinema hall to join the sea of humanity making its way into the hall, of settling into the front row with great relief and vicariously participating in the catcalls, whistles, hoots and parallel commentaries that was the prerogative of the frontbenchers. It could equally be the exclusive privilege of purchasing the seats in the most expensive category in advance and being whisked away, along with accompanying family members, to the box by attentive ushers. The pleasure of walking down with family and friends to the late night show in the neighbourhood theatre, with young adults and senior citizens tucked safely in bed, might be hard to explain to those unfamiliar with the restrictions of living in an Indian joint family. It was the sole refuge of young dating couples with small budgets, wishing to get away from intrusive stares. Visits to Jade inevitably trigger these memories of small town India or middle class neighbourhoods in big cities. Rather than the sensory quality of the images, the pleasures of going to the movies in Jade rest in the activation of the sensorium through contact with bodies with similar memories.

References

Abhay. "Response to Archana's Blog Entry, 'Air Conditioner in Jade'." blog (blog deleted; no blog name available, no URL available), 22 January 2010. website link missing (Last accessed 10 May 2010).

Anaida. "Response to Archana's Blog Entry, 'Air Conditioner in Jade'." blog (blog deleted; no blog name available, no URL available), 1 December 2009. website link missing (Last accessed 10 May 2010).

Archana. "Air Conditioner in Jade." blog (blog deleted; no blog name available, no URL available), 8 November 2009. website link missing (Last accessed on 10 May 2010).

Banaji, Shakuntala. *Reading 'Bollywood': The Young Audience and Hindi Films.* Basingstoke: Palgrave Macmillan, 2006.

Barnard, Timothy P., and Hui Lin Ho. "'World' Cinemas in Singapore before World War II." Unpublished conference paper presented at "Singapore Cinemas: The Locations of Film Exhibition." Singapore: Asia Research Institute, 22 May 2010.

Bhattacharya, Budhaditya. "At a Theatre Not Near You." *The Hindu,* 20 August 2012. www.thehindu.com/features/friday-review/art/at-a-theatre-not-near-you/article3795419.ece (accessed 5 September 2015).

170   *Anjali Gera Roy*

Chakravarty, Sumita S. *National Identity in Indian Popular Cinema 1947–1987.* Austin:University of Texas Press, 1993.

Derné, Steve. *Movies, Masculinity, and Modernity: An Ethnography of Men's Filmgoing in India.* Westport: Greenwood Press, 2000.

Desai, Jigna. "Bollywood Abroad: South Asian Diasporic Cosmopolitanism and Indian Cinema." In *New Cosmopolitanisms: South Asians in the US*, edited by Gita Rajan and Shailja Sharma, 115–37. Stanford: Stanford University Press, 2006.

Devadas, Vijay. "Rethinking Screen Encounters: Cinema and Tamil Migrant Workers in Singapore." *Screening the Past: Journal of Screen History, Theory & Criticism* 32 (2011). www.screeningthepast.com/2011/11/rethinking-screen-encounters-cinema-and-tamil-migrant-workers-in-singapore/ (accessed 4 September 2015).

Devadas, Vijay, and Selvaraj Velayutham. "Cinema in Motion: Tracking Tamil Cinema's Assemblage". In *Travels of Bollywood Cinema: From Bombay to LA*, edited by Anjali Gera Roy and Chua Beng Huat, 164–82. Delhi: Oxford University Press, 2012.

Dudrah, Rajinder Kumar. *Bollywood: Sociology goes to the Movies.* New Delhi: Sage, 2006.

Ekta. "Even Chandan Cinemas is Better Than Jade!" *INoutDIA* (blog), 12 June 2011. http://inoutdia.blogspot.in/2011/06/even-chandan-cinemas-is-better-than.html (accessed 5 July 2011).

Fuller, Matthew. *Media Ecologies: Materialist Energies in Art and Technoculture.* Cambridge: MIT Press, 2005.

Gillespie, Marie. *Television, Ethnicity and Cultural Change.* London: Routledge, 1995.

Guy, Randor. "He Brought Cinema to South." *The Hindu*, 29 April 2010. www.thehindu.com/features/cinema/he-brought-cinema-to-south/article417856.ece (accessed 4 September 2015).

Holmberg, Erik. "Cinema in Singapore from 1896 to 1910". Unpublished conference paper presented at "Singapore Cinemas: The Locations of Film Exhibition." Singapore: Asia Research Institute, 20 May 2010.

Hughes, Stephen Putnam. "When Films Came to Madras". *BioScope: South Asian Screen Studies* 1, no. 2 (2010): 147–68.

Jaikumar, Priya. *Cinema at the End of Empire: A Politics of Transition in Britain and India.* Durham and London: Duke University Press, 2006.

Kaur, Raminder, and Ajay J. Sinha, eds. *Bollyworld: Popular Indian Cinema through a Transnational Lens.* New Delhi: Sage, 2005.

Larkin, Brian. "Itineraries of Indian Cinema: African Videos, Bollywood, and Global Media." In *Multiculturalism, Postcoloniality, and Transnational Media*, edited by Ella Shohat and Robert Stam, 170–92. New Brunswick: Rutgers University Press. 2003.

Marks, Laura U. *The Skin of the Film: Intercultural Cinema, Embodiment, and the Senses.* Durham: Duke University Press, 2000.

Mishra, Vijay. *Bollywood Cinema: Temples of Desire.* New York: Routledge, 2002.

Narayanan, Sheela. "Time for Cleaner Halls." *AsiaOne News*, 6 March 2009. http://news.asiaone.com/News/Latest+News/Showbiz/Story/A1Story20090306-126612.html (accessed 5 September 2015).

New Tamil Cinemas. "Tamil Cinema." *New Tamil Cinema* (blog), May 2011. http://new-tamilcinemasrs.blogspot.sg/2011/05/tamil-cinema.html (accessed 5 September 2015).

Parciack, Ronie. "Appropriating the Uncodable: Hindi Song and Dance Sequences in Israeli State Promotional Commercials." In *Global Bollywood: Travels of Hindi Song and Dance*, edited by Sangita Gopal and Sujata Moorti, 221–40. Minneapolis: University of Minnesota Press, 2008.

Parikrama. "Bhaag.. Bhaag.. Monday Blues." *Parikrama: Get Busy Living, OR Get Busy Blogging* (blog), 5 July 2011. http://parikrama.blogspot.in/2011/07/bhaag-bhaag-monday-blues.html (accessed 5 July 2011).

Plantinga, Carl. "Movie Pleasures and the Spectator's Experience: Toward a Cognitive Approach." *Film and Philosophy* 2, no. 2 (1995): 3–19.

Going to the movies in Pardes   171

Plantinga, Carl. *Moving Viewers: American Film and the Spectator's Experience*. Berkeley: University of California Press, 2009.

Plantinga, Carl, and Ed Tan. "Is an Overarching Theory of Affect in Film Viewing Possible? – Interest and Unity in the Emotional Response to film." *Journal of Moving Image Studies* 4 (2007): 1–47.

Prasad, Madhava M. *Ideology of the Hindi Film: A Historical Construction*. Delhi: Oxford University Press, 1998.

Rai, Amit S. *Untimely Bollywood: Globalization and India's New Media Assemblage*. Durham and London: Duke University Press, 2009.

Rajadhyaksha, Ashish. "Who's Looking? Viewership and Democracy in the Cinema." *Cultural Dynamics* 10, no. 2 (July 1998): 171–95.

Rajadhyaksha, Ashish. "Viewership and Democracy in the Cinema." In *Making Meaning in Indian Cinema*, edited by Ravi S. Vasudevan, 267–96. New Delhi: Oxford University Press, 1999.

Rajadhyaksha, Ashish. "The 'Bollywoodization' of the Indian Cinema: Cultural Nationalism in a Global Arena." *Inter-Asia Cultural Studies* 4, no. 1 (2003): 25–39. www.isites.harvard. edu/fs/docs/icb.topic1218620.files/All%20Readings/rajadhyaksha.pdf (accessed 4 September 2015). Earlier version with the same title also in *City Flicks: Cinema, Urban Worlds and Modernities in India and Beyond*, edited by Preben Kaarsholm, International Development Studies, Roskilde University Occasional Paper No. 22, 2002.

Rajadhyaksha, Ashish. *Indian Cinema in the Time of Celluloid: From Bollywood to the Emergency*. New Delhi: Tulika/Bloomington: Indiana University Press, 2009.

Singh, Bhrigupati. "The Problem." Seminar 525 (May 2003): Unsettling Cinema – A Symposium on the Place of Cinema in India. www.india-seminar.com/2003/525/525%20the%20problem.htm (accessed 11 December 2009).

Siva. "Introduction." *75 years of Tamil Cinema* (blog), 23 June 2008. http://tamilcinema75years. blogspot.sg/2008/06/introduction_23.html (accessed 5 September 2015).

Srinivas, Lakshmi. "The Active Audience: Spectatorship, Social Relations and the Experience of Cinema in India." *Media, Culture & Society* 24, no. 2 (March 2002): 155–73.

Srinivas, S.V. "Devotion and Defiance in Fan Activity." In *Making Meaning in Indian Cinema*, edited by Ravi S. Vasudevan, 297–317. Delhi: Oxford University Press, 2000a.

Srinivas, S.V. "Is There a Public in the Cinema Hall?" *Framework: The Journal of Cinema and Media* 42 (2000b), online edition. Previously available at www.frame-workonline. com/Issue42/42svs.html. Now at www.academia.edu/558095/Is_there_a_Public_in_the_Cinema_Hall (accessed 4 September 2015).

Tamil Cinema Online. "Introduction." *Tamil Cinema Online homepage*, n.d. http://tamilcinemaonline.hpage.co.in/introduction_32415448.html (accessed 5 September 2015).

Vasudevan, Ravi S., ed. *Making Meaning in Indian Cinema*. Delhi: Oxford University Press, 2000.

Vasudevan, Ravi, S. "Geographies of the Cinematic Public: Notes on Regional, National and Global Histories of Indian Cinema." *Journal of the Moving Image* 9 (2010).

Filmography

Advani, Nikhil. *Chandni Chowk to China*, 2009.
Das, Nandita. *Firaaq*. Mumbai, India: Percept Picture Company, 2009.
Deo, Abhinay. *Delhi Belly*. Mumbai, India: Aamir Khan Productions, 2011.
Kapoor, Raj. *Awaara*. Mumbai, India: RK Films, 1951.
Kapoor, Raj. *Sangam*. Mumbai, India: RK Films, 1964.
Khan, Kabir. *New York*. Mumbai, India: Yash Raj Films, 2008.
Khan, Sabbir. *Kambakkht Ishq*. Mumbai, India: Nadiadwala Grandson Entertainment, 2009.
Murugadoss, A R. *Ghajini*, 2008.

Interviews

Doe, June [pseudonym]. Personal communication with the author. New York, 12 April 2009.

Edward [pseudonym]. Interview with the author. Singapore, 19 July 2010.

Manas and Geetishree. Personal communication with the author. Singapore, 8 October 2011.

Maria [pseudonym]. Ticket salesgirl at Jade. Interview with the author. Singapore, 8 October 2011.

Sahara [pseudonym]. Interview with the author. Singapore, 8 October 2011.

Sunny, owner of Sunny Videos. Personal communication with the author. Bangkok, 12 July 2009.

Index

7 Letters (series of Singaporean short films by Eric Khoo, Boo Junfeng, Royston Tan, K. Rajagopal, Jack Neo and Kelvin Tong) xxi–ii, 52

Alfian Sa'at 4, 8, 18, 139; playwright of *Anniversary* 139; *see also* Royston Tan *Anniversary*
Ang, Cecilia *see Purple Light*
Army Daze 105
assemblage 111, 142, 156–7, 163, 170–1
Australia 57; cinema attendance rate 144; National Film and Sound Archive 57, 62

bangsawan 5, 29–30; role in Malay cinema and Malay-language films 3–19; in P. Ramlee's *Seniman Bujang Lapok* 5–6, 30–32; in *Hang Jebat* 29–30, 32
Beautiful Thing (book by Jonathan Harvey, film by Hettie MacDonald) 135–136, 143
The Blue Mansion 105
Boo Junfeng xi, xxi, xxiv, 44, 139; *7 Letters* xxi; *Sandcastle* xi, 38, 45–47, 49, 133, 142–3; *Tanjong Rhu* xi, 132, 136–7, 142–3; *Things that Makes Us, Us* xix

The Carrot Cake Conversations 52
Cathay Organisation, cinemas and cineplexes x, xxiv, 35, 78, 145; Cathay-Keris production studio 3, 20, 36, 51; Cathay's Hong Kong produced Chinese-language films 78; ownership and management of the Cathay Building and The Picturehouse 145; operation of Jurong Drive-in Cinema 147, 149; studio productions of *Mambo Girl/Manbo Nülang* 78, 96; studio

productions of *Air Hostess/Kongzhong Xiaojie* 78, 97; studio productions of *Wild, Wild Rose/Ye Meigui Zhi Lian* 78, 97–8
Chan, Jasmine xi, *Eating Air* (film with Kelvin Tong) xi
Chen, Anthony xxiv, 82; *Ilo Ilo* xix, xxiii–iv, 82
Chew, Javior *see Purple Light*
Chia, Lincoln xxiv; *Sisters* 132–3, 143
China xxiv, 18, 35, 45–6, 77, 96, 100, 102, 152, 154, 164–5; China-India film production (*Chandni Chowk to China*) 164; Shanghai 145, 154
Chuchu Datuk Merah 146
Crime does not Pay 51
cultural materialism xxiv, 3, 6–13, 16–18, 67–79, 81–3

The Days 52
Dhavamanni, T. T. 105, 107–10, 112, 116; *Guru Paarvai* 109; *Guru Paarvai 2* 109; *Guru Paarvai 3* 109; *Gurushetram – 24 Hours of Anger* 105–17, 121–5; *Match' Stick – The Musical* 109
diaspora xxiv, 18, 156; Indian 112, 124, 156–67, 169–170; Chinese xxiv, 18, 77–78, 154
Digital filmmaking 51; as part of film archiving and preservation 51–63; as part of cataloguing and preservation process by the Asian Film Archive (AFA); as part of film preservation in the Australian National Film and Sound Archive (NFSA) 57–8; as part of film preservation in the Hong Kong Film Archive 57; as part of film preservation in the National Archives of Malaysia 57; as part of film preservation in the

174 *Index*

National Archives of Singapore 57; as part of film preservation in Ngā Taonga Sound & Vision in New Zealand 57–8; as part of film preservation in Singapore's National Library Board (NLB) 60–1; in Singapore's independent film industry 51–53, 56–7, 60–1; locations showing films through DCP 52–53; online through video streaming websites 53; screening films through Digital Cinema Package (DCP) 52, 54–5; storage and preservation formats and software 52, 57–59; 60–63; through 35mm film stock 52, 56; through Adobe Premiere Pro and Final Cut Pro 52; through Blackmagic Cinema Camera 52; through Canon 5D Mark II 52; through digital single-lens reflex cameras (DSLR) 52; through EOS C300 52; through professional camcorders 52
Dhool 108
Dynamite Johnson 51

film archiving 51–64; by Asian Film Archive (AFA) xxii, 51, 54–6, 59–63
Forever Fever (also known as *That's The Way I Like It* in USA) 51, 95–102; directed by Glen Goei 65, 103

Goh Chok Tong 24–6, 35, 92, 101, 103
Goh, Colin *see Singapore Dreaming*
Gurushetram – 24 Hours of Anger 105–17, 121–5; directed by T.T. Dhavamanni 105, 107–10, 112, 116; with Gunalan Morgan as Karthik in *Gurushetram* 112–4; with Karthik Moorthy as Sundeli in *Gurushetram* 112–3; with Mathialagan Manikkam as Anbarasan (CNB officer) in *Gurushetram* 106, 110, 112; with T. Nakulan as Marsiling Baby in *Gurushetram* 109–11; with Prakash Arasu as Subra in *Gurushetram* 112, 114, 122; with Sivakumar Palakrishnan as Vinod (drug ringleader uncle) in *Gurushetram* 106, 112–6; with Vishnu Andhakrishnan as Prakash (the nephew) in *Gurushetram* 106, 109–116, 122

Hang Jebat (film) 29–30, 32–33; by Hussein Haniff 29–30; based on Malay folklore 29; based on *Sejarah Melayu* 29; based on *Hikayat Hang Tuah* 29; *Taming Sari*, Hang Jebat's legendary keris 29; musical elements in 29–30

Hollywood x, xiv, xv, xix, 3, 29–30, 107–108, 145, 161, 164–5, 167; American cinema attendance rate of films produced in 144; *American Graffiti* 98; *Boogie Nights* 99; *Jaws* 161; *The Kids are All Right* 129, 140, 142; *The Last Days of Disco* 99; *Saturday Night Fever* 95; *Summer of Sam* 99
Hong Kong 3, 78, 144, 154; actress Ge Lan (Grace Chang) 78, 96–8; *Air Hostess/Kongzhong Xiaojie* (movie) 97; cinema attendance rate 144; cinema and films produced in xv, 3, 78, 96–8, 100, 103, 145; comedy actors 78; Great Wall Studio x; Hong Kong Film Archive 57; *The Loving Couple/Xin Xin Xiang Yin* (movie) 97; *Mambo Girl/Manbo Nülang* (movie) 96; melodramas x; *The Hole* 97; popular music 96, 100; *The Wild, Wild Rose/Ye Meigui Zhi Lian* (movie) 97
The Hypocrite 51

Iceland cinema attendance rate 144
India 45, 111; *Anjathe* 112; *Billa* 107; I *En Swasa Kaatre* 108; Indian film and cinema 156–7, 159, 163–4, 166–7; Bollywood 161–8; *Chandni Chowk to China* 164–5, 171; *Delhi Belly* 163–4, 168, 171; *Firaaq* 167, 171; Hindi movies 156, 159, 161–4, 166–8; *The Hindu* (newspaper) 109; Indian movies in America 161, 167; in cineplexes and multiplexes 161–9; Indian movies in Singapore, Malaya and Malaysia 158–67; Indian movies in Singapore theatres 159, 161, 164–169; Indian films and cinemas on Internet chat and blogs 156–7, 162–6, 168; Jade cinema/ theatre xxiv, 150, 161–72; *Jaggubhai* 108; *Kadhal* 112; *Kambakkht Ishq* 167, 171; *Karupaayee* 108; *New York* 167, 171; *Paruthiveeran* 107; *Pattiyal* 112; popularity of Indian films among non-Indians 160–1, 163, 165–6; *Sangam* 159–60, 171; *Subramaniapuram* 112; Tamil movies 29, 108, 157, 159, 161; tent cinema showing Indian films 158–9
Indonesia xv, 38, 45, 49, 78; cinema and films 38; Suharto 38

Jalan Ampas Malay Film Productions and Shaw Brothers (Singapore) Studio 3, 6–7, 15, 18, 20, 36, 51, 154

Index 175

Japan 39; Tokyo 145, 154; in films 39; Japanese Occupation in Malaya and Singapore 39, 96; Tokyo International Film Festival 107

Kampong 5–7, 20, 30–1, 146, 153; *kampong* in Jack Neo's films xxi, 79; *kampong* in P. Ramlee's films 5–7, 15–16, 20, 31–2, 36
Khoo, Eric x, xi, xxiv–v, 17, 38, 71, 82–3, 105, 107, 116–17, 120–1; *7 Letters* xxi; *12 Storeys* (film) 22–4, 26, 29, 51, 104, 121, 142; *Be With Me* 131–2, 135, 142–3; *Mee Pok Man* x, xvii, xxi–ii, 3, 22, 142; *In the Room* xi; *My Magic* 82, 105–107, 109, 116–25; *My Magic* with Bosco Francis as Francis 106–7, 116–21; *My Magic* with Jathishweran as Raju 106, 116–22
Koh, Sun 132; *One* 132, 134, 143

Lee Hsien Loong 38, 47, 49
Lee Kuan Yew xx, xxii, 23, 39, 42–5, 147; People' Action Party (PAP) Singapore xx, 4, 37, 39, 41–4, 46–8, 70–1, 85, 103
Leila Majnun 3
Lim Yew Hock 44
Lion City 146
Loo Zihan xxiv; *Solos* 132, 140, 143; *Threshold* 132, 138, 143
Lucky 7 (omnibus Singaporean short film collection) 52

Malay cinema and Malay-language films 3–5, 8; decline in Singapore 3, 8, 15–18; in Singapore 3–15; in Malaysia 3–19, 83; *Leila Majnun* as part of 3; role in Singapore cinema 4–13, 15–18, 68–69
Malaysia/Malaya xix, xxi, 3–7, 12–19, 22, 32, 39, 43, 74, 78–80, 108, 111–13, 115–16, 122–4; cinemas and theatres in 159; Da Huang Pictures 52; films based on *bangsawan* tradition *see bangsawan* films; films based on Malay folklore, *Sejarah Melayu* and *Hikayat Hang Tuah* 10, 29–30, 32; films by P. Ramlee *see* P. Ramlee; horror films with *potianak*, *orang minyak* and *toyol* 10, 29–30; in films 111–13, 115–16, 122; Islamic law 11; National Archives of Malaysia 57; separation from Singapore xvii, 3–4, 22, 43–4, 79
Marks, Laura U. 163, 167, 170

Mathialagan Manikkam 106; as Anbarasan (CNB officer) in *Gurushetram 106*, 110, 112; as well-known actor on Singapore's *Vasantham* TV channel 108
Merdeka Film Studio in Kuala Lumpur 6–7, 10, 13
musicals in cinema xx–i, 12, 29–30, 78, 87, 96–7, 109

Neo, Jack x, xi, xxi, xxiv, 8–9, 17, 37, 67–83, 107; *7 Letters* xxi; *Ah Boys to Men* xix, 71, 74, 80, 104; *Ah Long Pte. Ltd.* 70; *Being Human* 70–1; *The Best Bet* 70, 73, 80, 100; cinematic successor to P Ramlee 8, 17, 67–9, 75, 78–82, 104; cultural materialism in contemporary Singapore cinema 8–9, 17, 37, 67–83, 99, 102; Hokkien, Singlish and Mandarin lingo in Singapore movies 20, 67–83, 94, 99; *Homerun* 72, 79–80; *I Not Stupid* 70, 74–5, 79, 99; *I Not Stupid Too* 70; *Just Follow Law* 74; *The Lion Men* 80; Mandarin, Singlish and Hokkien music soundtracks in films of 94, 99–102; *Money No Enough* x, xvii, 17–18, 22–23, 25–6, 29, 51, 70, 74–5, 78–80, 99–100, 102, 122; *Money No Enough 2* 70, 80–1, 100–1; populist nature of Neo's films 68–73, 82; *That One Not Enough* 70, 79; *Where Got Ghost?* 70
New Zealand 57, 63; Ngā Taonga Sound & Vision (New Zealand Archive of Film, Television and Sound Ngā Taonga Whitiāhua Me Ngā Taonga Kōrero) 57
Ninaithale Inikkum 146

One Leg Kicking 105

P. Ramlee xxiii–iv, 3–19, 30–1, 35–6, 68, 146; *Ahmad Albab* 10, 14–15, 81; *Anak Bapak* 10, 13–14; *Anak-ku Sazali* 11; *Ali Baba Bujang Lapok* 4, 10, 79, 81; *Antara Dua Darjat* 9–10; *Bujang Lapok* 9–11, 16, 30–2, 35, 75, 79; cultural materialism in films by 8–16, 69, 75, 78–82; *Do Re Mi* 10, 15–16; *Hang Tuah* 10; *Ibu Mertuaku* 10–14, 81; *Kanchan Tirana* 10; *Labu dan Labi* 4, 10–11, 30, 80; *Laksamana Do Re Mi* 16; *Madu Tiga* 10–11, 15, 79; Malay culture and values 4–6, 13–15, 69; *Masam Masam Manis* 10; Malaysian productions of 7, 10, 12–17; *Musang Berjanggut* 10;

176 *Index*

music in films of 7, 11–12, 14, 16–18; *Nasib Do Re Mi* 16; *Nujum Pak Belalang* 10; *Patah Hati* 146; *Pendekar Bujang Lapok* 10, 79; *Penarek Becha* 4, 10–11, 35, 79; *Putus Sudah Kasih Sayang* 10–11; *Semerah Padi* 10; *Seniman Bujang Lapok* 4–5, 10–11, 18, 30, 35, 79–80; Singapore productions of 3–4, 10, 13, 15, 37, 104; *Sumpah Orang Minyak* 10; *Tiga Abdul* 10–11
Pang, Adrian xx; in *LKY the musical* xx; as Hock in *Forever Fever* 95–6
Pickles 123
Plantinga, Carl 156, 170–1
Pleasure Factory 52
pleasures of viewing films 156, 168–9
Purple Light (film by Cecilia Ang, Javior Chew and Charlene Yiu) 132, 143

queer films and Singapore queer cinema 129–143; *Anniversary* 132, 139; *Be With Me* 131–2, 135, 143; biopolitics and geopolitics in 130–1, 133, 135–6, 138–140; Foucault and otherness in 129–130, 132–42; *One* 132, 134, 143; *Purple Light* 132, 140, 143; *Sandcastle* xi, 133, 143; *Sisters* 132–3, 143; *Solos* 132, 140, 143; *Tanjong Rhu* xi, 132, 136, 143; 逃离思念 132, 137, 143; *Threshold* 132, 138, 143; *Transit* 132, 139, 143

Rajagopal, K. *see 7 Letters*
Ring of Fury 51

Saint Jack 51, 104
See, Martyn xxiv, *Singapore Rebel* (film based on Chee Soon Juan) 42; film on Said Zahari *see Zahari's 17 Years*
Sex.Violence.FamilyValues xviii; film by Ken Kwek xviii
SG50 and commemoration of 50 years independence in Singapore xvii–iii, xix–xii, 3, 39, 47, 146
Shaw Brothers Organisation x, xxiv, 78; studio and productions in Singapore under Malay Film Productions 3, 6–7, 15, 18, 20, 36, 51, 154; studio and productions in Hong Kong under Shaw Brothers Organisation x, 78; ownership and operation of entertainment complexes in Singapore 154; Shaw cinemas 52, 150–2; Shaw Tower and Jade cinema/cineplex xxiv, 150–2, 161–170, 172

Singapore x, xi, xvii, xx 3–7, 12, 32, 79–80; acceptance of homosexuality in the family in 134; the Arts House in 146; Astra and Army Kinema Corporation in 146, 149–52; campaign against video piracy 144; Cathay-Keris production studio in 3, 20, 36, 51; cinema attendance rate in 144; cinemas and movies and theatres in 145–54; cinema locations in x, 149–153, 159; cineplexes, multiplexes and cinemas in entertainment complexes in 147, 152, 154; challenging dominant narratives in politics and history in filmmaking in xviii–xx, 37–50; Chinese dialects in Singaporean movies 67–83, 94, 98, 99; drive-in theatres and cinemas in 147; ethnic Indians, Tamil language and speakers in 104–126; heteronormativity according to Asian values, Confucian values and the penal code in 131, 133, 136–41; golden age of cinema in xxiii–iv, 20, 29–36; Housing and Development Board (HDB) flats in 23, 28, 35–6, 88; Indian representation in Singaporean films 104–126; Malay films and cinema in 3–13, 15–18, 68–69; Mass Rapid Transport (MRT) subway in 88–90, 152; Media Development of Authority (MDA) of Singapore xix, 52, 62, 63, 76, 109; movie snacks in 147; national Tamil Language Festival in 106; *Oli* (Tamil radio station) in 123; open-air mobile film units in 146–7, 149–53; planned economy in 136; post-national cinema in xxiii–iv, 20–9, 33–6; racial categorisation in 104; separation from Malaysia xvii, 3–4, 22, 43–4, 79; sites of gay socialisation in 134–6, 138, Singapore film and cinema x, xviii, xix, xxi–v, 7–9, 12–13, 15–19, 20–36, 84–93, 94–103, 129–143, 144–155; Singaporean films in Tamil 104–26; Singaporean Tamil film *Gurushetram – 24 Hours of Anger* (directed by T.T. Dhavamanni) 105–17, 121–5; Singaporean Tamil film *My Magic* (directed by Eric Khoo) 105–107, 109, 116–125; *The Straits Times* (newspaper) in 108; the Substation in 146; 140; *Tamil Murasu* (newspaper) in 108; *Uncle! Taxi Engeh Poguthu* (TV show) in 108; *Vasantham* TV channel in 108, 116–17; *Vettai: Pledged to Hunt* (TV show) in 123

Singapore Dreaming (film by Woo Yen Yen and Colin Goh) 77, 82; sensuous citizenship and cultural vernacular in contemporary Singapore landscape and cinema in 84–93

Sivakumar Palakrishnan 106; as Vinod (drug ringleader uncle) in *Gurushetram* 106, 112–6; as Mr Raju in *First Class* 108

Soundtracks in Singapore movies 94–103; diegetic music 94; non-diegetic music 94–5, 102; extra diegetic music 95; featuring *Jajambo/Shuo bu chu de kuaihuo* (song) 97; *Jive Talking* (song) 95; featuring *Kung Fu Fighting* (song) 95; featuring *Sneezing/Da Pen Ti* (song) 97; *Vixen/Yanzhi Hu* (song) 97; featuring *We are Singapore* (song) 101; featuring *We are Jing-kang-khor* (song) 101; in affecting nostalgia 94–99; *I Don't Care Who You Are/Wo Bu Guan Ni Shi Shui* (song) 97; *I Love Cha-Cha* (song) 97; *I Love Calypso/Wo Ai Ka Li Su* (song) 97; *I Want Your Love/Wo Yao Ni De Ai* (song) 97; in *The Best Bet* 100–2; in *Forever Fever* (also known as '*That's The Way I Like It*' in USA) 95–6, 98–9, 102; in *Hock Hiap Leong* 97–8; in *It's a Great Great World/Da Shi Jie* 95–9, 103; in Jack Neo films 94, 99–102; in *Money No Enough* 100–2; in *Money No Enough 2* 100–2

South Korea 144; cinema attendance rate 144; Pusan/Busan International Film Festival 107

Taiwan 78, 100; popular music 96; films and cinema 100, 145; Taipei International Film Festival 107

Taming of the Princess 146

Tan Pin Pin xi, xx, xxi, xxiv, 49–50, 53, 63; *To Singapore with Love* xi, xix, 47; *Invisible City* 38–40, 44–5, 47; *Singapore GaGa* xi, 84, 86–7; destabilising the narratocratic mode *in Singapore GaGa* 88–9; Gn Kok Lin in *Singapore GaGa* 88; Juanita Melson in *Singapore GaGa* 88; Margaret Leng Tan in *Singapore GaGa* 88; Melvyn Cedello

in *Singapore GaGa* 88; narratocratic mode in the voice of the MRT in *Singapore GaGa* 90–1; performance in the panoptic space in *Singapore GaGa* 89; quotidian sounds in the alienated space of the void deck in *Singapore GaGa* 89–90; reaching for a collective and individual Singaporean identity in *Singapore GaGa* 91–3; Victor Khoo and Charlee in *Singapore GaGa* 88; Yew Hong Chow in *Singapore GaGa* 88

Tan, Regina 132; *Transit* 132, 139, 143

Tan, Royston xi, xxi, xxiv, 17, 38, 82; *15* (film) xi, 26–29, 82; *881*(film) 30, 82, 104; *7 Letters* (series of short films) xxi; *12 Lotus* (film) 30; *Anniversary* 132, 139, 143; *Hock Hiap Leong* 97–8; *Old Friends* xix; *Old Places* xix; *Old Romances* xix

Thailand xix, 38, 50, 78; cinema and films 38

They Call Her ... Cleopatra Wong 51

Thia, Henry 97; as Ah Boo in *It's a Great Great World/Da Shi Jie* 96–7

Tong, Kelvin xi, xxi, 17, 82; *Eating Air* (film with Jasmine Chan) xi, 35, 51; *It's a Great Great World/Da Shi Jie* x, 82, 95–9, 103, 154; *7 Letters* xxi

Truth Be Told 52

Two Sides of the Bridge 51

Wee Li Lin 77, 82; *Gone Shopping* 52, 77, 82

Won, Jerome 132; 逃离思念132, 137, 143

Woo Yen Yen *see Singapore Dreaming*

Xiang Yun 97; as Mei Gui (Rose) in *It's a Great Great World/Da Shi Jie* 97–6

Yiu, Charlene *see Purple Light*

Yon Fan 22; *Bugis Street – The Movie* 22

Zahari's 17 Years 37–40, 42–44, 47; film by Martyn See xxiv, 37–40, 42–44, 49; featuring Said Zahari and based on his books *Dark Clouds at Dawn* and *The Long Nightmare* 38–44, 47

Zombie Dogs xx, film by Toh Hai Leong xx